I Love You,
LET'S
WORK
IT OUT

by

DAVID VISCOTT, M.D.

SIMON AND SCHUSTER

New York London Toronto Sydney Tokyo

Published by Simon and Schuster
A Division of Simon & Schuster, Inc.
Simon & Schuster Building
Rockefeller Center
1230 Avenue of the Americas
New York, NY 10020
SIMON & SCHUSTER is a registered trademark of
Simon & Schuster, Inc.

Designed by Irving Perkins Associates
Manufactured in the United States of America

10 9 8 7 6 5 4 3 2 1

Library of Congress Cataloging in Publication Data
Viscott, David S., date
  I love you, let's work it out.
  1. Love.   2. Interpersonal relations.   I. Title.
HQ801.V62 1987   646.7'8
ISBN 0-671-62531-4

TO KATHARINE,
WHOSE UNDERSTANDING
AND LOVE
BROUGHT ME
TO THIS PLACE

Contents

Contents

He loves not who does not show his love.

—William Shakespeare

How I Found Love and Worked It Out

THERE ARE some books that can be written only at a certain time in life. This is one of them. Throughout my professional life I have tried to help people understand their feelings and build loving relationships. I knew the principles for living together, but I'd had an unhappy marriage that eventually led to my own separation and divorce. I needed love. I was like everyone else in that respect, but, as a psychiatrist, I was also trying to help other people who needed love. While what I understood about love was correct, I had never felt completely loved and, therefore, could not speak from that special knowing that comes only with experience.

I wrote *How to Live with Another Person* in the hope of answering this riddle. As a professional I made correct assumptions about love, but something was missing from my understanding because something was missing from my life.

It was not until I found Katharine—miraculously, it now seems, in a ski line in Vermont—that I discovered the difference that being loved made in my life. My prior understanding of love, I also realized, was like that of a person thinking in a second language, just a bit removed from the truth. In learning to think and speak in the language of my own heart, I discovered that love was far more important than I had ever realized, more important than I could

11

have admitted to myself when I did not have love. The pain of not loving can make anyone cynical.

It was not always smooth. The arguments and the negativity Katharine and I sifted through often overwhelmed us. We sometimes lost our belief that we loved each other and became disillusioned and discouraged. We both considered calling it quits, but we realized that only people who are as close as we are could have such power to hurt each other. We came to accept that we were both still growing and that we needed to build self-confidence and trust and to hold our arsenals in check so we didn't retaliate, even when deliberately provoked. We believed in each other, and our love prevailed.

Being loved, feeling loved, and working out the difficulties between us proved to be the most important part of my own emotional growth. I was challenged at my weakest points and encouraged to become my best. I was supported in taking risks that previously I had barely dared to think about. If a goal made me happy, it was important to Katharine that I reach it. I learned that being loved was like having another self that loved the *best* in me and insisted on seeing and communicating with it even when I had lost sight of it. I discovered that love was about being your best selves together.

After moving to California with Katharine to start a new life, I began to broadcast on ABC's Talkradio network, practicing psychotherapy on the air. Now I truly believed in the possibility of love. But I discovered that almost *everyone* I dealt with had a problem with loving themselves or someone else. My experience has given me the opportunity to evaluate thousands of people and to speak to millions. Still, the deepest truths I discover about love— the truths that I hope to be able to share—continue to be those I learn in loving Katharine and growing together.

We are both imperfect, childlike, open, and sensitive. We are also fragile, vulnerable, caring, devoted, totally trusting, supportive, and committed. We have only one rule in our relationship. We both must be free.

We are truly in love.

I hope this book will make it possible for you to say that as well.

INTRODUCTION:

Working It Out Together

W HAT IS the secret of making your
relationship work and living happily
together?

When things go smoothly the partners hardly notice, but when
a relationship gets into trouble it is difficult to see clearly or to
understand the events that led up to the problem. When times are
rough partners fumble in the dark, trying to make sense of the
confusion that alienates them. Each partner clings to his hurt and
tries to make a case for being right and proving the other wrong.
The scene is set for further confrontation rather than real problem
solving and reconciliation.

All relationships, even the best and most loving, experience bad
times. When they happen, it is easy to forget that you love each
other.

Often motivated by a desperation to make things better, the
partners make peace superficially rather than reach a true understanding. Then, when the problem recurs, the partners are disappointed and lose faith. They often lack the courage to bring up the
questions that bother them; they're afraid they'll make the situation
worse or discover that the other person really doesn't care.

This book specifically addresses the many problems that come
between people who love each other and offers an effective step-

by-step method for identifying and resolving them. None of this information has been watered down. It is the simple truth presented in a clear and direct fashion. It may not always be easy to grasp these thoughts, but understanding them is necessary for you to be happy together. So take your time and let the ideas take hold of you and direct your thinking. You will find it especially valuable to read sections of the book aloud, either to your partner or to yourself. Doing so will help clarify your problems and give you the strength to take the steps to solve them.

Throughout the text are exercises designed to raise your understanding and free you. They can either be completed with your partner or by yourself. You can write out your responses to the questions in each exercise, dictate them into a tape recorder, answer them aloud, or simply read and answer silently to yourself. However you choose to complete these questions, do not rush. They are designed to broaden your attitude and free your thinking. So take the time to ponder. Listen carefully to your innermost responses. The questions will guide you to the answers within.

While they are all part of an integrated process, each chapter is also designed to stand alone and to serve as an aid in solving a specific problem. You can follow the sequence of the chapters as they are presented, or you can begin almost anywhere, using the issue that concerns you most as your point of departure. Taken all together, what follows is a series of windows that look out on the vast and varied landscape of a relationship.

There is no secret to building a happy relationship. It is a matter of working together in love and belief in each other. A relationship has no point unless you both try to make it the best it can be. This book will define the steps that will take you to that point.

You deserve to be happy together.

Part One

FINDING OURSELVES TOGETHER

CHAPTER ONE

Being Free Together

A RELATIONSHIP is a commitment to another person.

If you don't have a commitment, you don't have a relationship. It is impossible to discuss committing to another person without talking about committing to yourself. In fact, the strength of your commitment to anyone else is qualified by the firmness of your commitment to yourself.

You cannot love another unless you love yourself. You cannot stay for long in a relationship that does not allow you to grow into your best. While you may hide in a relationship and avoid the risk of testing yourself, the day will come when you feel cramped by your limitations and need to grow. You will then be forced to take the very risks you've been avoiding. Your relationship will come under stress as the imperative to move forward pulls you away from the same ties you once counted upon to keep you securely in place.

Yet a relationship must be the glad accompaniment to *both* partners' development. If each partner is not committed to his own growth, he cannot offer the sustenance necessary for his partner to grow, for he will see his partner's growth as a threat and his partner's success as an embarrassment to his own shortcomings.

If the partners are not committed to their own and each other's

17

growth, they tend to undermine each other. This may not be intentional, but anything less than wholehearted encouragement is seen as an unwillingness to support the other. You are either allies or adversaries; there is no middle ground.

All growth is overcoming doubt.

You either risk or stagnate. You either decide to do it or you waste years thinking about it and making empty plans. If you commit, you discover and confront your shortcomings and grow; if you do not, you lose faith in yourself. In its early stages, the act of risking is especially tentative. The depth of commitment by each partner to the other must be complete so that when one partner seeks out the other and makes eye contact, he feels the fullest undaunted support coming in return. A nod suggesting "What are you waiting for?," a believing smile to give courage, and the expectation of optimism is all we want from a partner. "Go for it!" is what we want to hear.

Shouldn't we be able to find the courage on our own, prod ourselves and reach for the stars? Of course. Most great accomplishments come from the self. No partner, however beloved, can remove our struggle or give us the determination to find the right subject for our creation, the words for our poem, the notes for our song, the courage to reason eloquently in court, or the finesse to negotiate a business deal. Still, finding our best intention positively reflected in our partners' eyes matters as much as anything else.

It is our partners who keep faith with their memory of our best, who bring it to our attention through an attitude of positive expectancy. They remind us constantly that we can do it. We want our partners to have faith in us and to reflect this belief by their presence alone. This does not mean that our partners cannot criticize us. In fact, we value their criticism most, for they have been our closest companions on our life journey. They have seen us struggle, fail, and triumph. They know our talents and our capabilities. They know when we are trying to get away with less just to have a sense of completion rather than accomplishment. They encourage us because, more than anyone else, they know what we are like to live with when we have risked everything and have succeeded. We are fuller, happier, more giving, better lovers, more committed to them, and more fun to be with. They have a vested interest in our being our best. Their enduring, supportive presence fills in the gaps of our own resolve.

When partners are not committed and one partner takes risks, there is a great temptation for the unrisking partner to use the privilege of closeness to undermine the other, thus reinforcing the risking partner's worst fears by focusing only on the danger involved while omitting support entirely. The undermining comes from the thinly veiled suggestion that the other cannot make it. This lack of support causes the greatest injury. If it is intended to curtail one partner's search for himself, it is always doomed to failure because it goes against nature. Every person is endowed with gifts and has an imperative to develop and express them. To attempt to dam up this flow of energy is to risk a tidal wave. Each partner must be committed to himself and must also be able to express his belief in the other, especially at those vulnerable moments when the other has forgotten his worth.

CHAPTER TWO

Committing to Each Other

COMMITTING IS acting on belief.
Whether or not you are committed is the issue that determines the depth of your relationship. If you haven't committed to each other, committing is the issue you continually discuss or avoid discussing.

Louisa and Peter each divorced their spouses in order to be together. However, once free they found reasons for staying apart. Peter even accepted a job in a city five hundred miles away just at the point when they were about to move in together. They professed their love and demonstrated their caring openly, but they could not commit to taking the final step.

It seemed as if every romantic evening they planned slowly degenerated as the subject of committing inevitably reappeared. Each time it did, they both became hurt and frightened and blamed the other for bringing up the subject.

Disappointed and angry, Louisa then tried to force Peter to decide by withholding her love. Peter responded by being even more aloof. All of the good between them began to fade until finally the love that had once been their reason for being together became a hindrance to being free, and their relationship eventually unraveled.

The fear of committing causes pain and disappointment. It inspires partners to run away or to precipitate crises that dissipate closeness and lead to a disheartening cycle of intimacy and regret in which each gives second chances to the other based more on hope than reality. Both partners end up feeling used or entrapped.

If you haven't committed to yourself, it may explain why committing to another has been such a problem. Sometimes committing to the person you love gives you renewed belief in yourself. But you cannot commit to another person unless you know what you want out of life. People do a lot of pretending about this; they form unequal bonds based on unrealistic hopes and mistaken appraisals of the other person's worth, sincerity, motivation, and capacity to love. If you have not found yourself, it is unlikely that you will find the person who is right for you. How would you know if you did?

FALLING IN LOVE WITH LOVE

People are always looking for someone who represents an ideal— to have the perfect mate implies that you are perfect. Because such people are few, we tend to idealize others and fall in love with our idealization. Then, when we get close enough to see their faults, we reject them, for in our insecurity we fear that our partner's weakness reveals that we are flawed as well.

When we were young and in the green days of our reason, we committed to others because we saw in them what we needed to see. Those commitments were often one-sided. We fell in love at a distance and held our hearts in check, secretly thrilling whenever we passed close to the other in a crowded school corridor. We walked miles out of our way to go past her house, hoping to catch a glimpse of her in the window. We found ourselves interested in a sport he played and, in response to the slightest criticism, defended it with embarrassingly misplaced passion.

First commitments are physical, born of ideals, a search for perfection and an awakening to feelings, both unfamiliar and arresting. That nose, the angle of the neck, that wonderful chest, those breasts; and that face, sought out in crowds, seen in dreams; and that laugh, the way he or she dances, or those eyes; and that rear end that moves to a silent drum; and those delicate hands, those legs and the adjacent places whose fullness evokes the need for exploration. What would he say if I approached him? Would she refuse me if I asked?

First loves preoccupy us, dilute our thoughts, capture our time. First loves make us become something other than ourselves. We pursue what we think we should be to appear lovable. We act differently, embarrass ourselves, and cover our comments with transparent avoidances. We play roles, now confident, now overly serious. But beneath it all, we wonder if anyone will ever be there for us as we really are.

The problem for many people who claim they "like the chase" is that they never quite get over this initial stage of being in love. They mistakenly label the intense eroticism and carefree romanticism of this period as real love. They seek relationships that contain the same feelings as they imagined in the past, but they can't find them. They pursue an impossible ideal and age in their disappointment. How could they know that what they are seeking existed only in the state of mind they brought to love years ago?

These people seek not only a person like those in their past, they are also trying to recapture their own youthfulness, their carefree days when they were protected. They want a love that reflects a life full of promise that still lies ahead of them, and an optimism untainted by failure, limited only by their capacity to dream. They want a person who inspires them to wonder again.

The world has other plans for us. The perfect mate never comes. We are left with our unfulfilled dreams and the knowledge that we are getting older. But somehow the miracle happens again, or so we believe. We find in another person a trait that we once cherished years ago, and suddenly, almost without our encouragement, we view the new person in stage lighting from another era. We are older, but we feel youthful again. In this loving context we forgive the shortcomings we should question and imagine a completeness that does not exist. It is easy to see how such a relationship quickly comes to mean more than it should, more than it can ever deliver.

But we don't want to know this. We just want to believe that love exists. It only takes one hurtful comment to cut through our self-deception and bring us down to reality again. Our partner puts us down without realizing it. He belittles something we care about or mocks a value we cherish. We are stunned! The other person is not what we thought, and we are different as well. Before we were sure of everything, now we have deep doubts. The commitment we made seems trivial. We don't even understand what we saw in the other person. In fact, we reject them for the same superficial traits to which we once were drawn. His strength is now seen as controlling. Her spontaneity is seen as flirting. The whole business is an embarrassment. It is easier to break up and run away than admit how our needs distorted our perception and contributed to our own betrayal. And so we move on, resolving never to allow ourselves to be hurt this way again.

LETTING GO OF MAKE BELIEVE

Some people leap into love again, trying to prove their former partner wrong, replacing one number with another. Others play distant and hurt and seek to avoid any situation that will bring them into close human contact. But most of us pick up the pieces and move on. We shop the world in our own changing style. Our shopping list of desirable features gets longer out of defiance, then shorter out of desperation. We want someone who makes us look good, someone we can take anywhere. Beauty, money, personality, and charm rank high as we pursue the love we think we want. But then, if we are lucky, and usually only after we have lost belief in the possibility of realizing our ideal, we find someone in whose presence we can simply be ourselves, tell the truth easily, and so we begin to work out our lives together. Whatever we discover in this relationship starts with the realization that what we imagined to be right for us is not quite the same as what *is* right for us.

We pass through many stages of growth before we are willing to commit either to ourselves or to the relationship in which we presently find ourselves. Moving in together, sharing finances, having children, supporting each other through triumph and failure, illness and aging are parts of a continuum of committing. In the most deeply committed relationships, commitment is never an issue. It is a fact. In uncommitted relationships, commitment is an unsettled account that continually demands collection. No matter how positive, each experience in an uncommitted relationship leaves the partners asking each other, "Where do we go from here?" Committing makes the world you share more real. Knowing that you are there for each other gives you the emotional freedom to enjoy life and linger a little longer to savor the happy moments, without raising the question of what the future will bring.

Commitment to each other is both the beginning and the future of a relationship.

The essence of commitment is acceptance and understanding of your partner and your self.

TAKING THE STEPS TOWARD COMMITMENT

The rest of this chapter is designed to give direction to your relationship by helping you define the obstacles that still stand between you and your partner. No matter where your relationship is now, the exercises that follow will make clear exactly what areas need work in order to make the relationship a happy one.

While talking about commitment here may seem a bit premature, making a commitment should be your ultimate goal. Defining the issues that separate you and your partner is the first step in reaching a commitment. In the following exercises, you will look at your fears, your needs, your ideals, and your objections to making a commitment and share them with your partner. You will also examine how committed you are at this point in your relationship.

Finally, as you look at the issues that face you, you will determine what kind of a commitment, if any, you can make. It may not be possible to reach the commitment you desire at this point in time. But do not lose faith—a growing relationship is *always* exploring its commitment. Approach the questions in the exercises knowing that they just skim the surface; they are simply making you aware of the road ahead.

The Crucial Issues

Should I commit?
Can I commit?
Will I commit?

EXERCISE 1
*Why Are You
Afraid of Saying Yes?*

This exercise is designed to help you pinpoint the fears that prevent you from committing. Each partner should complete it by reading and answering the following questions aloud:

Is this relationship right for me?
How do I know?
What changes would make it right for me?

List all the things you would like to change in your relationship in the order they come to mind. Be honest. Include *all* the things you need but are not getting from your partner. For example, do you think your partner should:

Lose twenty pounds?
Indulge you more sexually?
Give you more money?
Listen to you or pay more attention to you?
Care more for your relatives or friends?

Say what you want without any attempt to protect your partner's feelings or keep yourself from appearing petty or crass. What prevents you from getting closer needs to come to the surface now. If you are not honest in answering this question, your true resistance to committing will not be discussed.

What Would It Take for You to Commit?

Clue: Most of your excuses have become bigger obstacles than they really are. Sometimes they hide other doubts you are afraid to mention. Take another look at your reasons for keeping your distance.

How important are each of your concerns?
What changes are necessary for you to say yes to this relationship without reservation or doubt?
What are the chances that these changes will happen?
What does each change depend upon?

What would it take for each to happen?
Would you commit then? If not, why not?

What Are You Really Afraid Of?

Consider again:
Do any of the obstacles you mention make you feel secure?
Is it possible that you feel comfortable knowing they prevent you from committing?
What makes you feel uncomfortable about your relationship?
List these concerns and indicate what you fear about each.
What would make you feel more comfortable together?
How often do you discuss these points?
Even if your partner makes you uncomfortable by bringing up unsolved problems, your partner is doing you a favor. If you cite your partner's insistence on discussing painful issues as the main reason you avoid committing, you are really afraid of getting close to yourself.
It's fine to be afraid. Just admit what you fear and why.

Perhaps You Fear Being Trapped

How much in control of your relationship do you feel?
Do you feel manipulated by your partner?
How much control do you think you would have to give away if you committed to the other person?
Sometimes we hold on to obstacles as safety valves in our relationships. Louis, for example, was a prominent real estate investor who had been separated from his wife for ten years without getting a divorce. He found that staying married provided him with an impenetrable shield that protected him from making another mistake. While many of the women who dated him over the years complained about his failure to make himself available, they clearly were glad that they were also freed from making a commitment. They fought with Louis over it. They complained about it. They threatened to leave because of it. But it actually made them comfortable. They knew a relationship with him could never be serious, so they felt safe demanding a commitment.

We tolerate the obstacles because we need them to protect us from ourselves. If the other person seems unwilling or unable to commit, how much do you depend on their resistance to keep from being trapped? Why else would you choose someone who did not want to get close?

Your Ideal Partner

To help you define your needs, make a list in order of importance of the ten qualities you desire most in a partner.

After you have completed this list, indicate next to each quality how your partner measures up to that ideal. Is your assessment accurate?

How do *you* compare with your own standards?

How well suited are you to each other?

Accepting Each Other's Imperfections

You may be in a relationship, even married for years, and still be uncommitted. To be committed means that you accept the other person without waiting for something to happen to make him more acceptable. You commit to him as he is because you see that being together makes each of you better. You commit to her without waiting for events to change, finances to improve, parents to give permission, or the divorce to be final. You commit when your heart reigns over your doubts. You commit with all your faults in full view. Though you are both imperfect, you make a perfect commitment based on acceptance of each other.

We avoid forming relationships and making commitments because we are afraid of being hurt, of finding ourselves deeply involved without any way of getting out uninjured. We fear becoming bonded to someone who is only average, where we would like them to be exceptional. We fear that our important needs will go unanswered. Even when they are not, we want our partners to be easy to talk to, to show sensitivity to our feelings, to return our affection, to listen with interest, to have sexual adventurousness, to display intellectual curiosity, to show gentleness and caring with children. Sometimes we deceive ourselves into believing we have what we need just so we can avoid being alone. We may claim we are committed to the other person, but deep down we know we are not getting what we want. When our commitment is tested, we find ourselves holding back, and often can't understand why.

Knowing what you now know, would you still choose the person with whom you are involved?

If so, why?

If not, why?

DISCOVERING HIDDEN OBSTACLES

The questions in this exercise define a process for thinking about and solving complicated problems. They are designed to help you break through the obstacles to commitment. Allow yourself to react freely to them. Let the answers that appear in your mind take you as far as they can. They will direct you toward a new understanding and a workable solution. Keep a record of your thoughts by writing notes as you complete the rest of the exercises. Sometimes a simple question can lead to a startling revelation. It's also a good practice to reread your notes and share them with your partner.

Marge and Bill have been living together for six years without a commitment. Bill's electronics distributorship was thriving. He'd become a minor celebrity by starring in his company's television ads, where he often appeared in ridiculous costumes smashing stereos with a giant hammer to illustrate how he crushed his competition's prices. Marge was a great beauty, but her small gift shop barely could meet expenses and it survived in a fashionable shopping mall only because Bill lent her money. They were one of those couples with great sexual chemistry. You could tell from a hundred feet away that they were attracted to each other. But every time she brought up the issue of commitment, Marge became needy and accusatory and the discussion degenerated into an ugly fight in which Bill, who was generally affectionate, pulled away. They had separated twice over committing. Marge always returned tearfully professing her love. Bill always accepted her with open arms.

These are Marge's notes:

Working on this exercise, I realize that Bill doesn't want to get married and that I feel weak without him. And I've learned that my continual pushing to get him to commit so we can have a baby before I turn forty is a false issue. I'm not even sure I want a baby. It's just been a handy way of setting a time limit and it didn't work.

Going through the list of all the things a partner could object to has made me realize that he has used practically everything on this list at least once as an excuse. But I know he loves me and that none of his objections really matter to him.

I think he just doesn't want to commit to anyone. Period.

Maybe my mother was right after all, and he is just using me. But how could he be using me? He's put thousands into my company. It doesn't make sense.

He thinks I'm using him. That's what he tells me when we fight. He says I wouldn't have a decent place to live or a car without him and that he makes our life-style possible. We always fight over this. I tell him I am self-supporting, but the way the business is going maybe I'm just kidding myself.

Maybe I *am* using him. In a way I guess I am. But we love each other. Every couple uses each other. We share a lot. I give to him. I accept what he gives and provides. I am grateful. I appreciate all he's done for me.

But I never tell him!

I never tell him.

Why?

Maybe I'm pretending to be independent. This is embarrassing! I pretend I'm a successful businesswoman doing it all by myself. I'm $40,000 in debt! I didn't even have an American Express card till I met Bill, and I have never thanked him in so many words.

Maybe that's what he backs away from. I can understand that. I wouldn't want to be with someone who took from me and was so insecure that she couldn't even thank me. No wonder he finds all these silly things to object to. Most of them are just made up. He's really afraid of telling me the truth, that I'm an unappreciative phony.

When Marge shared her realization, Bill was stunned. It immediately rang true to him and allowed him to understand his own reluctance. "I knew I was trying to tell you something," he said, "but I just didn't know what. I was angry, but I was always afraid to hurt you. I just drew a blank."

Sometimes people can't make a commitment because they feel trapped in the other person's self-deception and do not know how to confront it. Instead, they object to safe flaws that are easy to discuss.

It's hard to commit to someone who believes in something you know is not true.

WHY YOUR PARTNER WON'T COMMIT

In each of the following categories, list the specific excuses your partner gives for not committing. What do you think of each excuse?

Your Behavior: Does your partner object to your behavior and bad habits, such as excessive drinking, gambling, drug use, or inability to earn a living? These are important objections because they are fatal to growth and success in a relationship. No relationship can survive unless these problems are solved, and no person who values himself can commit to another unless both are committed to solving these problems. Many people do bond to mates with severe problems in the hope that their love will give their partner the strength to change. Unfortunately, this is often wishful thinking born of desperation. Most of these relationships cannot bear close scrutiny, and fail.

Your Style: Does your partner object to the way you do things, to your style, to your manner? It is only natural to object to a person with a controlling nature and a tendency to manipulate. And it's hard to commit to someone who clings or puts you down or refuses to be open with his feelings. Just because you have never heard such objections spoken openly does not mean they do not exist. You can sense such objections. They give you the feeling that you must change to be accepted. They form a major obstacle to committing and to being happy together.

Your Taste: Lesser problems—such habits as snoring, nail biting, or smoking, and issues of taste (for example, poor table manners, one's style of dressing or taste in friends, sports, movies, and restaurants)—may seem trivial, but they can create friction that can take a lot out of a relationship. Partners who love each other but don't express their deepest feelings sometimes use these annoying characteristics as easy targets for releasing the deeper negativity they feel toward each other. Such displaced resentment can build and, over time, become a sore spot that never heals because it does not address the partner's deeper concerns.

In summary, to which of your characteristics does your partner most object?

Finally, what traits do you dislike most about your partner?

You need to accept your partner's faults so you can love without reservation or regret. The power of love can bridge over imperfections, but not over dishonesties.

ACCEPTANCE BEGINS
WITH HONESTY

Sam was a young man who had written several novels but had not been published. His girlfriend, Vicki, was the weatherperson at a local television station and had become extremely popular for her good looks, perkiness, and sense of humor. She often appeared in advertisements and was a minor celebrity.

Sam, who was orphaned at twelve, attached himself to Vicki and her two daughters and almost instantly became part of the family. But for all their closeness he would not commit to her. He gave a lot of excuses, including that she had obnoxious phony friends who were trying to use her and that she did little to separate herself from them. He also objected to her insistence on knowing his every thought. Under close questioning, Vicki got Sam to admit that he was secretly jealous of her success and did not want to feel inhibited in his writing by being around her. This prevented him from committing.

Vicki offered to change her friends but refused to give up her career. Indeed, Sam said he never wanted her to, but it was still an obstacle to committing because he had to write and just couldn't in her house.

They began to drift apart. Each accused the other of insincerity. Finally, after an emotional argument, Sam admitted that the real reason he could not live with Vicki was that she was controlling. Vicki recoiled and demanded to know how. Angrily, Sam pointed out how she used her attractiveness and charm and even her giving to make herself appear perfect to everyone. He felt manipulated by her representing herself as always being right. He felt that she surrounded herself with phonies to make it easier to carry that off. Sam even admitted that he was a phony, but that he needed a partner who could sometimes admit imperfection.

Vicki tearfully admitted that she was always trying to control Sam and asked why he had never spoken about it before.

"It was the way you were, and I was afraid of rejecting you and losing my relationship with your kids," Sam said.

After this, Vicki and Sam were able to relate honestly to each other and finally commit.

If you want to make a genuine commitment, you must discuss what you really object to no matter how much you fear it may hurt the other person or what you may risk losing by doing so.

TAKING STOCK OF YOUR RELATIONSHIP

Think about your answers to the questions in this exercise, look again at your notes and lists, and go over them quietly by yourself.

This is a time for honest reflection.

Do you have the relationship you want or are you trying to create a relationship based only on need and circumstance? Don't be afraid to admit this if it is true. You have to begin with the truth to make things better.

There is nothing more damaging to a relationship than pretending you are happy. You always pay for self-deception. Silent regret and unspoken pain cause partners to drift apart. Whenever alienated partners talk, deep feelings of resentment over not being accepted and hopelessness over the future intrude. The way to avoid this is to accept your own and your partner's limitations and risk speaking truthfully together all the time.

The main reason people feel they cannot commit is that they fear they will lose their freedom in doing so. No one wants to be trapped in an untruthful relationship. No one wants to give up their right to choose what is best for them. If you commit to a relationship, you should at least get what you want from it.

What *do* you want from your relationship?

Can your partner give it to you?

Should or can you give it to yourself?

If you are the only one in your relationship who can give you what you need, you cannot commit to the other unless you are free to take care of yourself.

PREPARING TO SHARE

Before you meet with your partner to share your responses to these questions, you need to feel comfortable with yourself.

Keep in mind that a committed relationship is real, flexible, and nurturing. It feels like home, accepts you as you are, and allows you to make mistakes, to be forgiven, and to grow. If you don't have a committed relationship you'd probably be better off alone. In an uncommitted relationship, you waste time and energy trying to fit together pieces of two different puzzles. If you don't fit, don't force it. Allow your differences to speak for themselves.

When you share your responses, you will be tempted to make concessions for unacceptable differences just to keep the peace or to avoid hurting the other person. Ignore the temptation—don't say anything that is not the truth. You don't have to give up anything you really want or need.

Remember, you are free, so act like a free person with your partner.

If you both can speak honestly about the differences dividing you, you have the best chance to close the gap. But if you cannot work it out, at least you will know where you stand and your energies can go into looking for a relationship that holds better promise for making you happy.

EXERCISE 2
Updating Your Commitment Together

To complete this exercise, you and your partner should be in a quiet place, free from interruption. You'll need at least an hour together, but you might take an entire weekend or repeat the exercise every few months or on your anniversary. Allow the natural dialogue that these questions inspire to flow. Let your curiosity guide you. Be brave and, again, be truthful.

Each of you should take turns answering all of the questions that follow one at a time. Be sure you answer aloud. Before your partner takes his turn, he should reflect on what you have just told him and you should respond to his concerns. It's not necessary, but it can be helpful to have a tape recorder running. Taking notes will also be valuable. But make the conversation more important than the notes! If your partner refuses to participate, complete the exercise alone and reflect on the way you feel afterward.

What Are the Persistent Obstacles to Our Relationship?

The *main* reason I am afraid to commit to you is:
Other reasons are: (List these without editorial comment.)
What stands in the way of my making a genuine commitment to you?

Can I Be Myself with You?

If I commit to you, I feel I will have to give up:
I need to be free because:
If I were completely free right now I would:
Would this be all right with you?

What Are the Things I Really Need from You?

I need support from you in the following areas:
I need to know how you really feel about:
I need to know the answers to the following questions:
I need to know that you are telling me the truth about:

How Do I Really Feel about Myself?

This is what I cannot compromise, yield, or in any way diminish without losing myself:

Can I have this and still have us?
I must be true to the following:
Can I be true to this and still be with you?
When I am my best I am:
Can I be this way and be with you?

What Are the Changes I Would Like to Make?

I would like to remove these rules from our relationship:
I would like to renegotiate the following contracts:
I no longer believe in the following agreements:
I would like to remove the following old conditions:
I require these new conditions:
These additional changes would make me happy:

What Are the Loose Ends in Our Relationship?

I would like to reclaim these things I gave up for you:
These issues still disappoint me:
These are my desires that still go unmet:
The issues I cannot discuss with you are:
The doubts I still have are:
I feel trapped because:

ACCEPTING THAT YOUR
PARTNER HAS GROWN

The answers to all of the above questions should be stated simply as fact, not threats or accusations. Partners in a relationship change and grow, and the relationship itself must change and grow to reflect that reality.

Nevertheless, changes in your partner's personal needs can often seem like a betrayal, especially if you yourself have not grown. So before responding to your partner's requests with anger and hurt, try to understand the risk he has just taken in expressing his true feelings. Real growth is only possible if you accept the ever evolving reality that you share together.

Pretending that nothing has changed over the course of your relationship, or insisting that your old agreements be ironclad, is unrealistic. It reflects a wish for inflexible standards to apply to maturing human values. We often seek such stability when we are young, but we all change. You are not the same person you were ten years ago. If you are fortunate, you put away the weaker parts of yourself and grew stronger, discarding the crutches you thought you needed until you felt confident enough to be self-supporting. Your partner's growth is also a testimony to the love you share and the strength that was derived from your care and support—even if that support was reluctant, forced, or offered only because you felt you would lose your partner if you withheld it. Accept the condition of your relationship as it is right now and build on the best of it.

MAKING A COMPROMISE

It is impossible to make a commitment without compromise. But when a compromise limits your ability to grow, it places both of you in jeopardy. You always need to be free to be your best in order to make your relationship work.

NEVER COMPROMISE YOUR FREEDOM

It takes two free partners to make a relationship whole. When the partners question each other's right to act freely, the relationship is filled with testing and resentment. It is not in our nature to forgive another for playing on our weaknesses and coercing us to give up our freedom. Worse, the resentment one feels toward oneself for being weak and yielding this right often becomes the basis for defiance and rebelliousness and an overstated need to prove one's own independence. Doing things just to prove you are still free to do them is not the act of a free person.

Compromise becomes evolution when partners relinquish control over each other and grant each other the freedom to do whatever they want. When you allow your partner to be free, you also free yourself from being his keeper.

36

If you reject this idea because you find it too threatening, your self-doubt stands in the way of achieving a workable compromise. In the best relationships the partners are always free to do what they want but they choose, on a daily basis, to be with the other. A forced compromise is a loose bond that easily comes undone. After a while, "Am I *free* to do this?" becomes a more important question to the trapped partner than "Do I *want* to do this?"

Doing what you want and wanting what is best for you is the sign of a mature person who loves him or herself and is therefore capable of loving like an adult. Relationships in which rigid restrictions abound are like relationships between children and parents. One partner has the power and the other is intimidated into obeying. Excessive rules turn such relationships into a replay of the conflicts each partner experienced while growing up. They encourage rebellion rather than real growth. The mistrust and self-doubt that spawned these rules create a climate of continuing hurt and resentment, not a place of love.

If the freedom to choose is always available, real loyalty builds. How can you be disloyal to someone who is committed to your freedom?

And yet some compromises must always be made.

Just remember, if you ask your partner to give up part of his or her identity, friends, or sources of support, you also sacrifice part of your relationship. If you diminish your partner's strength, you also undermine his ability to give to you.

When a partner compromises his or her chances to grow, the issue will come back to haunt the relationship. A partner who feels incomplete can only love incompletely. So when a partner has second thoughts about making a compromise for the sake of your relationship, he must be permitted to express his doubts. And while expressing them may cause pain, hiding disappointments always makes matters worse. If the compromise causes pain, it's not the right solution and a new understanding needs to be reached. For a relationship to work, both partners must win.

WHAT CAN YOU COMPROMISE?

Some things are easy to compromise—taste in sports, food, vacations, and schedules. Be flexible. With other things—sexual needs, allocation of money, irritating habits, household chores, and parental responsibility—there will be discomfort and conflict. And on still others you can compromise only with great upheaval—your religious faith, racial boundaries, your friends or attachment to place, education, and life-style. But both partners have to make their needs known. If resistance is in the open, it can be resolved. Compromising to avoid conflict is harmful, not helpful, to a relationship. Be sincere.

WHAT YOU CANNOT COMPROMISE

Some things you cannot compromise without losing your self: your honesty and your sense of what is right or what is real. You cannot compromise your own happiness. You can never give away your right to defend yourself, to say what is best for you, to express your thoughts or your feelings. You have to be your best. You can never compromise your sense of fair play, your generosity, your innocence, or your natural affection for others. You have to live with yourself.

COMMITMENT ALWAYS REQUIRES SOME COMPROMISE

Your answers to the following questions will help you evaluate the compromises that may be necessary in order to make a lasting commitment to your relationship.

What will I absolutely *not* compromise?

Am I being asked to make that compromise in order to be with my partner?

What am I most afraid of losing by making a compromise?

What compromises would I like to reconsider?

Why did I agree to give my partner what I gave in the first place?

Am I asking my partner to make an unacceptable compromise?

How much of myself do I think I will have to give away to make this relationship work?

After that, will there be enough of me left, and enough freedom of choice, to enable me to make a genuine commitment to this relationship?

EXERCISE 3
Drafting a Commitment You Can Grow With

After you have answered all the questions in Exercises 1 and 2 and discussed them honestly with your partner, each of you should write a letter to the other in which you reflect upon the nature of the commitment you feel you are now willing to make to your relationship.

Indicate what you can commit to with an open heart, lovingly, and without reservation. Tell the truth. Do not let the passion you feel—either positive or negative—influence you to make outlandish concessions or statements. Passions change. You want your relationship to endure.

Indicate those things to which you would like to commit but still have reservations about.

Indicate the points on which you can compromise and those you cannot.

Indicate the compromises you need your partner to make.

Indicate the kind of commitment you need your partner to make.

Indicate the circumstances under which you will take back your commitment. That's right. You should and do have certain limits; define them.

Reread your letter and correct it so that it reflects your most sincere intention. Then exchange letters with your partner and discuss them together.

ROOM TO GROW

For many people, writing a letter is the only way they can put their feelings into words. That was true for two people whom I will call Tom and Elsa. Their twenty-three-year marriage had been tumultuous, punctuated by successes and failures in both of their careers

—his as a writer and hers as a lawyer and city councilwoman. Tom had supported Elsa through several political campaigns, including one unsuccessful attempt to run for the U.S. House of Representatives. Following her defeat she had become reclusive, stopped working entirely for several years, and totally rejected him. Tom had several affairs and a problem with alcohol that he finally controlled after going to AA. They endured four long separations, including one in which Tom moved in with a much younger woman.

But then, following the second anniversary of his being sober and Elsa's rejoining her law firm, they resumed a very tentative and guarded relationship. Both seemed to want something more, but somehow they couldn't talk about it. So they wrote letters to each other.

Dear Tom,

I am shaky and frightened as I write this. The last thing I want is to get trapped in the old cycle again. I want a new start this time and want you to promise to be there for me. No more placating me or lying to my face. That only worked when I didn't feel good about myself. I'm a lot better now, so you'll have to be better, too. I know this sounds like I am putting it all on you. I guess I am in a way, but some of the hurt of those lonely nights worrying about you still comes back to haunt me.

I know this ruminating on the old is a bad habit of mine and I am working hard on letting go of the past. I can see that you were right when you said that it was my unwillingness to take responsibility for my life that makes me look into the past seeking to blame others for my failures. I admit that freely now and I am willing to accept my own shortcomings. If I slip into the old ways I want you to let me know. Only when you do, this time, please show a little gentleness. You take such delight in showing me up. It's not good for my self-esteem. I know this is focusing on the past again, but I need to tell you how I need to be talked to. I want to listen to you. It's just that when you accuse I can't let anything in.

I need to know that I am as important to you as your work. I know writing is your life. I guess it's still hard to accept that sometimes I don't mean as much to you as your writing does.

I guess my insecurity in accepting this relates to what my work means to me. And I am sad to tell you that after much sober introspection I can admit I have used my work to get praise and public approval rather than to fulfill myself. I know I am often pretentious. I realize I can't find happiness playing to the crowd and that trying to please everyone is flirting with disaster. I just take rejection too seriously.

I am trying to tell you that I have a lot more love for myself and therefore I think I am capable of loving you like an adult. I am quite imperfect. Don't laugh. I know that you are always trying to tell me that, but now I admit it freely. I don't want to be perfect. I just want to feel I can be loved by you and that when we are having problems you won't become sarcastic or go running out looking for someone else.

I want to be my best living together with you this time, but not just for you, for me. I know I sometimes made myself appear weak and needy to keep you close. It was bad not because it didn't work, but because I convinced myself that I needed you in order to be me. I know better now.

So I guess this all means that I am willing to risk making another commitment to you. That means I will be open to discuss all of this and I want you to do the same. I love you, but only when you are sober. I need you, but only to complement me, not to sustain me. I need you to be there for me. I need you to notice that I am as important as anything you are writing. I am a good character with an interesting story line and I want to write a happy ending together.

Dear Elsa,

I need love and acceptance.

I cannot report in to you. I need to be free. I need you to be without suspicion. I need you to be able to accept that I am often preoccupied, that it's my process, and not take it personally.

I want us to maintain separate financial accounts as we have been doing. We'll both contribute equally to a house account and pay expenses out of that.

I need to be alone in the writing when I must.

I need to be able to work without being accused of neglecting you.

I realize this sounds a bit guarded, but I guess I've been hurt by your guilt-producing behavior in the past and still resent being manipulated by your helplessness. See, I guess I can hold on to the past, too. I will try not to encourage your desperation. I confess I know how to get to you.

I apologize for doing so.

If I can be free to do my work and love you as I love you—sometimes more, sometimes less—without you becoming frantic, I think I can commit to being together again.

I admit that I am frightened. I know how hard it is to change and admit that I probably won't, but I promise to be more open and let you in.

I'm willing to give it another try.

I must be nuts . . . (just kidding).

Elsa and Tom still had a lot of problems, but they got back together in a mutual commitment to try to work things out. Their letters to each other opened the door to that commitment. The letters you exchange with your own partner will help do the same thing. There will still be differences between you, but you can make a temporary commitment that reflects each of your aspirations at this moment in your relationship. Disputed issues can be discussed as you grow and the commitment becomes permanent. You need to accept your differences as part of the growth process.

In fact, the only commitment that you should ever make is an open-ended one. All agreements must be flexible and permit both partners to grow and choose freely. But if neither of you is ready at this moment to go forward together, then no agreement that tried to force that could possibly work. Remember, it takes a commitment to work out a commitment. So if you can find any ground of mutual agreement in your relationship, it's a positive sign. You've made a beginning.

CHAPTER THREE

Communication: Open Hearts, Open Minds

THERE IS nothing more painful than being unable to talk to the person you love. We are vulnerable—we need to share our fears and be reassured. When we hurt others we need to ask their forgiveness. When others hurt us we need to share our pain and come to an understanding that makes it safe for us to trust again. When we fail to communicate such feelings, minor hurts spur us to hurt the person we love. Our silent hurt turns into anger, and when we finally express it it seems exaggerated. It may make sense to us, but its exaggerated expression is obscure to others. In our pain we are often cruel, and even though our hurt is real, we become the villains in our relationships.

We need to share our love as well. Love that is not shown is not love. Sharing our hurt and negative feelings makes it possible to love again. In fact, the reason we love someone is because we can be ourselves with them without fear of rejection. Love is possible only when we can tell our partners how we really feel.

THE OPPRESSION OF A
SILENT PARTNER

People who fear rejection always seem to have excuses for not speaking what is in their heart.

It feels like punishment when a partner lapses into gloomy silence. Responding to the question "What's wrong?" by saying "Nothing" may reflect a wish to be drawn out, but instead it causes most people to recoil. Still, people who are desperate for love and attention often struggle endlessly to get silent partners to talk. Unfortunately, lavishing that kind of negative attention only gives the silent partner more power and little motivation to change. People who are silent have usually been hurt, but do not want to take responsibility for their anger. Their sullen silence plays on anxiety and the fear of rejection. It isolates their partners, conceals weakness, and avoids admitting one was wrong, angry, or hurt. This passive silence is a cowardly form of retaliation— anger that silent partners can easily deny. After all, they've said and done nothing.

Contrary to what we are taught, silence is not safe. Silence, in the face of a sincere appeal to know the truth, widens the gap between partners and undermines goodwill. Not paying attention, refusing to listen, and not asking obvious questions because you fear what will be uncovered are the worst forms of silence. Words designed to conceal, that make only casual contact, or that serve only to fill the space of television commercials convey little of the feeling between partners and, like a drug, deaden what transpires between them.

EMPTY WORDS

One can talk and say nothing. Conversations that are superficial, pretending everything is all right, are largely a waste of time. A life filled with them is boring and flat. Some couples only feel safe discussing the outside world. It is fine to debate this performer's skill and that author's cleverness, but these are impersonal exercises in small talk unless they are invested with a shared passion.

If your world is not made personal by sharing your feelings, your life might as well have been lived by someone else. You make your life your own by expressing your feelings. And if the words that flow between you and your partner are not invested with caring, nothing that happens between you really matters.

The language of the heart must be on the tongue. If your relationship is to work, it must find words. It takes a secure person to listen openly, take in what is said, and understand without interrupting. Asking irrelevant questions under the pretense of clarifying details is often just an attempt to stifle the other person or throw him off track. Insecure people are afraid to let others speak and prove them wrong or bad. They also try to show that others are wrong to feel the way they do, telling them they are too sensitive or are exaggerating. When self-worth is low, even the mildest criticism is devastating. It is no wonder that we are more likely to confide in people who are secure. Insecure partners find it easier to presume guilt in others than to accept their own shortcomings.

Without sharing, partners become entrenched and seek to justify their positions rather than forgive. The opposite of communicating is insisting that you are right. Communication between partners is not giving orders or making unilateral pronouncements. Communication, like love, requires equality and understanding.

WHAT ARE PEOPLE AFRAID TO SAY?

People are afraid of saying "I love you" only to hear "I don't care" in response.

They fear exposing their weakness by admitting their hurt.

They fear being abandoned if they express their anger.

They fear telling the truth and hurting their partner.

They fear revealing their ignorance, starting a fight, opening old wounds.

And yet ignorance comes from withholding inquiry, fights occur because consensus has not been reached, and old wounds fester because they have not been exposed. Learning to talk takes bravery and trust. The rewards are worth the risk.

SPEAKING THE SIMPLE TRUTH

Being with another person without being able to communicate feels more lonely than being by yourself. There is nothing worse than being unable to speak the painful feelings brimming within you. You want to be heard and you want the other person to know what you feel. You just don't want to be alone in your pain.

Listening is a simple gift and knowing you will always be heard the greatest treasure of a relationship. Without being heard there is no real understanding, no basis for growing together, and no acceptance. If your partner doesn't know your feelings, he doesn't really know you, and you lose a part of yourself whenever you are in his presence.

To be heard, speak from the heart. Speak directly, simply, straightforwardly, and honestly. Say what you mean, speak your words just as they are formed. Express the truth that lives within you. Once you have spoken be silent and listen carefully to your partner's response. Or, if there is silence, observe your partner—his reply may not be in words. You do not always need words to read each other's feelings.

If the other person reacts silently, share your impression of that silence in your own words. Observe your partner's pulling away, acting closed, or smiling. Don't analyze his actions. Speak only for yourself and share your response.

It is common, when expressing negative feelings, for obscure positive feelings to begin to surface as well. Express these feelings, even in the middle of your anger. Encouraging their reappearance is the reason you risk telling everything, the reason you and your partner are together in the first place. These positive feelings are proof that the other person matters to you. Letting the other person know that you still care or that you are suddenly feeling love or close again in the middle of a confrontation is a wonderful confirmation of the good in your relationship.

Nothing is as powerful a talisman as love appearing through anger.

If you share everything, in time your negative feelings will subside and your positive feelings will show themselves everywhere. You will no longer feel trapped in your partner's presence. Most of all, you will feel your freest being together.

The following exercises will help you understand the obstacles that block clear communication between you and your partner. Being together should not be an inhibition, but a relief. Only when partners can say everything on their minds to each other can they feel free being together.

Some of these exercises in communication involve close observation of momentary behavior and lend themselves to the use of a tape recorder in order to study the problem in depth. But you can also write your responses in a notebook or speak them aloud and share them later.

EXERCISE 1
What Matters to Us

This exercise is designed to help you understand what is important for you to share.

Part One: What I Need to Tell You
(To be completed individually by each partner.)

Imagine that it is 1940 and you and your partner are in France escaping from the invading German army. The two of you are separated and are racing in different directions to reach the border and safety. You hope to be reunited in a few weeks, but the situation is dangerous and there is a strong likelihood you may never see each other again. At great personal risk you have arranged what may be your last telephone call. Unfortunately, the connection is poor and you cannot hear your partner, so you have to do all the talking. Or, you are writing a letter and you have only a few minutes to tell your partner all of the important unfinished business of your life, to set matters straight, to clear up any remaining misunderstandings between you by saying what you really mean and intend.

Your relationship is in precisely the same condition that it is now.

Turn on your tape recorder or open your notebook. Pour out your heart and tell your partner what he or she needs to hear for you to be at peace.

Hurry!

Say exactly what comes into your mind. Do not edit. Just let it all flow.

When you have finished, answer the following questions. Be brief. Remember, this may be the last chance you have to speak to each other. Respond as honestly as possible.

What do you forgive?
What do you want forgiveness for?
What would you like to take back?
What does your relationship really mean to you?
What are the major problems in your relationship?
Why do you think you haven't been able to work out these problems?
What has kept you from saying all this before?

Sheila and Aaron were married at her insistence. She interpreted his passivity and quiet ways as gentleness and for many years denied that he was unresponsive. They went to several couple weekends in an unsuccessful attempt to get closer. Aaron was hard to reach and Sheila's speaking up for him and putting words in his mouth made it difficult for anyone else to get through. He would just agree. In spite of the frustration Sheila felt and the desperation that brought her into counseling, she would shower praise on Aaron merely for mumbling "yes" or nodding agreement with her, only to feel frustrated again when she got home. She was always on the verge of giving up her denial and accepting the problem, but backed away, answering her own questions with bland affirmations.

The following is a transcription of a part of Sheila's response to this exercise:

I can't think for a minute. This is odd. It's funny but talking into a tape recorder actually feels like one of our conversations. And you're not even here. I mean, you don't say very much. Wait. Am I doing this right? The directions say that the connection is bad and I can't hear you.

I can't hear you? I never can hear you. I never know if you really are listening to me or can hear me. I always feel as if the connection is broken. This is terrible. I always feel like I am alone and carrying on both sides of the conversation when we are together. Just like now. You don't even need to be there. Do you? I just heard myself say, "I know you agree."

The truth is I don't know if you agree. I don't know anything about what is going on inside you and I don't know what to tell you in this phone conversation. I'd have to begin by starting to share my whole life with you. I feel like I've been keeping company with myself.

I'm tired of it. I guess I really am. I feel so lonely with this tape recorder. I need a friend. I need someone to talk to me. You know I don't think you've ever asked me a personal question. This feels so weird. I don't even know where to begin.

If you complete this exercise in earnest, it can repay you with great insight. It will help you see your priorities and point out the risk you need to take to improve communications with your partner.

Part Two: The Obstacles That Get in Your Way

(To be completed together.)

When you and your partner have completed part one of this exercise, play back the tapes or read your letters to each other one at a time. Each partner should then comment on what he has just heard and take turns answering the following questions aloud:

How did it feel to put yourself in this imaginary position?

How did having a last chance to talk affect what you said? Did it make it harder or easier? Why?

Compare the way you just shared your ideas and feelings with the way you presently talk to each other.

49

How can you bring this urgency into your life now?

What keeps you from being as open in real life as you are on the tape or in the letter?

Why do you withhold information from your partner?

What are you most afraid of sharing? Why?

How do the two of you differ in the subjects you each chose to bring up in this exercise?

What did you learn about the issues, problems, or feelings you each consider important in your relationship?

Looking at your life together, what obstacles do you allow to inhibit you from speaking freely: schedules, fatigue, work?

What does it usually take to get the two of you to talk?

Is that what you want? What other arrangement for talking would please you?

What do you need to hear from your partner that would allow you to be more open, feel more at peace, or more loving?

How can you grant each other's request?

What risks must you take to keep your communication timely and alive?

Even if your partner has not taped a message or written a letter, you can ask him to listen to your tape or read your letter and then respond. Anything that opens communication is positive. Even if your partner just listens, it is a step forward. But ideally, you should exchange messages, for communication in a relationship must always be a two-way street.

EXERCISE 2
When Talking Is Difficult

When they were first engaged, Rita attributed Perry's silences to shyness and had accepted them because she too felt comfortable keeping to herself. After the children were born, Rita began to feel more and more isolated. Whenever she brought up problems with the children, Perry shrugged, saying it was her problem and usually left the room. When Rita asked about fixing the leaky roof, Perry would mumble something about her nagging and Rita would chastise herself for being pushy, finding it easier to blame herself than recognize Perry's problem. No matter what Rita wanted to discuss, Perry cut her off, making her discontent seem like a personal flaw. Rita swallowed her hurt.

A wonderful knitter, Rita managed to start a successful business selling sweaters at home. As her confidence grew, she began to see how she had been making excuses for Perry. She realized he was hiding his low self-esteem and that he felt inferior. Secretly he dreaded anyone pointing out his shortcomings.

Rita's exposure to a world of communicative people opened her eyes. Finally, she openly admitted that Perry's silence was bothering her and began to insist that he talk to her. Although at first he refused to open up, she persisted, telling him that she had outgrown the silences and needed human companionship. If she did not get it, she threatened to leave.

In a panic, Perry told Rita that he loved her and was afraid of losing her, but was even more terrified of being rejected if he expressed himself.

It was the first step. Rita had to make Perry's silence seem more dangerous to him than his talking. She professed her love for him, but reminded him that she had limits and needs of her own. Even though she insisted on his being open, he often slipped back into his silent ways and once she even left home for a few days to prove her point. The anger Perry showed when she returned was expressed freely, and they reunited, communicating openly for the first time.

There are times in every relationship when it is difficult to be heard, when the subject being discussed is frightening or causes embarrassment. No one likes to hear accusations or have his shortcomings pointed out. It's easy to shut the other person off when her style is offensive or his tone angry. Attacking the messenger for his message or misreading his intentions only block communications further.

If you persist, however, even closed people begin to open up, but the first emotions they express aren't always pleasant. Patience, love, and understanding of the silent partner's fears are essential.

Giving support and encouragement while stating your own needs works best.

The following exercise is designed to help open the lines of communication between you and your partner. Again, prepare a message for your partner, either by talking into a tape recorder, writing a letter, or simply sitting down and talking to each other in turn. If the silent partner is reluctant to participate, ask him or her just to listen to what you have to say.

Part One: Learning to Listen to Each Other

To begin your message, tell your partner you'd like to make it easier to talk. If you've been having difficulties communicating, it's likely he's heard that before, so you will have to be a little more convincing this time. Without blaming, say that you don't always understand what gets in the way of your speaking openly together and that you'd like to find out how each of you contributes to the problem.

Each of you should then make a list of at least three points you would like to discuss with the other—these can be complaints, plans, needs, or hurts. It's best to avoid subjects that are inflammatory, but don't make the list bland. There should be a little emotion when two people begin to open up to each other.

Now pick a place and set a time when the two of you can talk undisturbed. Do not set any rules about how to go about this. Your discussion should represent your usual style of interacting. Ask your partner to bring up the points on his list first. To keep the conversation moving, ask questions or make comments that will encourage your partner to open up. For example:

I don't understand. Please repeat that.

Why is that important to you?

What do you want? Why?

What would make you happy?

What do you want from me that will help you get what you want?

Notice that these remarks are all open-ended, motivated by love, not criticism. They are directed at understanding how your partner feels, what he believes, why he believes it, what he wants and why. Your goal is to understand.

Do not try to prove a point during this exercise. Your object is to create an atmosphere in which you and your partner can talk freely and openly, without feeling threatened. You may disagree with what your partner says, but do not allow yourself to be dragged into a fight. If you feel you are being pushed in that direction, say to yourself, "There is no way to win. I must observe how my partner pushes me, how I feel when he does, and remember what we were discussing at the time because that is what he is trying to avoid." Make a mental note of it and consider why it is threatening to him.

Part Two: What We Find Difficult to Hear and Why

If your discussion does become heated, you may feel timid about continuing immediately with this exercise, but it will be easier to understand each other's reluctance to talk about certain subjects if you proceed right away.

If you made a tape of your conversation, replay it. If you took notes, refer to them. Or simply remind your partner of the times either of you seemed to have difficulty getting through to each other, then ask him to answer the following questions aloud. Listen to your partner's response without commenting.

> What did you want me to hear that I didn't?
>
> How did you feel when I shut you off? Were you angry or threatened?
>
> Do you think I was avoiding your opinions or your feelings?
>
> Did I say something that made you uncomfortable? What?
>
> Do you feel that anything I said was wrong, unreasonable, or selfish and that it was useless to listen?

Again, the object of this exercise is not to start an argument with your partner, or prove that he is wrong and you are right. If you don't liked to be yelled at, corrected, accused, put down, or diminished, say so. But the most important thing to demonstrate is that you have heard what your partner has said, even if you disagree with it. You are willing to listen and you are trying to understand.

Generally, people have trouble listening when they are afraid. We tend to deny anything that makes us appear less lovable. We try to control a conversation when we fear the other person will reject us. We pretend not to care or listen when we are trying to avoid being vulnerable.

We are all protective when we don't feel good about ourselves. A loving relationship allows each partner to express self-doubt, offer reassurance, and accept hurt and anger as natural feelings without seeing them as a sign of betrayal.

COMMUNICATING SPONTANEOUSLY

Rick was a free spirit who married his wife, Ellen, after she got pregnant and refused an abortion. Though Rick loved Ellen, he found her to be closed and preoccupied. Whenever he tried to share his ideas and fantasies with her, she redirected the conversation to their budget, carpool problems, or social calendar. Rick appreciated her concern for these details and was secretly relieved that she assumed responsibility for them, but he missed the special intimacy of just talking about little things, of sharing ideas, feelings, and dreams. Ellen always had something more practical to discuss.

Rick felt trapped into being a father and provider. He yearned to be free and share his imagination and secret thoughts. To his surprise, he found himself becoming infatuated with other women. As soon as he was about to become sexually involved, however, he would break it off and move on. He loved the chase, the courting, but mostly the conversation.

Then one night he called Ellen, tearful and angry, explaining what he was feeling and the extent to which this inhibition of his spirit had driven him. He had just consummated an affair and he didn't even like the woman. Ellen had never valued openness, and only when she saw the danger in which her attitude placed her did she feel motivated to change.

Not everything that is communicated between partners needs to be important, but it's important that everything can be shared. Real intimacy is not necessarily heavy. At best, it is playful, innocent, and childlike, celebrating the openness between partners. It is wonderful to know that you can say anything you think or feel, and that you don't have to be anything but open to be loved.

EXERCISE 3
Sharing Your Inner Soul

There is in each of us a voice that speaks in the language of our most simple selves. It speaks without inhibition. The best relationships are those in which the partners feel free to express themselves in this voice. These are trusting relationships between people who accept themselves, for you cannot hear that voice unless you feel comfortable with yourself.

This inner voice tells you when a situation is dangerous and when it is safe to move forward. It tells you the truth, so you are limited by your own honesty in your ability to hear it and you are limited by your trust of the other person in your ability to speak it.

Learning to speak in your inner voice and encouraging your partner to speak in his should be your goal. Relating to others in this voice with the immediacy and openness of your first reaction makes you free. Using your inner voices to communicate with each other creates the greatest closeness in a relationship.

The following exercise will help you and your partner communicate your intimate selves.

Part One: What I Am Really Like
(To be completed individually by each partner.)

Each of you should answer the following questions privately. Write down the first answer that occurs to you. Do not edit. Be absolutely open. Be brief and proceed quickly.

What faults do I dislike most about myself?
If I could relive any moment of our relationship, which would I choose?

If I could erase any moment of our time together, which would it be?

What are the things about myself that make me feel childish?

When things aren't going well between me and my partner, what do I think about?

What am I most disappointed with in our relationship?

What am I most disappointed with in myself?

How do I feel I have let myself down most?

How have I let down my partner?

When do I feel most in love?

When do I feel like calling our relationship quits?

What silly things crossed my mind this week that I have not shared?

Part Two: How We Inhibit Each Other from Telling the Truth
(To be completed together.)

Have your partner ask you the same questions you just answered privately in part one of this exercise. Do not refer to your list when answering. Be spontaneous, and your partner should listen without comment to your answers.

As you respond, mention any inhibitions you feel about speaking in your partner's presence. Explain the risks you feel you are taking in being open and what you fear in being candid. Also, note any time you appeal to your partner for reassurance or approval, or look to see his reaction.

Note especially any hurdle you feel you have to overcome to answer honestly in your partner's presence. Describe this hesitation each time you encounter it. You may feel concern over hurting your partner. You may be ashamed. You may fear appearing bad, weak, petty, or wrong. Share these feelings.

Now ask your partner the same questions; he should also respond without referring to his written list, and you should be silent as he speaks. Once he has answered all of them, go through the list of questions with each other again, but this time read your written responses.

When you have finished, discuss whatever differences you recognized between the written answers and the verbal ones. To define the differences carefully, take turns answering the following questions:

Which responses were freer? Why?

What did you conceal or change? Why?

Were you seeking approval by altering some of your answers? Which ones?

How many of your true feelings did you change or edit out in your partner's presence? Why?

What did you try to protect?

Is there anyone with whom you are more open?

What is the difference between that relationship and this one?

What makes it easier to share with that person?

The way to become more spontaneous and open with each other is to tell the truth at all costs. It may be frightening at first, but raising the level of spontaneity, openness, and honesty in communicating with your partner always pays off by increasing the spontaneity, openness, and honesty of the expression of love.

Before you go on to the next exercise, is there anything you omitted that you feel more open about sharing now? Share it. If you can do that, you are taking the next step toward a committed relationship.

EXERCISE 4
Revealing Your Needs

The essence of communication is to be open with your needs. Some people respond to their partner's needs with an inborn intuitive ease. They follow their instincts and track their partner's yearnings with a loving eye. They are present for the other person and anticipate their needs.

Other partners are preoccupied—with self, financial concerns, the children, the house, the job—and are unaware of anything but their own immediate needs. It is easy to assume that such preoccupation stems from a lack of interest, especially if you present your needs at a time when your partner is absorbed by his own concerns. But when a person has passion for his own life and career, he generally has passion for the love of his life. Trust in that and make your needs clear.

If you want your needs to be met, you have to risk rejection.

What We Want—What We Need

In this exercise, each partner should ask the other to answer the following questions aloud, one question at a time. Do not comment until all the questions have been answered.

What fear do you keep from me?
What do you find difficult to tell me?
What do you want most from me?
What pain do you keep to yourself that you would like to share with me?
What do you secretly worry about the most?
What disappointments have you kept to yourself?
What can I do to make it easier for you to tell me these things?
When do you feel the most love for me?
When do your loving feelings fade?

No matter what response you and your partner have heard, tell yourselves that if it is a new truth, it has created new room to grow. The most precious gift in a relationship is knowing that you and your partner have no secrets from each other.

WALKING ON GLASS

At one time or another all of us conceal our critical thoughts and feelings from our partners because we don't want to harm them. Sometimes this happens when life's struggle seems to be overwhelming our partners, at times of depression and great upheaval. And yet these are the very times when our partners would benefit most from hearing exactly what we think and feel, even if it is critical of them. Having to humor your partner when you are confused and need to know the truth only compounds your pain with added confusion and distrust. Knowing the truth—even if it hurts—has the power to make any situation clear. Pain clearly seen is a great motivator.

If we are to be of any worth as friends and lovers, we must be able to count on each other to tell the truth, even if it is unflattering, even if it hurts. Honest relationships hold no surprises, no blind sides. Each partner knows he is imperfect, and that his partner knows it too and loves him in spite of it.

HELPFUL HINTS FOR IMPROVING COMMUNICATION

Risk Telling the Truth

If you can't tell your partner the truth, indicate that there is something you feel uncomfortable discussing. Sharing this awareness is a step toward open communication.

Anything you think you want to tell the other person should probably be shared.

Honesty can sometimes be cruel if it is not motivated by love.

If your communication is based on love, there is nothing you can't share.

If you can't share your hurt and anger, you can't share your love.

Observe your partner when he is listening to you. Actions may speak louder than words.

Don't give a speech. Resist making pronouncements and ultimatums.

Learn to Listen Openly

Take the time to hear, to allow what you have heard to sink in.

Wonder about what your partner is saying. Ask why you are being told these things in this way.

Does what your partner says hurt you? If so, share the reason why with your partner.

59

Have you heard this before? Why wasn't this settled earlier? What still needs to be expressed?

Resist the impulse to interrupt, but try to understand why you feel the way you do.

When you miss something, ask your partner to repeat it.

When you don't understand, ask your partner to explain. Giving your partner room to speak is often all that is needed to allow him to hear himself and rethink what he is saying.

Avoid being argumentative. If what your partner is saying is obviously false or farfetched, be patient and ask her to help you make sense of it.

Give your partner the benefit of the doubt. Assume that she believes what she is saying and is saying it with love.

The purpose of communication in a relationship is to discover what both partners need and want, what they feel and believe, and why. Only when both partners understand this can they find ways to give each other what they want.

Only then will they feel free and safe in making a strong commitment to the relationship.

Part Two

HOW WE FEEL

CHAPTER FOUR

Sharing Feelings —the Language of Love

LOVE IS the most vulnerable of all feelings; it is fleeting, capable of evaporating
like mist in the morning sun. A little insincerity makes us doubt it.
An argument over little things can threaten it. Sometimes it seems
much easier not to struggle to love another but to be content just
to love ourselves.

And yet we want to see ourselves and the world through a partner's loving eyes. We want a relationship in which love makes us
feel safe enough to be ourselves. Yet it is in such a setting of the
deepest togetherness that the greatest trespasses and injuries can
take place. While lovers' quarrels may seem silly to a bystander,
the betrayal of vulnerability and the depth of hurt that occur can be
overwhelming. What can be lost is more than trust in a lover, but
trust in love itself. It is no wonder we want to run when our love
turns sour—we want to preserve our belief in love.

Love is a state of heightened awareness and sensitivity. Lovers
see so much good in each other that they lower their usual protective barriers and open themselves to being hurt. They trust that no
one who loves them this deeply would ever hurt them, but it may
take only one incident to destroy this belief. When that happens,
their first instinct is to retaliate, to hurt their partner as they have
been hurt. Thus, a minor disagreement can escalate into a devastating battle.

Understanding and accepting each other takes time. At the beginning of a relationship you often feel as if you have known the other person forever, but you really haven't. Mostly, you know how the other person reacts when everything is going well. But his reactions under stress—when he is irritable, insecure, closed, and distrusting—reveal an entirely different side. It is difficult to overestimate the disappointment lovers feel when they first become aware of this. But with understanding and experience, you can withstand even the rockiest times in a relationship. For if love makes you vulnerable, it also makes you strong.

A LOVER'S QUARREL

Nearly ruined financially by his divorce, Edgar had sworn off women. He felt his wife never loved him and just wanted a free ride through life. So it was with great reluctance that he agreed to go on a Caribbean vacation with his friends. Perhaps it was the balmy evening and the palm trees, or maybe the moon over the water, but when he met Natalie at the welcoming beach party, he got lost in her eyes and they fell in love.

At first, Natalie, who until recently had been living with an abusive man, was skeptical, but she could not find one single negative point about Edgar. Her doubt, which seemed almost obligatory at first, simply dissolved by their second day together. Edgar extended his stay to match her reservation and they flew back to town on the same flight.

In the weeks that followed all they talked about was each other —that is, in the rare moments they were not together. They moved into Edgar's apartment at the end of the first month. They thought their happiness would never end.

Edgar felt generous and full being with Natalie and wanted to give her the best. In a moment of irresistible love, he promised her a new car. They set the next Saturday to pick it out. But Edgar was already strapped financially, and because his new relationship had taken his mind off work, his supervisor gave him a stern warning on Friday. It shook him, but as with the rest of his financial difficulties, he did not share it with Natalie. He did not want to dampen her spirits. He just wanted to make her happy.

Unknown to Edgar, Natalie, bubbling with anticipation, had been visiting automobile showrooms all week, and since Edgar said she could have whatever she wanted, she allowed the salesmen in a dozen dealerships to show her around. She had collected a stack of brochures and couldn't wait till Saturday morning to take test drives with Edgar.

But early Saturday morning Edgar awoke to the doorbell and was being served a summons to make payment for an expensive watch his ex-wife had charged to him out of spite. He called his wife's lawyer to say he wouldn't pay, but was coldly told that he'd go to jail if he didn't. He was also reminded that his alimony payment was late. Furious, feeling cheated, and doubting his lovability and financial stability, he sat down to a beautiful breakfast Natalie had just prepared. Natalie took out a brochure, and full of innocence and anticipated gratitude, said, "You can get me the Porsche."

Edgar, who had counted on Natalie for his strength in a time of adversity, stood up, ripped the brochure to shreds, and knocked the breakfast dishes to the floor. "You women are all alike," he shouted. "Out for all you can get."

Natalie was stunned. She couldn't believe what was happening and found herself calling Edgar the same names she had called her abusive boyfriend. He called her even more hurtful names, and for every moment they fought, each saw more terrible traits appearing in the other until, finally, Natalie burst into tears and Edgar stormed out of the apartment.

She was packing when he returned, and only then did Edgar begin to confide his stress over his financial concerns. Natalie said she knew he was worried about something but had been afraid to ask because she wanted everything to be perfect. They began to open to each other's love again and came to terms with the fact that they were both only human. Because they loved each other, they knew they could share their weaknesses as well as their strengths.

Natalie learned that Edgar was no less deserving of her love because he was not perfect. And they both discovered an equally important truth: Since love does not flow freely again until a threat is removed, the pain expressed, and the anger resolved, they had to learn to love each other even more deeply for whatever kindnesses they gave when settling their differences and to accept and forgive without recrimination.

THE IMPORTANCE OF
EXPRESSING FEELINGS

Disagreements occur in the most loving relationships. If the partners do not resolve their negative feelings completely, the love
between them gradually erodes. Even if they promise to be better,
their hidden feelings will not let them keep the peace. Saying "I'm
sorry" means nothing unless the injury is understood as well as
admitted. Unresolved hurt and anger only lie in wait for trivial
incidents to trigger them into awareness again. This produces emotional brittleness, fosters distrust, and shatters the vulnerability on
which the innocence of love depends.

If you do not understand how and why you hurt each other, you
are not free to love. But what really happens when people hurt each
other? What are the dynamics of emotions? How do feelings work?
What do they mean? A greater understanding of your feelings will
go a long way toward making your relationship flow more
smoothly.

Although people find it difficult to identify their emotions in the
heat of the moment, the feelings felt are easy to understand. A
feeling is the direct response to something that is said or happens
to you. You do not *think* about this response, it just happens. And
it is always your most truthful reaction.

When feelings are not expressed the moment they first occur,
they must be concealed and so they immediately become more
complex and difficult to understand. Withholding both positive
and negative feelings distorts our view of the world and isolates us
from others. When our feelings are not shared, we feel lonely and
resentful.

When we are open with our feelings we are willing to share
ourselves with the world as we find it. When we withhold our
feelings because we are angry, in pain, or fearful of expressing
them, we begin to search for evidence that justifies our reaction.
Our withheld feelings lead us to become prejudicial, to believe that
the world is against us, and to back up our case with slanted reasoning. When we hold in feelings, they become blown out of proportion and lose their relationship to the events that caused them.

Each time we do this it becomes more difficult for us to let go and express our true feelings. We want to be right and the other person wrong. So we continue to react to the negative past rather than be open to the present.

When we hold in feelings, we distort the world around us. We really do not believe what we profess to be true and so we doubt our judgment. We make villains out of the people we love and begin to lose belief in ourselves as well. We become more interested in being right than in making peace. Although we hold feelings back to stay in control, doing so makes us feel fragile and at risk of going out of control. Our anger builds. We struggle to keep from exploding. We take it out on innocent people. We are easily triggered by minor frustrations.

Expressing both positive and negative feelings openly is the most important business of a relationship. How receptive your relationship is to sharing emotions determines its strength and worth. Everything else is a distant second.

Without the expression of feelings, relationships crumble, sex becomes mechanical, giving becomes manipulation, hurts become grudges, and love becomes loathing.

UNDERSTANDING FEELINGS— THE KEY TO UNDERSTANDING EACH OTHER

The Feeling Cycle

It is impossible to understand your partner or to be truly intimate without caring about his or her feelings.

There are two kinds of feelings: positive and negative.

Positive feelings—love and joy—represent the honest fulfillment of real needs. They are not a problem unless they are inappropriate —for example, if you feel sad when something good happens to you.

All negative feelings are derived from pain. All pain comes from a loss or injury. The age of the pain often determines the depth and intensity of negative feelings.

Anxiety

Anxiety is pain in the future, the expectation of loss or injury.

It includes all forms and degrees of fear and worry whether real or imagined, remembered or anticipated. It ranges in intensity from wondering if you heard the phone ring to paralyzing feelings of panic, from alertness to terror.

You cope with anxiety by asking yourself what you are afraid of losing and why it is important to you. Then you take steps to prevent the loss to minimize your pain. In this way anxiety is seen as a warning. You do not run from it but face it openly, assessing your strengths and weaknesses to determine whether you should put up a struggle or save your strength for a better moment. Ignoring anxiety is similar to ignoring the smell of smoke in your house. Anxiety requires open and honest evaluation. It always gets worse when you try to hide from it. If there is something about your relationship that you fear will cause you loss or injury, air your anxieties as soon as possible.

Hurt

Hurt is pain in the present, the experience of loss or injury caused by something that is happening now.

Hurt feels like sadness, being depleted or disappointed. Its intensity depends upon how seriously you feel you have been hurt.

You cope with hurt by expressing the pain to whoever caused it as soon as possible. It's always best to be straightforward and direct. If you are afraid to tell your partner that he hurt you for fear that he won't take you seriously or that he doesn't care about your feelings, you need to ask yourself why you are involved with someone who does not care about you. If a person does not care about his own feelings, he cannot care about anyone else's. If a person doesn't care about *your* feelings, he doesn't care about you. If you conceal your hurt because you do not want to reveal your vulnerability, your pride is in the way of your happiness. Don't pretend you are above feeling hurt—you'll only lose touch with yourself. Be honest. If the source of your hurt is your own disappointment in yourself, deal with it by admitting your shortcomings and seek to improve yourself.

68

As soon as you've been hurt in some way by your partner, say, "Ouch. It hurt when you did/said that. I'm not happy about it."

If your partner ignores you, say, "I want you to know you just hurt my feelings."

If your partner starts to make excuses or still ignores you, say, "Look, I'm the one who has been hurt. A simple acknowledgment of my hurt and 'I'm sorry' will settle this."

If your partner refuses, tell him you resent being hurt and it makes you angry to be treated like that.

If your partner says, "I'm sorry," tell him you're glad you could express your hurt openly and then let go of it.

Don't be deceived by the obviousness of this example. You'll have all you can do to keep it in mind the next time you are hurt.

People who are unable to cope with a great loss sometimes keep their hurt alive for years and feel it a little bit at a time. This is characteristic of anniversary reactions when, on the date or season of a loss, people mourn the residual part of the loss for which they still haven't fully grieved.

Keeping hurt alive by wallowing in self-pity is a self-destructive act that eventually alienates those who love you. The person who will not let go of a hurt often uses his suffering as a way of punishing others. If you find that you are feeling sorry for yourself, just admit it matter-of-factly and decide to stop. Even if that seems oversimplistic, it is the necessary next step to feeling better. You can postpone or prolong the moment when you decide to let go of your hurt. You can wait for therapy or revenge, but you will still have to come to the same decision. Decide to be your best, to forgive, and move on.

Anger

Anger is pain in the past, the resentment over a loss or over having been hurt. The wish to hurt back is always implied.

The mildest form of anger is irritation, the most extreme is rage. Anger is usually directed toward the person who has caused you injury. However, when its direct expression is blocked, anger leaks out and attaches itself to innocent activities, investing them with negative energy. Closing a car door can become an angry slam, good nature fades as irritability replaces patience. Voices are raised, sarcasm increases, and the family dog goes into hiding. To the person with a chip on his shoulder, retaliation feels justified, even deserved, since everyone seems short with him.

To cope with angry feelings, express the hurt that underlies them to the person who caused you injury. Explain that you resent being hurt. You do not need to blow up. Just indicate that you feel hurt and why. You can talk to the person who hurt you face-to-face or over the telephone, or you can write. You can pretend that the person is sitting in a chair and shout what you feel. You can throw darts at a picture of the person or write his name on a wall and throw stones at it. Anything that will mobilize your anger and start its outward expression helps. The cycle of feeling hurt, holding in the anger, and feeling remorse must be broken. Again, figuratively saying "Ouch" is the first step.

Roland married Gretchen when he graduated from optometry school. He had failed to get into medical school and whenever tight finances were a problem, he would begin to apologize for not being a more aggressive businessman. Gretchen always soothed him. She taught modern dance and was a highly expressive person. They had children and she contributed her earnings to the family and was everyone's emotional support. Roland could not stand to be criticized or to have anyone think he was inadequate. In the early years of their marriage, Gretchen easily forgave his business failures and aloofness, but she swallowed a lot of anger in order to do so.

Not surprisingly, the bright fire that had been their mutual attraction began to cool. Their growing children took most of Gretchen's attention and Roland resented this. His defensiveness also drained her energy. Whenever she expressed her hurt, Roland became deeply wounded and used his unrelenting pain and guilt as a shield, thus inhibiting her further. No matter how much Gretchen had been hurt, Roland's painful reaction to her anger always outdid her and stopped her in her tracks.

When Gretchen discovered that Roland was having an affair she confronted him, and Roland became severely depressed on the spot. When she persisted in expressing her anger, Roland started talking about suicide. Stunned by the reality she had not fully grasped until that moment, Gretchen exploded, "You're not the one who's been injured. I am! I'm not your mother. I'm your wife. All you do is take from me, and when I catch you cheating on me, you play for my sympathy. I have a right to be angry. You've been a creep, pretending to be fragile and despairing all these years just to cover your unfaithful escapades. Let me get angry. You've hurt me!"

"It doesn't mean I'm bad," Roland protested, not hearing her at all.

"No, it just makes it impossible for me to love you."

"That's why I had the affair," Roland explained. "I never felt you really cared."

"No one can love you enough to make you feel good about yourself," Gretchen said. "That's not the point. You want to have your girlfriends, be a sloppy businessman, leave all the responsibility to me, and then *you* feel hurt because I don't approve of your hurting me. The only way I can win is to lose. I'm leaving."

"It'll kill me," said Roland.

Gretchen suddenly started to laugh at the ridiculousness of it all and especially her own gullibility. For the first time in years, she felt relief.

Bottling up your partner's anger will undermine the love in your relationship.

Guilt

Guilt is the pain of unexpressed anger.

Again, to contain anger one must block its expression and redirect it inward. Such anger has no place else to go. Often we try to handle our anger mentally by building fantasies of vengeance. But such gruesome thoughts cause us to lose faith in our own goodness. Our thoughts and dreams become filled with our repressed emotion. Our sleep becomes troubled and we feel burdened. The anger festers there, hurting us.

Guilt is being angry with yourself. Sometimes guilt feelings are justified—when you hurt others or have broken the law. Should your anger lead you to hurt innocent people unintentionally, it reinforces your belief that you are bad.

Coping with guilt requires believing on faith that you are a good person. Next, you need to admit that you feel angry because you were injured. As always, the critical step is to make the person who hurt you aware of your feelings. Merely saying "I'm angry with you for hurting my feelings" will do wonders. When people have held in anger for a long time they fear that expressing any part of it will prove to the world they are bad. Try to remember that everyone makes mistakes. Everyone deserves a second chance. You're only human. You still need to grow. Admit whatever role you played in what went wrong and move on. Make amends, repair hurts, seek and grant forgiveness. To begin with, risk being open with your hurt and let go of it. It will help the most.

Depression

Depression is a chronic pattern of reacting to all hurt by holding it inside.

Since anger is an active feeling that naturally seeks expression, people erect defensive barriers to contain it. Thus, holding in anger depletes your energy, leaving less to activate your belief in yourself, to do positive work, or energize your body. This depletion of energy is called depression.

Depression ranges from a passing discouragement over a specific and recent loss to a chronic immobility that is the result of distant and obscure events. The depressed person holds in the smallest hurts. Life hardly feels worth living to a person bursting with anger.

Coping with depression is similar to dealing with guilt. It is important to realize that your anger results from being hurt. What depression teaches you is to say how you feel whenever you are hurt. Be aware that as you begin to express your current feelings, past feelings may also come to the surface, making your expression seem a bit exaggerated. Even so, persist in letting your partner know how you feel so you can be free to be yourself again.

Your relationship is the best place to risk being open with your feelings because, more than anyone else, your partner should care about your feelings. Every good relationship is "therapeutic" in that partners help each other deal with the disappointments of life in the belief that the good that is still to be experienced together is worth it. Understanding feelings is a prerequisite to mastering the expression of love. Coping with our losses together frees us to give.

DEFENSES AGAINST THE PAIN
OF LOSS

The losses that cause pain fall into clearly defined categories.

The loss of love: This is the loss of belief in your lovability and includes the loss of health, life or limb, or the loss of your worth or goodness. It also includes the loss of someone you love or the loss of someone whose love you need in order to feel lovable.

The loss of control: This includes the loss of power, position, influence, money, potency, or strength.

The loss of esteem: This includes the loss of looks or the ability to perform and the loss of rank or reputation.

Defenses act as buffers between a loss and our fullest realization and acceptance of it. They allow time for us to adjust to a painful reality. To accept a loss and cope with the pain we must eventually give up the defense and feel the pain fully. We mourn a loss by feeling the hurt, expressing our resentment and regrets, accepting our lot and moving on.

Denial: The first defense against loss, especially rejection, abandonment, and the loss of love, is denial. When we suffer such a loss we say, "No. It can't be." Gradually this denial subsides and we allow bits and pieces of the pain to filter in as we try to comprehend our hurt.

Denial is not a subtle defense. We employ it to block out the unthinkable. A good example is when you discover that your partner is having an affair and carry on as if nothing has happened. The hurt festers beneath the surface, building into anger and leading you to fear you will lose control of your emotions. But since you are denying the truth, you also have a fear of the unknown. Denial usually gives way to an admission of the facts—then the pain slowly settles in on us. You feel sadder, but more open. When denial has passed, you can direct your anger at your partner instead of holding it in. Your fear of the unknown disappears.

Although everyone uses denial to soften the blow of an overwhelming loss, it is the defense most commonly used by dependent people. They feel too helpless to deal with a loss of love so they

deny that it is happening. This explains why some dependent partners will put up with outlandish abuse rather than face the truth
and risk taking action that might result in their being on their own.
People who use denial don't want to be abandoned. They need to
realize that they must be independent, must grow and risk if they
are to enter into a relationship as anyone's equal.

Excuses: Excuses describe a broad class of intellectual defenses.
Whenever we rationalize, justify, or blame others for our actions
or losses, we are using excuses and are *measuring* a loss rather than
feeling it. Much of the fighting over money that characterizes bitter
divorces is an attempt to express anger at the spouse rather than
to resolve one's own hurt. The sadness and hurt still seek expression, and to release these feelings, the partners must admit that
they still care for each other. Unfortunately, this is often too vulnerable a position, so the partners stay far removed from their
feelings and humanness. It is no surprise that so many divorces are
cruel.

Intellectual defenses are used to deal with the loss of control.
Controlling partners are most apt to use excuses to explain their
shortcomings. They give every reason imaginable for hurting their
mates, but won't admit that they did so in anger. Controlling
partners blame the other person in their relationships. Rather than
accept responsibility for their disappointments, they are motivated
to hold grudges, act punitively, and use the silent treatment while
nurturing their resentment. They frequently blame their failures on
their partner's lack of support or encouragement. They feel unappreciated, claim they are only working for their mate's happiness,
and continually seek indulgences that relieve them of the need to
be companionable and friendly. This attitude of self-importance
isolates and alienates them further. They need to learn that their
partner deserves to be forgiven and that it's possible for their partner to hurt them and still be a good person. Unfortunately, those
who use intellectual defenses are generally critical and accuse their
partners of being unreasonably angry no matter how they have
mistreated them. Because they seldom admit they are wrong, they
cannot accept others' anger as making sense.

Blaming others for your hurt suggests you are powerless. You
can only fix the mistakes you admit you made. You don't have to

be perfect to be good, but you have to admit your shortcomings to grow.

Pretending: Pretending is a defense to deal with a loss of self-worth or self-esteem.

To save face, competitive people pretend they don't care. By pretending they didn't really try or weren't really interested, they seek to avoid anything that suggests they are not deserving or good enough. By pretending, they postpone judgment about their performance or true worth. Partners pretend they don't care anymore to avoid dealing with rejection. They also pretend they didn't give their best effort on the job in order to avoid having to take their failures seriously. They say things like, "It doesn't matter if you apologize," or "So what, I don't love you anymore," or "So you're having an affair. I'm glad someone finds you attractive," rather than face a hurt that implies they are not loved as they would like to be.

Partners who pretend can be difficult to live with. Just when you think they are about to admit that their feelings have been hurt, they pull away and don't seem to care. Or when you tell them they have hurt your feelings, they take your comment as an attack on them.

It would be easy to admit that you cared if you knew the other person felt the same way. It would be easy to accept your shortcomings if you really believed in yourself.

I use the term "emotional debt" to describe any incompletely expressed hurt. Whenever you withhold your feelings you are in debt to your emotions and limited in your ability to be free. The defenses that guard your negative feelings also imprison your spontaneity. You fear that if you were open, you would spill your secret hurt. Still, little fragments of hurt always break through like an overdue bill, reminding you of your emotional debt.

You need to free yourself to live at your best just as you are. The way to resolve emotional debt is always the same: express your hurt honestly to the person who caused you pain. The shorter the time between your injury and the expressing of your pain, the greater your peace of mind. Arguments will be fewer and shorter, and your relationship will be more loving. When one partner is in emotional debt, the entire relationship is imprisoned.

LEARNING TO SHARE FEELINGS

If your partner is right for you, learning to express your emotions will do wonders to stimulate feelings of love and spontaneity. When two people share their feelings, they build trust. When partners conceal their emotions, fear of the unknown grows, creating suspicion and doubt that tarnishes what's good between them.

The following exercises will help the truth flow between you and your partner. They will enhance intimacy and encourage openness in your relationship.

EXERCISE 1
Understanding What I Feel

Understanding others requires understanding yourself. The defenses that insulate you from your negative feelings also limit your ability to identify with others. Your capacity to empathize with your partner is the measure of the depth and meaning of your relationship.

The first step in sharing feelings with your partner is to understand what *you* feel and why.

A Feeling Diary
(To be completed individually by each partner.)

For the next week, you and your partner should each carry a small notebook in which you record your feelings. Although you can collect your feelings for three or four days to do this exercise, a full week—including work and leisure time—will give a more accurate picture of your emotional life. You should both start on the same day so you can compare how you react to the same events. The ideal diary starts on Monday. Use a new page for each day, and every time you have a positive or negative feeling—especially about your partner or your relationship, but also about anything you consider important—enter it into your notebook. For all entries note the date, day of the week, the time, and place. Then use the following guide to identify your feelings.

Negative Feelings:

Fear: Expecting injury or loss

Hurt: The sadness of being injured

Anger: Resentment over being hurt

Guilt: Anger for yourself or remorse for hurting another

Depression: Feeling depleted and hopeless

For each feeling you record in your diary consider:

What triggered your feeling? An event? A memory? Someone's actions or failure to act? Your performance? What were you doing or what was said when the feeling started?

What is the age of the feeling? Was it old, new, recurring? Did it remind you of anything? What?

What did you do about the feeling?

What could you have done? Why didn't you?

How did you express the feeling? Completely, partially? Did you hold it in? Bury it in work? Take it out on someone else? Drink, take a drug, eat, go shopping, work out, cheat, or feel sorry for yourself? Did you blame someone, make excuses for their action, deny your hurt, or pretend you just didn't care?

How long did the feeling last?

Did you feel blocked in expressing the feeling? Why? Tell your diary all about it.

Positive Feelings: You feel love, happiness, and joy when your real needs are honestly met. In noting your positive feelings in your diary, ask yourself:

What needs were met? How?

How could you have enhanced your feeling of pleasure?

Did anything interfere with your enjoyment? What got in your way and what could you have done about it?

Analyzing Your Own Feelings

After you have completed your diary, reread each day's entry, feeling by feeling, as curiously as if you had found a stranger's notebook. As you do, answer the following:

What kind of a person is this?

What is troubling this person?

What negative feelings recur?

What are the sources of this person's pain?

What is this person doing about the things that hurt him?

What would he like to do?

What stops him?

Is this person doing enough of what makes him or her happy?
Why not?

Also consider the following:

How truthful were you in keeping the diary?

What did you change or omit and why?

In the margin, write what you *really* felt but don't erase your original comment.

Can you see any pattern to these changes?

When and why do you distort by denying, making excuses, or pretending?

Looking back on your diaries, how much of your hurt is still unexpressed?

What were you afraid of sharing?

What have you held back?

Sharing Your Diaries

After you have reviewed your diary, meet with your partner to go through your diaries together.

Take turns reading aloud from your diaries, one day at a time. As you read, feel free to explain or elaborate on your experience. If you have questions, ask your partner to expand on his report. Use the following questions as a guide.

What apprehension or discomfort do you feel in sharing your diary?

As you read through each day, how do the two of you differ

in what you feel and how you express it, especially when you share a highly emotional event?

How quickly do each of you get over a feeling? Does a feeling linger and seek expression throughout the day or is it over once you've acknowledged it? Is there a tendency to exaggerate, play down a situation, not care about or ignore a problem?

When you have a bad day, what feeling dominates? How open are each of you in admitting hurt, anger, responsibility, and regret? Does either of you bear a grudge, become silent, act overly sensitive or feel sorry for yourself?

After you have gone through your diaries together, each partner should share his understanding of what hurts the other and try to correct whatever misunderstandings or distortions still exist.

Remember, the object is to get to know each other through learning what each of you feels.

Painful Subjects

Unresolved Feelings: Are there unresolved or inhibited feelings in your relationship?

Inhibited feelings become the silent sponsors of negative attitudes. Because the events that caused these feelings are often remote, these attitudes seem irrational. They complicate our understanding of present events. People suffer over these past hurts because they don't believe in themselves enough to be open.

If your fear of hurting your partner keeps you from being honest, you are making your partner's feelings more important than your own. That is a high price to pay for peace. If you or your partner inhibit the discussion of any particular subject, your relationship is confining and you run the risk of starting a war just by being open.

Taboos: Are there issues that are forbidden to be mentioned in your relationship? What happens when you try to talk about them? Most such taboos are one-sided. Compliance is enforced by intimidation: one partner acting irrational, exploding, or retaliating whenever a particular subject is brought up. A taboo demands that you share your partner's avoidance of a subject he perceives as threatening even though you may not share his insecurity.

Trying to enforce a taboo is a dangerous tactic because it compromises the other partner's right to be himself. This restriction of freedom is a bigger issue than any subject you're trying to avoid because it weakens the relationship.

Some typical taboo subjects:

Avoiding admitting that a friend, relative, or child has problems—a touchy subject especially when the child is from a previous marriage.

Refusing to admit one has been injured as a way to avoid confronting others or testing how much others really care.

Avoiding admitting that one is being used or manipulated in a relationship.

Discussing or admitting a partner's addictive behavior, alcohol or drug abuse, compulsive gambling, eating, or shopping.

Money problems, including refusing to accept responsibility for financial failure, especially when a partner's strength in the relationship depends on it.

Emotional instability.

Neatness and hygiene.

Sex.

In discussing your diaries, consider the emotions and subjects you and your partner try to avoid. It's important because they reveal your vulnerabilities. Then ask each other the following questions:

Why do you fear expressing your negative—or positive—feelings openly about any subject?

How does this affect the way you feel about me?

How does this affect the way you feel about yourself?

Why are you willing to put up with such avoidance?

EXERCISE 2
Sharing Your Concerns and Your Affection

What's the point of living together if you don't know what your partner is concerned about? It's easy to misinterpret feelings when you don't know their source. When a subject is taboo, the frustration created finds expression elsewhere, distorting feelings and making other hurts seem exaggerated. This exercise is designed to make you aware of these distortions so you can solve the underlying problems more directly.

Each partner should make a list of *all* the problems he or she can think of that matter or cause discomfort—whether they originate in your relationship or elsewhere. Write each problem on a separate card and set aside a time to meet to share them with your partner. Each should arrange his cards in order of importance and place them in two columns side by side: his and hers.

Start with the first card in your column and take turns, one card at a time, explaining to your partner the pain or loss that each problem causes you. Say why each issue is important and what it means to you. Share the feelings you have about it, even if they seem small or petty. If you have feelings you haven't expressed before, tell why you held them in. Then indicate what you would like your partner to do about this problem.

When it is your turn to listen, do not argue or offer any rebuttal. If your partner says a particular issue is painful, accept it without question. Listen and indicate that you understand. If you do not, ask your partner to explain; after listening, indicate what you can do to help make the situation better.

Go through the entire pile of cards in this manner. Then each of you should take a few minutes to summarize what you know about your partner that you hadn't realized before. What is your partner concerned with most? What does that tell you about him? What concerns do you share? What are you willing to do to lessen your partner's hurt? How can you resolve the concerns that bother each other?

Making the Problem Clear Is Part of the Solution

Bert and Carol had been drifting apart. Bert seemed more involved with his work and Carol had lapsed into complaining. They completed the exercise above; here's what they came up with.

81

Bert's list:

She spends money unnecessarily.
She's always too tired for sex.
She never listens to my problems.
Worrying about layoffs in my department.
Behind in tax payments.
Her mother still makes trouble.
The boss is not aware of my contribution.
Do I need to learn computers?
Sometimes I want to start over, be single, have no responsibilities.
She's too busy to cook.
I need a real vacation.
Making these cards depresses me. I want to be like we were.
We need more time together.
All the financial burden is mine. I need her help.
Carol never asks how I feel.

Carol's list:

We need a burglar alarm!
The baby's room needs weatherstripping.
The bedroom window won't open.
The smoke detectors need to be upgraded.
He's too busy to talk.
He's demanding sexually.
I feel inferior to my friends.
I hate working part-time; filing is boring.
My contribution around the house is not appreciated.
I get very little help with the house.
My mother is always negative, finding fault with me.
My car is a junkbox.
I want more romance.
We hardly go out.
He watches too much TV.

After sharing their lists, Bert and Carol were both surprised to discover how many of their complaints shared the same root. They realized that they were expecting the other to read their mind. Bert saw that Carol felt insecure and that he did not take her seriously enough. Carol was surprised that Bert was unsure of himself and that she could make a positive contribution to his life by organizing their home finances better. Carol decided to look for a better job and Bert decided to take advantage of the company's educational program, increasing his skills and lowering his anxiety about success. They also decided to spend more time together. The changes they made were painless and positive, and their relationship grew stronger.

Looking at your problems and sharing them with your partner produces powerful results. The obvious is sometimes hardest to see. But in solving the problem, do not promise to do anything you do not want to do. Do not withhold anything out of spite. Be as generous as you can, but give without any expectation of getting anything in return.

It is important for you to understand the pain each of you feels and what you are willing to do to help solve each problem. There is great comfort in accepting reality. If you know the limits of each other's giving, you stand the best chance at arriving at a solution that works and lasts. You need to have a clear picture of what can and cannot be changed so you can make decisions based on what is real. It's much better to *know* that you are all alone and have to solve a problem by yourself than to be continually disappointed when expected help is not there. At least when you know it is up to you, you can motivate yourself and do what you must. The solutions that are most likely to fall apart are those insincere concessions that are made to placate or manipulate a partner just to silence his complaints. What you've got in your relationship is what you've got. Understand and accept it.

Note: Exercise 2 can be repeated as often as you like. It can also be used to assess all of the positive parts of your relationship. Just make a list of traits, actions, or help that you appreciate, and share them in the same way.

EXERCISE 3
The Aftermath of an Argument

This exercise is designed to help you understand in greater detail how each of you reacts after a disagreement. If you are aware of the emotional effect you have on each other, you will be clearer when you disagree and less likely to hurt each other needlessly.

You need to agree in advance that the next time you argue, you will both keep a feeling diary for at least one full day and later review it together.

Charting the Injury

When you have a conflict, follow the directions in Exercise 1 on page 76 for recording your responses in a diary. Be sure to note the time of day for each entry and indicate how long your emotional response lasted. In addition, make an entry for each of the following reactions:

Whenever you thought about the other person. Indicate what you felt or yearned for.

Whenever you felt remorse. Describe in detail what you regretted.

Whenever you considered getting even or hurting back.

Whenever you discussed the problem with another person. Indicate what you said and to whom. The details are not as important as the point you were trying to make. What were you looking for: sympathy, understanding, comfort, support of your position? Did this sharing help?

Whenever you felt disheartened.

Also include times when you had romantic thoughts for your partner again. Sometimes people become more sexual after an argument, especially if a blocked emotion has been released. But sex can also be used to manipulate. Sometimes partners wishing to end hostilities will try to make repairs erotically before a real understanding is reached. This reassures them that love is still there. Even if that happens, you still have to resolve the disagreement.

84

Also, share expressions of avoidance, such as the wish to run away, call an old lover, or live alone.

Indicate whenever your train of thought was broken, your work interrupted, or your mood sullen or irritable because you were preoccupied with the disagreement. Just be sure you don't exaggerate a hurt to make your partner feel guilty.

Estimate the total amount of time this conflict took out of the twenty-four hours covered by the diary.

Reviewing the Damage

Share your diary with your partner the day after you have had a serious disagreement. Read your diaries to each other one at a time without interruption. Then, when you're finished, take turns answering the following questions:

Are you surprised about the way you reacted? At the way your partner reacted?

Are you still feeling hurt?

Are you still bearing a grudge?

Are you still denying your pain, making excuses for your actions, or pretending not to care?

What new understanding did your partner's diary give you?

What did you learn about your partner's style of dealing with problems?

Is there any point your partner has not yet understood about your reaction? Make it clear now.

What irrational behavior can you admit to now? What concessions can you make?

What specifically did your partner say to trigger your anger?

What could you have done to decrease your own or your partner's suffering? (Could you have called, said you were sorry, admitted something you previously denied? What kept you from doing so? If you are like the rest of us, the reason you withheld a comforting hand was that you were still hurt.)

You need to assume you still love each other. If you know your partner is suffering and has difficulty expressing feelings, consider the impact that a telephone call, a kind word, or a hug will have in relieving the stress. Just show that you believe in your love and that you care enough to maintain contact. That, alone, is often enough to help resolve the disagreement between you and put your relationship back on an even keel.

Remember that while neither partner can possibly know everything the other feels or thinks, the gap in this understanding defines the distance between them. Closing this gap by trust and sharing is the rightful goal of both partners and the source of the growing love between them.

LET YOUR DIARY MAKE SENSE OF YOUR LIFE

Christopher's son Glen was a high school dropout who did odd jobs, but mostly hung around the house. Christopher felt guilty about leaving Glen when he divorced. So, in an attempt to make up for the disrupting effect his divorce had had on his son, Christopher welcomed Glen into his new home with open arms. Although Glen was a sweet and charming boy, he was also lazy and used his father's guilt to manipulate him to get a car and expensive audio equipment. Glen spent most of the day in his room with the stereo blaring. His life was at a standstill.

After a heated confrontation during which Jessica, who had been like a second mother to Glen, threatened to leave, Christopher agreed that Glen would be self-supporting by his twenty-first birthday, and he also agreed to give Glen ample warning so he could get a job, an apartment, and make arrangements to start life on his own. Then several weeks later, at breakfast, when Christopher innocently asked Jessica for suggestions for celebrating Glen's birthday, Jessica asked how the arrangements were coming. No progress had been made. Christopher became defensive. Jessica felt defeated and accused him of acting in bad faith and betraying her. She ran out of the house after a half hour fight that set them both off on the wrong foot that day.

Jessica's diary:

8:45 Sped through traffic. Cut off two cars. Missed my exit. Took the wrong turn at the next intersection and found myself heading in the wrong direction to work. Stopped to get gas and gather my thoughts. Christopher is a spineless jerk and deserves to live with that bum of a son. Left front tire looks unevenly worn says the attendant—he's only 19. Why doesn't Glen work in a gas station?

10:30 I've been bummed out since I got into the office late. Chris doesn't take me seriously. Why am I in this relationship? Why is Chris coddling Glen?

11:45 Feeling very sad about Glen. He really doesn't have much going for him.

12:30 Lunch with client; bragging about his two boys in college. I can't compare Glen to other kids. I just want him to support himself. Not very effective at lunch. I let the client do all the talking. He probably didn't notice.

1:45–3:00 Forget to call D. F. Bender Inc. about a contract renewal. I'm a model of efficiency today!

Running to make up for lost time . . . I can't seem to get involved.

Does Christopher really love me?

4:00–5:00 I put down two perfectly good suggestions by one of the juniors—not like me. If I keep this up, I'll be the office bitch.

I'm so angry!

5:30 Lost patience with Emma for misplacing a file. I called her "unhelpful." I apologized . . . this comment was directed at Chris. I know it!

6:00–7:00 Unhappy all the way home. I don't want to go home tonight.

Christopher's diary:

8:30–10:00 Exploratory laparotomy on a fifty-four-year-old obese white female revealed stones in the common bile duct.

Surgery took twice as long as usual and I was behind schedule all morning taking complaints from patients in the office and from both of my nurses. I feel everyone is piling up on me.

I'm angry. I try to do the best by everyone and if I think Glen needs a little more time, why can't I be entitled to my decision? I pay the bills. I should have some say in what happens to money in this house!

12:00 Canceled lunch with Ed Marcus, M.D. All I needed today was to have the hospital pathologist tell me what's wrong with my technique. Eating at my desk to catch up. Looking at a vacation folder for a surgical convention in Greece. Maybe I should go alone. I don't want to go alone.

3:00 Found a two-centimeter mass by rectal exam in Genevieve, my best friend Calvin's wife. It feels hard like cancer. Called him, scheduled her for a lower GI series. I probably should have referred the case. She's been looking terrible for the last six months . . . that pasty gray complexion. Why did I choose this specialty?

5:00 Got short-tempered with an incredibly lazy medical student on rounds. Where the hell are they getting them these days? Talk about the bottom of the barrel. Doesn't he realize medical school is a privilege?

Started to think about Glen and his laziness. . . . Maybe I was too rough on the medical student?

6:30 Stuck in single-lane traffic behind a near comatose kid. He's probably on drugs. Honked at him, but another driver turned around and made a face at me! What am I so impatient about?

Maybe I am irritated with Glen.

Maybe Jessica is right.

I don't know, I just want this to work.

Why do I always have to be the heavy?

Why does Jessica take this out on me?

I wish Glen would move out on his own. I just don't want to be rejecting like his mother.

I feel torn. I have to do what I want to do, which is . . . ?

I want Jessica to love me and let me make my own decision.

And I want Glen to leave.

How do you like that? She's right.

AN EMOTIONAL BILL OF RIGHTS

Each partner has the right to express what he or she feels or thinks.

Each partner has the right to tell the truth.

Each partner has the right to be trusted and believed.

Each partner has the right to be listened to and be understood.

Each partner has the right to admit weakness without being ridiculed.

Each partner has the right to express his or her needs and desires and to be taken seriously.

Each partner has the right to be heard in the context of the moment without being reminded of the past.

Each partner has the right to grow.

Each partner has the right to seek help, friendship, and support.

Each partner has the right to be forgiven.

CHAPTER FIVE

Closing the Distance Between You

W HAT IS a relationship worth if you don't feel close?

Is there anything more painful than sensing a gulf between you and the person you love? When you're separated from the person you love you feel as if you're separated from the loving part of yourself. When an unresolved hurt distances you from your partner, it also alienates you from your best.

We invite such distance when we are afraid, when we cannot admit our mistakes, when we feel unloved or unlovable, when we feel unforgivable, and when we do not want to forgive. We use distance like a moat to shield us from pain, but only end up isolating ourselves from the love we need.

WHEN WE FEEL DISTANT

When something, no matter how small, comes between us and the one we love, we mourn the loss of the closeness we once had. We no longer feel free to speak, to share, or to love. Our desire to be close only causes us greater pain. We despise the distance between us. We hate not loving and not being loved. We want to abandon our pain even if we must forsake our love to do so.

We build a case against loving. The same love we once revered for its perfection, we now reject for its flaws. We try to reduce our investment and limit our involvement by suspending belief in each other. Unfortunately, the openness we withhold from our relationship we also keep from the rest of our life. We become preoccupied and have difficulty concentrating on our work. Our access to creative ideas and positive feelings is diminished, and we start to feel badly about ourselves. Our memory of ever being in love fades. We feel depleted and cheated. The world seems bland and robbed of its magic. All we can think of is the love that is missing.

The openness that once created a sense of wonder all around us seems gone. We feel discouraged and cynical about love. We'd rather be alone than try to convince ourselves that we don't love the person we love. We just want to be close again.

Being close is what love is all about.

LEARNING TO BE VULNERABLE

Closeness depends on vulnerability. You feel vulnerable to another person when you trust they will not hurt you. You develop trust only when you feel safe. Your capacity to trust is limited by your ability to forgive, to share your feelings, and let go of your hurt.

Being vulnerable means being open to all feelings. No matter how much you love the other person, you cannot promise you will never hurt them or be sure they will not hurt you again. The best you can hope for is that once your partner knows your weakness, he will not hurt you intentionally.

In the best relationships the partners continually work to become as open as possible. No one likes to hear that they have hurt their partner or have done something wrong. Learning to listen openly to all of your partner's hurt and anger is the best way to build and preserve your closeness. If, even when obviously provoked, you can stay detached and simply ask your partner to reveal the hurt behind his anger, you not only maintain your vulnerability, but you convert a potential conflict into an opportunity for giving.

Learning to be vulnerable even in the face of open hostility is the best protection. It is a powerful way of rebuilding closeness. Allow your partner to express his emotions without taking them personally or judging him. To do this, listen dispassionately and immediately admit whatever hurt you have caused. Say you are sorry he is hurting and that you wish he had told you about the pain sooner. Then ask your partner why he allowed his feelings to grow out of proportion. Indicate that holding in feelings creates distance and is not fair to either of you.

To be vulnerable means to be open in sharing your pain.

WHY BEING VULNERABLE IS DIFFICULT

If you feel threatened by your partner, it is unlikely that you can be vulnerable together. You feel threatened when you feel unsure of yourself. It is always your responsibility to feel good about yourself. However, if your partner uses the knowledge he has gained through being intimate to play on your weaknesses, your sense of security is undermined—you fear being attacked, rejected, or shown up, all good reasons to feel threatened.

Partners are less likely to pull away when their mate is sad than when he is hostile. Sadness is less threatening than anger. Depression, however, does create pain in others. Since depression is a closed state in which anger is being withheld, it alienates the sufferer both from himself and his partner. You also become angry with a depressed partner for diminishing the person you love.

You can tolerate witnessing a great deal of pain in another person if that person is open, but very little if he is closed. You can be vulnerable about expressing everything you feel if you accept yourself and trust that your relationship supports you.

What keeps you from exposing your heart? If you are like most people, you fear rejection or not being taken seriously. You fear discovering that your partner doesn't care about your feelings or you're afraid of starting an argument. You fear being hurt, and even open people pull back after being hurt. Hurt destroys trust. The function of hurt is to teach us what is safe. Accepting that our partner can hurt us is the first step in building genuine trust.

Paradoxically, only when you do not need your partner can you completely trust and accept him. Only when you can accept your partner's deficiencies can you fully accept the good. Only when you know what you cannot trust about your partner can you know what you can believe in.

All relationships undergo trials in which trust is tested. Do not despair whenever your relationship goes through difficult times, but see it as an opportunity to accept and settle the differences between you. You can agree out of desperation to anything just to make peace and persuade someone not to leave you, but you cannot live up to any promise but to be yourself.

If your relationship is worthy of trust, it must reflect your strengths and weaknesses. You need to create a place where each of you can be at home just as you are. You deserve to be loved for yourself, and you can only love another for the way he or she is. You can't love a promise. Real love is always based on reality.

WITH WHOM CAN YOU BE OPEN?

You can only be open with a partner who will not take advantage of the secrets you reveal, who is not suspicious and trying to prove you wrong. It is difficult to be yourself with someone who has a preconceived notion of how you are, were, or should be. You would always be apologizing and explaining yourself. Your partner cannot accept your growth if he has not grown himself. Closed relationships are the most painful, for when it is not safe to be yourself, you soon become drained and demoralized.

THE RISK OF BEING OPEN

When Richard suggested to Adrian that they move from their small rural community to a large city, she was reluctant at first, but the idea of going back to school and getting a degree in social work appealed to her. Richard had always been a good negotiator, and making a strong case by arguing the benefits was how he had gotten his way in their marriage. When he was done, Adrian was convinced that they were making the move just so she could resume her career and Richard was giving up the most just to give her the chance.

Adrian felt uncomfortable about the arrangement, but couldn't put her finger on what was bothering her. She was concerned about giving up a support system that had taken a lifetime to develop, a support system that made up for deficiencies in her relationship with Richard and made it unnecessary for her to discuss her needs with him. What she did not get from him, a friend or relative supplied. She had some fears about depending just on Richard, but could not voice them.

They moved into an apartment that Richard had acquired on an earlier visit to the city. It immediately made her feel cramped. The two children were forced to share the same bedroom and fights between them increased. The city seemed threatening and restricting. Adrian was accustomed to large open spaces and going wherever she wanted. Now she worried about crime and violence, and traffic and smog, and feared that the graduate-level classes she was taking would be beyond her capabilities. To make matters worse, finding a reliable day-care center was also difficult.

Richard had persuaded her to move by promising that life would be better and that his new job would give them more money and opportunity. It was a better job, but it preoccupied him, and he seemed even less aware of Adrian's feelings than before. He also ignored his promise to help out more around the house, thus making it difficult for Adrian to feel comfortable about spending time at the university. She felt more alone in her marriage than ever.

Because the day-care center she found did not measure up to her standards, leaving for school each morning tore at her. Each morning the kids pleaded not to be dropped off at the center. She could not concentrate. She did not think she was being a good mother. Her grades suffered and her belief in her ability fell with them. Because Adrian believed that her education had been the deciding factor in the move, she felt to blame for everything that was happening to her family. She tried to conceal her disappointment, afraid Richard would chastise her for being unhappy, especially after all the sacrifices they had made for her career. But Richard did not even notice she was unhappy.

The more miserable Adrian felt, the more she tried to hide her feelings. She blamed herself for everything that was wrong between them and apologized for being a wet blanket. Richard responded by telling her that she shouldn't worry about interfering in his career. It was going well. He reassured her that she should just focus on school. He didn't even ask what was bothering her.

After one of the children sprained an ankle while Adrian was at school, she became despondent with guilt and anger. In desperation, she swallowed a bottle of aspirin to try and bring attention to her pain. With his usual unruffled ease, Richard took the suicidal gesture in stride. He reassured Adrian that she didn't need to feel bad about what she'd done. After all, he and the kids had not been hurt. Still, she spent her time apologizing for doing such a stupid thing, embarrassing and annoying him at the same time.

All through their marriage Adrian had been afraid to risk being vulnerable and tell Richard how she really felt. She withheld her disappointment over the move and concealed her anger at him for not paying enough attention to her. Mostly she was angry because he was only concerned with himself. He tried to make it seem as if she were the selfish party and he the long-suffering husband. Because she did not trust Richard's love, much of her self-injury was an attempt to test his caring indirectly.

Adrian had not yet learned to be vulnerable. She felt she could not trust Richard and could not risk knowing the truth. When she sought my help, I pointed out that she'd been hurt by Richard and needed to be open and tell him how she felt. She wasn't sure she could do it, but would try. She confronted Richard, got angry at him, and explained her pain. To her surprise, she discovered that Richard did care, but that was not nearly as important as the relief she felt just by being open and knowing she wasn't crazy. Even though she was openly angry, she felt closer to Richard and able to deal with him as an equal. Though he was stunned by her accusation, he was able to address her needs and admit how he had manipulated her through her weaknesses. Adrian and Richard began to learn to trust each other.

You can only be open with a partner who seeks the best in you. The best self is not perfect, but is perfectly aware of its own faults. This is the essence of the evolving personality. The wiser you grow, the more willing you are to acknowledge your shortcomings. Once you admit your weaknesses, they won't block your growth. When you have no need to hide your faults, you can perceive yourself—and others—as you really are.

Your relationship should be a safe place to admit shortcomings. Overcoming your dishonesties together is the first step to being more open. Attacking the other and trying to force an admission of weakness or wrongdoing only makes matters worse. You need to let your partner know that you see a better self within by addressing that better self.

It's too easy to be negative. You can identify with your hurt and your belief that you are being cheated. You can focus on how little you are getting or how much better you could have done with someone else. You can complain and accuse and put your partner down, but in doing so you may be overlooking the realization that every crisis presents an opportunity. Before you follow the path of blaming and recrimination, you owe it to yourself to address your partner's best self and help bring it out. Believe that there is still good between you, and act to salvage it.

OVERCOMING SELF-DOUBT

When we do not believe in ourselves, we forget that we are good. We feel that being our best seems like too much work. We do not want to take responsibility, we just want to be rescued or escape. We believe that we are hopeless and undeserving. Our reasoning and judgment are prejudiced and distorted. We feel pessimistic about everything. We may give lip service to the idea that we can be better, but our actions only deny it.

Most people have occasional, brief lapses of belief in themselves, but longer periods are also common. The more a person challenges himself, the more he finds himself lacking. A life full of growth and risk is also filled with excitement and questioning. As you struggle to be better, you become more willing to take responsibility for yourself. Still, no one is immune to self-doubt. It is when we are closed and do not share our doubts that we allow them to create a negative world around us. We push others away, find flaws in their supportive comments and undermine their giving. We insist that we are no good and that it is useless for us to try.

From time to time every partner suffers self-doubt. It's best not to become alarmed at your partner during these times, but rather remind him of the good he has done and that such episodes are part of growing. Also remind your partner that he always has a choice to doubt or to believe in himself.

SEEKING TO BELIEVE IN YOURSELF

Remember, no matter how overwhelmed you may feel, there is always a part of you that is able to deal openly with your problems. Seek it by assuming there is something you can do to make things better. Focus on the good in your life and permit yourself to be nurtured by it. Your best self finds good in the world but does not deny the pain. Trust your feelings. Trust yourself. That will allow you to be open about your pain and still be strong. The more you believe in yourself, the more that belief will grow and the stronger you will become. Just say to yourself "I will get through this somehow" rather than saying "I will never get through this."

SEEKING TO BELIEVE IN YOUR PARTNER

Doubt about your partner is just as destructive to a relationship as self-doubt. If you believe your partner can also be better, address your comments to his better self as if it were already operating. Trust him and he will trust you in return. Should your efforts be rebuked, give your partner the benefit of the doubt. Seek to understand, not criticize. Be curious, not suspicious. Insist that you believe in your partner even if he does not seem to believe in himself.

Belief in yourself and your partner is the most powerful force in any relationship. As strong as it is, it is also easily occluded by negativity and doubt. So believe in the light, even when it's dark. Seeking to believe in others is also the best way to find belief in yourself.

BEING YOUR BEST IN
A RELATIONSHIP

A relationship is a living thing. It grows, changes, and evolves. At times it is close and the partners are inseparable, telephoning just to hear each other's voice. At times the partners find different answers to their quest. Worldly and isolated at the same time, they pursue separate directions, are drawn away, consumed by self or lost in their careers. Then, when losses undermine self-belief, the partners grow close again to lean on each other for support. Confidence returns and they venture forth in the world again, but this time in closer touch with each other.

A relationship must expand and contract to fit the love it contains. We need our partners to understand that we must continue to pursue our best and to trust in the love that flows between us so we can risk without the fear of being abandoned. In the best of all possible worlds, we would be asked to help when we felt full, our bills would come due when we had the money to pay them, and our lovers would respond to us when we felt amorous, but time and nature have other plans. It is in our ability to adapt that our closeness flourishes in a relationship.

Remember your love even when its recollection seems dim, but do not allow your needs to create belief out of desperation or intimacy out of yearning. You can convince yourself that you are loved even when you cannot remember the last time you were hugged and kissed in simple friendship. You can pretend that you are close even when you haven't shared a thought in months. You can live for years expecting your partner to change, but then you lose hope in your own future. More important is your survival as your best. You cannot create a relationship single-handedly and you cannot sacrifice your life to empty promises.

We feel most open in a relationship when we are most self-accepting. We let in criticism most easily when we are convinced of our own worth. Unfortunately, we need to be most open when we are under the greatest stress, the very time when we are most likely to be closed. If you can learn to trust yourself at these times and decide that whatever happens, you can face it, you set the stage

98

for being your best. However, being your best does not mean that you can't feel hurt or angry, or that you can't slip back and decide to be foolish or hurt yourself. Being your best means believing in yourself and choosing what is best for you. Being your best in a relationship means believing in your partner and working to achieve what is best for her.

The ideal conditions for that kind of relief are not when you are stress-free and have found safety, but when the road looks rough, the roof is leaking, the bills are piling up, and you realize that in spite of everything, you still have each other. Believe in the possibility of working it out together and share that belief. Believe in yourselves and each other. Solidarity is a quiet thing, born of love and acceptance. It all comes down to saying "I am here for you"— and meaning it. Those are the conditions that allow you to believe.

CHAPTER SIX

Giving

L OVE IS always a gift.
You do not earn it by doing some-
thing; you deserve it by being yourself. The essence of love is that
it is free. When love is used as a reward it become debased. When
love is used to acquire, it becomes an object of barter. It no longer
is a gift and, therefore, no longer love. You cannot love if you are
obligated to love. The only condition for giving your love is that
you are always free to love or not love. Where love is owed the bill
goes unpaid.

You always feel impoverished when you are bought off instead
of loved. How do you rationalize accepting gifts that were given
to possess you? No gift given to buy your affection ever wins your
full surrender. You always hold back something just to keep from
losing yourself. You resent yourself for selling out and distrust the
other person for playing on your weakness. The only thing you
resent more than having a price put on your love is agreeing to it.

Gifts should reflect love, not measure it.

When love is freely given, it enriches and gladdens the receiver,
making acceptance the only necessary response.

THE GIFT OF LOVE

Knowing that someone you respect and trust believes in you goes a long way toward helping you believe in yourself. Ideally, you shouldn't need anyone to raise your self-esteem, but from time to time we all doubt ourselves. The gift of love helps us overcome that doubt.

If that gift is withheld, or if it is offered only conditionally at times of self-doubt, your partner is taking unfair advantage of a vulnerable situation and making it less likely that you will be open in the future. Still, it is difficult to withhold negative comments when your partner finally begins to admit what you've been telling him for years. Resist the temptation. Allow your partner to voice his or her worst fears with total freedom from retaliation. If, during later arguments, you bring up these weaknesses, you will betray the deepest trust. Just as you are the greatest of all confidants when you are friends, you are the most unfair of all possible opponents when you are not. No one knows how to love or hurt you more deeply than your partner.

Insincerely expressing your belief in your partner is another way of saying you don't believe in him. It is demoralizing to tell your partner that his work is good when you feel it isn't. Being patronizing to avoid hurting your partner's feelings will only injure him further and reduce your credibility. The reason your partner feels self-doubt is that he sees his faults. It's always best to tell the truth with reassuring love.

Let your partner express his doubts without cutting him off prematurely with stock reassurances. Hear what he has to say. If your partner starts beating his breast and feeling sorry for himself, do not make too much out of it. Remind him that he has momentarily lost his confidence.

Ask him what he thinks went wrong. Have him indicate the possible solutions. Encourage him to follow his instincts in spite of his doubts. If he responds negatively, don't take it personally. Just remind him that his doubt will pass just as it always does.

Do not reward his negativity with a lot of attention. Simply listen and try to understand. Above all, express your love and belief honestly and sincerely. That is the greatest gift you can offer.

THE GIFT OF SECURITY

Support, whether it is financial or emotional, must be given freely. You support another person because you want him to be able to survive without you, not because you want him to be dependent on you. While a husband may wish to protect his wife by isolating her from financial concerns, he may be causing her needless worry because she knows she is not learning to prepare for adversity. In old-fashioned relationships, men controlled the money as part of their protective role. Today, men still tend to conceal their business activities from their partners. They wish to retain control and avoid such questions as: How much money did you put into this? How much will we get out and when? How safe is it and how do you know? Why can't we use that money to fix up the house? The more problems a relationship has, the more husbands tend to conceal such financial information.

Before a relationship can be equal, the partners must share control over money. Being supported financially is a handicap if it prevents you from developing a sense of independence. The ability to be flexible in adversity comes from facing adversity. Peace of mind does not come from being taken care of, but from knowing you will be able to take care of yourself. The best security in a relationship comes from encouraging your partner to develop his strength and to share in all the important decisions. It's the only way to be sure you have a partner you can count on.

THE GIFT OF TIME

Your relationship is all your times together. The good times, the bad times. The time yearning to be together, the time spent wishing you were apart. The time loving, the time fighting. The time giving, the time in need. The time of fullness, the time depleted.

The time of celebration, the time in mourning. The time in understanding acceptance, the time in suspicious jealousy. The time nurturing, the time undermining. Above all, the time you spend being yourselves together.

The reason you joined forces in the first place was to take the time to discuss your feelings. Your time together should not be defined by a rigid agenda; it should be free, shaped by your needs as you discover and share them. The demand that your partner not bother you with his or her concerns is a dangerous posture that quickly becomes a bad habit. It always increases resentment.

You are together even if it is not good right now.

Accept your time together as it is. Don't keep comparing it to what you wish it could be. The way to make the most of your time together is to clear the air of lingering negativity. That should always be your first priority. Trust in your love. It will appear again when the negativity is past. If you stay open during the difficult times and let your feelings out, the good times follow.

No excuse—work, kids, or meetings—that permits unresolved feelings to pile up is acceptable. The partner who sacrifices him or herself for the sake of the other, but does not give of himself to make the relationship work, is not really giving anything.

Still, you need to avoid making your time together seem like an outpatient clinic for disturbed couples in which you are continually ventilating your needs and don't seem to have any fun. These overly analytical relationships are more self-indulgent than therapeutic. You are together to live together, not to talk about living together. You do not have to resolve every difference; air every concern to be honest with each other. You have to seek a balance. You can be an adult and resolve your own personal concerns by yourself, or share them with your partner and take the time to enjoy yourselves.

There are no rules for this. Follow what feels right. Don't hide, but don't confide every bruise of your sensitive ego either. Try to have a good time by being honest. Remember why you are together: to share the love between you.

THE GIFT OF BEING THERE

Of all the gifts in a relationship none is as reaffirming as being present for your partner. Being present means being a witness to the other's feelings, staying in expectant contact without reacting or commenting. By being present you share the emotional impact of life. You make room for the other person's reactions without adding to them. You are glad for the intimacy of feeling together.

Listening to the other person, giving him time and room to express himself is a wonderful and necessary gift, but listening is only part of being present. Being present is paying attention to your partner's feelings and your inner responses without judging either. It is not even necessary to voice your responses to share them. Just being alert and interested in what your partner says creates the closeness you yearn for. Being present is experiencing through the other person. So don't let your mind wander. It's easy to tell when your thoughts are elsewhere.

When you have a need to share, there is no loneliness greater than finding that the person you need most to care is not interested in what you have to say.

Being present for your partner starts with being comfortable with yourself. You need to care, to be curious, and want to share, but you can only let in what is not threatening to you. You cannot fake being present merely by being silent. Being present requires active attention. You remain in contact with the other person, listening to the silence together, following your inner responses to his comments, staying sensitive to change and alert for discovery. Eagerness characterizes your silence. You are listening for the approach of an answer to a question you haven't enough information to ask. When you do speak, you speak as a friend, sharing your wonder and vulnerability, not as a rival trying to win a point.

The purpose of being present is to encourage your partner to share his most sensitive secrets by offering understanding. It is only at such times that you get to know each other. When you look back on the best parts of your relationship, the times you remember are the times when you were there for each other, the moments you were there together.

THE GIFT OF FREEDOM

You cannot give your partner the gift of freedom. Your partner can only free him or herself.

You can only diminish your partner's freedom by imposing restrictions, and they always damage a relationship. When your freedom is compromised, it is the only issue that matters. Your partner is more likely to leave the relationship to be free than for any other reason.

If you are not free to be yourself, you cannot love.

If you are not free to risk, you cannot grow.

If you are not free to reject, you cannot accept.

Unless each of you is free to make your own decisions and live the life you choose, your relationship is only temporary.

You cannot control the love and fidelity of another person.

You cannot make another person love you.

You cannot hold on to your partner out of fear. Your partner will break loose just to test his bonds.

You cannot restrict your partner's friends, hours, or career without setting the stage for betrayal.

You cannot compromise another person's right to be himself or make decisions for him.

You need to encourage your partner to take risks and be for himself not merely to help him be free, but to maintain your independence as well. How can you be free if you have to be not only your own person, but your partner's as well?

THE GIFT OF APPRECIATION

There is no gift as easy to give or as needed as appreciation, especially from the person you love. Love is the sincerest form of appreciation. You love someone because you are attracted to their giving, understanding, style, openness, and caring. And yet people often forget to express their appreciation.

We withhold our praise when we are disappointed, hurt, or

angry. We withhold praise when we do not like ourselves: We can only appreciate another fully if we are at peace with ourselves. We withhold appreciation out of envy, when we do not value ourselves and when we believe that what the other person has we will never get on our own.

Withholding praise and appreciation diminishes our love. Showing love is showing appreciation. Next to seeking freedom, most people leave their relationship because they do not feel appreciated.

Sharing appreciation should occur simply and naturally. Like the expression of any feeling, appreciation is best shared in the moment it is felt.

The best show of appreciation is a little ceremony of love. Take a moment to say "Thank you," "I like this," or "How wonderful you make me feel!" Avoid making an intrusive display that embarrasses or distracts. Remember, the key is to be timely, easy, and genuine. Insincere praise feels worse than no praise at all. It feels like a bribe. You don't need to go out and buy something to show your appreciation, but if you do, it should only be symbolic. Gifts wear out, appreciation builds love. Most important, be sure you take enough time to say thank you properly. Getting your partner's attention and giving a little hug or kiss whenever you feel appreciative works wonders.

When we first fall in love, we are filled with discovery and wonder, and eagerly show appreciation for our partner's good qualities. We all tend to get a little blasé over time and take each other for granted. So it is important that you stand back for a moment each day and look at the person you love. Allow his or her positive attributes to impress you anew and share your admiration.

Making love is a continual part of a good relationship. People who care express their caring all the time. They are willing to risk rejection by intruding on their partner's busy life to say "I love you." Their reward is knowing that they don't have to search further back than this morning to remember a moment they loved someone and someone loved them back. Your love is always the best way to show your appreciation.

THE GIFT OF ACCEPTANCE

At best a relationship should feel like home. It should be a place where you feel let in without fanfare or having to be something you are not. A relationship should always be your place. It is where you are accepted when you are not your best, when you have anxious days, when you feel and sound crazy, when you fail as well as when you succeed.

Being accepted doesn't mean that your shortcomings are condoned. It means, rather, that you are not being rejected because parts of you are unacceptable. And just as you want to be accepted, so you must accept your partner. Your partner's shortcomings embarrass you most when your own acceptability seems to depend on them.

Acceptance is not a compromise. What you accept, you must accept completely. You cannot permit what you do not accept to diminish your love. It is this gift of acceptance that allows us to love each other perfectly in spite of our imperfections.

In your relationship, you must accept:

This time: As much as you would like to return to the past to set things straight, or as much as you yearn for the day when you will have what you want, you only live in the present. You are only alive now. You need to accept how you are here, in this moment. It is when you are what you are, not what you were, not what you will be.

This place: This is where you are now. Don't daydream about where you want to be. Make plans to get there, but make plans from this place. Gather your forces here. Accept that you are here and take your next step from where you now stand. More false steps are made because people are mistaken about where they are than because they do not know where they are going.

This person: You are yourself. You are only yourself. What you will be does not matter nor does what you have been. Only your fullest acceptance of yourself as you are can give you the momentum to change and grow. Denying what you are, your faults and your needs, only clouds your ability to motivate yourself and give to yourself. You can only give to others from the truth of who you are. You are everything that has led up to your being what you are. To be whole, don't deny your parts. Accept yourself as good.

This other person: The person you love is also what he or she is, nothing more or less. Your failure to accept your partner is the burden of your relationship, the obstacle to your love, and the resistance to being happy together. Give your acceptance freely, without reservation. You don't need to like your partner's short-comings, but you need to accept that they exist. Do not diminish your acceptance with conditions. If your relationship is to work, it needs room for all of the parts of you and your partner.

Acceptance is the catalyst of growth, the greatest gift of all.

CHAPTER SEVEN

Overcoming Doubts

G IVING THE benefit of the doubt is easy
      if you trust your partner. It is impos-
sible if you do not. There is no way around this. If you do not trust
your partner, there is not much sense pretending that you do. If
you do not trust your partner, there are probably good reasons.

Perhaps you do not trust yourself, but find it easier to accuse
your partner than admit you doubt your own affections or that you
are already unfaithful either in spirit or in deed.

Perhaps you do not trust your partner because you do not value
yourself—your distrust is only a logical extension of your poor
self-image. In essence you are saying, "Why wouldn't someone
cheat on me or take advantage of me? After all, I'm not so hot."

Perhaps you have suffered and find it difficult to trust anyone. It
is hard to trust others when anger leads you to discover malice in
innocent actions or remarks. Angry people find anger all around
them. It is their own anger leaking out, but they cannot see its
source.

Expecting betrayal invites betrayal.

When you distrust without cause the person you love, you hurt
him deeply, for the greatest pain is not being believed by the person
you need most to believe you. If you are going to be doubted,
whether or not you are loyal, you have little incentive to be good.

So your lack of trust sets up your partner to retaliate. What better way for your partner to get even than to make your worst fears come true? He or she will do this because he feels abused by your suspicion, not because he is bad. Distrust makes your partner an outsider in your relationship.

You cannot love if you do not trust. You cannot trust if you cannot forgive. It does not matter how innocent you were or how cruelly others treated you. You need to forgive, not to set others free, but to free yourself to love without suspicion.

If you have reason for not trusting your partner, bring it out into the open. If your partner will not relieve your doubt or if you cannot believe what your partner tells you, you should question why you are together. You should not be with a person you cannot trust.

To give your partner the benefit of the doubt, react to situations in the present as if you had no past history together. For example, greet a late-arriving partner with relief rather than angrily confronting him with a fantasy you have been weaving. Say that you have been worried for his safety and then release your concern. After all, your partner is safe now. Don't seek alibis or try to trap him in a lie; accept on face value whatever reason he or she offers for being late.

Trust rekindles passion. Although the following story may seem hard to believe, it happened exactly this way. Jill was an insecure woman who continually cross-examined Ben, her long-suffering husband, over his activities. He dutifully reported in at prearranged times during the day to update his schedule. If he was five minutes late, she would be bitter and impatient. If he missed a call she would be in a rage. Once, when he had to go to the emergency room with a bad cut, he was out of contact for an entire afternoon and she was ready to leave him, even when he told her about his injury. Although Ben still loved Jill, her doubt alienated him and they began to drift apart. He threatened to leave. His needs were always overshadowed by her anxiety and distrust. He had had enough. She panicked. I suggested to Jill that the next time he called in she should express her appreciation that Ben loved her enough to call and allay her fears. I also suggested that she thank him for putting up with her insecurity all these years, something she had never done before. She followed my suggestions and Ben was shocked that Jill had any understanding of the pain to which she had subjected him. He immediately softened, lowered his defenses, and felt warmly toward her rather than guarded. Instead of arriving at the doorstep anticipating an argument as he usually did, Ben brought flowers and for the first time in years they spontaneously made love in the daytime.

FALSE ACCUSATIONS

Remember, while most delays are innocent, most accusations are not.

Again, most suspicion comes from self-doubt. If your partner starts to come home late, it more likely has to do with how you are together than what he is doing on the way home. So ask him what he is trying to avoid and have the courage to listen to his response. Be open and uncritical and you'll be told the truth.

The person you accuse your partner of wanting to be with is probably that part of him that he does not feel free to reveal in your presence. Whenever you have to withhold part of yourself from your relationship, you feel incomplete being together. Some people feel lonely when they are with their partner. They feel they are missing something, but cannot put their finger on it. They miss the part of themselves that their partner inhibits, perhaps the child-like self that wants to play, perhaps the poet, the stud, or the siren. People often mistakenly seek out others because of this loneliness, but they are really looking for themselves.

Unfounded distrust does more damage to a relationship than an actual betrayal. Partners are secretive more to avoid unwarranted criticism than to hide wrongful activity. When you falsely accuse your partner, you reveal that you cannot tell when he is being truthful. You are asking him to add something to the truth to make it acceptable to you. Anything that alters the truth between partners alienates them.

When trust fades, the relationship falters. So if you find yourself continually doubting your partner without cause:

Confess your distrust openly.

Do not accuse.

Give your partner permission to remind you of your tendency to doubt and accept it as your problem.

Allow him to declare his innocence easily, without contradicting him.

Again, in every relationship there is always evidence that could be used to make a case for distrusting the other person. So when you are looking for trouble, you can usually find it. But should you suspect something is wrong, say something right away. Make your point and be done with it. If you're not satisfied, pursue it further. If you find nothing, drop it.

When we doubt our partners, when we are hurt or angry, we remove our love from our relationships. Even if it's only for a moment, we retreat within to imagine other solutions to our discomfort. We may wish we were with another person and our eyes may wander as we cast our fantasies with real people. We may never get to the point of acting on these feelings, but we need to be free to express them. They simply reflect how we feel.

It is only natural to fantasize being with someone else when your relationship is in trouble. This can be a faceless person, an old lover, a stranger one fancies, or even a friend. You find relief in fantasy the same way your dreams process unexpressed feelings. It is similar to thinking about a different job when something goes wrong at work. You use your fantasy to gain distance to think over your problem.

Unfortunately, we can only express such fantasies to a secure partner. Having an insecure partner is a burden—you are not permitted to admit your natural feelings without risking rejection. These fantasies are not a sign of betrayal, nor are they declarations of future intent. They merely reflect your hurt and yearning. When you are not free to express these thoughts, you feel like a prisoner. When you can share them, you feel free and intimate together.

Sharing fantasies builds trust, hiding them undermines it.

JEALOUSY

Jealousy is the belief that you are not unique and that the feelings someone has for you can be easily bestowed upon someone else.

Jealousy is always a reflection of low self-esteem.

People who value themselves don't waste time worrying about being replaced, but when you need another person to feel good about yourself, you continually fear losing that other person. This borrowed self-worth is fleeting, the stuff of infatuation. It is fragile, the first casualty of doubt.

The desperate possessiveness of jealous lovers always has more to do with the fear of losing self-worth than it does with losing a partner. Jealous mates see their partners as necessary proofs of their worth, as adornments to their personality, not as individuals. Jealous people seek to possess their partners and display their ownership. They are not saying "Look what I have, how wonderful my partner is," but rather "See, I must be wonderful to have a partner like this." Their partners resent them for this lack of acknowledgment and for using them. Not suprisingly, a jealous person is easily embarrassed when his or her partner looks bad.

Being with a jealous partner almost always feels bad. When jealous partners feel insecure, they imagine you are rejecting them. And should you need their support, you're likely to frighten them or be rejected as an embarrassment. For life to flow smoothly with jealous lovers, everything must be perfect, for they misinterpret everything. Their insecurity prompts them not only to exaggerate their partner's faults, but to take offense at the slightest negative nuance. Getting a second-rate table in a restaurant is reason enough to precipitate a heated argument, the basis of which is often: "If you really loved me, you would have done better." They relate everything that happens to themselves. They are so self-conscious they think other people are watching their every move, and so any shortcoming they can perceive in their partners' behavior they immediately believe others also see and regard as an insult to them. To make matters worse, jealous people tend to be unforgiving and their memories long. Even when an old wound seems healed, the original pain can be recalled with minimal provocation and the distorted accusations begin again.

Jealous rage is like a child's panic in which the child feels abandoned, out of control, and unable to fend for himself. Partners, blind with jealousy, imagine abandonment and see it as proof of an unworthiness they only reluctantly admit. Jealous lovers often act out their insecure feelings by quickly taking the first replacement lover they can find. On the the surface they may claim they are doing this to get even, but they are really trying to placate their self-doubts and reassure themselves that they are still attractive. They dread abandonment.

Jealous people continually demand to be reassured that they are lovable but seem most unlovable when they are insecure and needy. Their demands are likely to be answered sarcastically, for their partners, long since exasperated by such requests, no longer take them seriously. The jealous partner reads further betrayal into this lip service and finds in it additional reason to doubt.

Understandably, the partners of jealous lovers continually consider leaving. They are weary of having their love tested. They resent every issue being reduced to whether they love their partner or not. The jealous person usually has no idea of how his insecurity monopolizes discussions and imprisons his partner. While the jealous person may be aware that his partner feels like leaving, he never sees that it is his jealousy that is pushing his partner away.

Having a jealous partner makes you feel as if you are being abused. You are always reduced in importance to their suspiciousness. Your feelings, your needs, and your desires are always secondary to your partner's insecurity. Their fears rule. In a word, the jealous partner's feelings are always more important than yours. Whatever the underlying dynamics of the situation, it does not feel like love. Any objections you make to being treated this way are greeted with such overreacting and panic that it hardly seems worth the attempt to make things better.

Everyone dislikes being mistrusted, but the partners of jealous persons eventually get to the point where they see their partners' anxiety and pain as punishment that fits the crime of their false accusations. Eventually, out of frustration, they become tempted to withhold reassurance, to create additional doubt, and permit their jealous partners to suffer a little bit more just to get even. If they stay together, both partners are imprisoned in the relationship. Of course, when the jealous partner also controls the purse strings, the imprisonment becomes unbearable.

COPING WITH A
JEALOUS PARTNER

To cope with your partner's jealousy:

Accept the situation and don't be embarrassed by it.

Remind your partner that the problem is his insecurity, not your unfaithfulness. This needs to be repeated over and over again.

Of course, when you also need your partner's love and he reacts to this suggestion by withdrawing, the scene is set for conflict.

Be patient, even if you must be a little distant to stay calm.

Accept your partner's weakness, but do not give in to it or allow it to interfere with your giving and support.

Keeping this observing distance without withholding your love is the most important and most difficult attitude to maintain in dealing with a jealous partner, but it works. Losing patience and becoming irritable, while only natural, is seen by a jealous partner as proof that you don't love him and will only aggravate the situation.

The Jealousy Cycle

Lowered self-esteem leads to the fear of being replaced.

Doubting your partner's love causes him to withhold love.

Feeling unloved further lowers your self-worth.

A CLOSER LOOK AT JEALOUSY

Because no one is always sure of himself and from time to time we all tend to depend upon another person for our self-worth, everyone has some tendency to feel jealous. Knowing when these feelings occur will help you understand and manage them. Even if you are seldom jealous, completing the following will help you understand a jealous partner.

A Jealousy Diary

Keep a diary of just when and why you feel jealous. If you are not a particularly jealous person, it is likely that you will have only a few entries for an entire week. If you tend to be jealous, you may have more entries in a single day than you can deal with. The following example shows how jealousy can totally consume a person.

Elena was eight years younger than Constantine. She divorced her husband to marry him and he left his wife and three daughters to be with her. Constantine was in the wholesale fish business and would leave for work at three-thirty in the morning. From the moment he left the house till he returned, he worried about Elena being unfaithful to him. It was with great reluctance that he agreed to keep a diary. This is a transcript from his portable tape recorder. Many entries are missing and some are incomplete.

4:30 A.M. Driving in. I don't see the point of this, Elena. All I want from you is to pay attention to me and give me what I deserve. I get up early, work hard to give you a good home. Do I complain that I can't have my own daughters in this house? I have made a sacrifice to be with you. I don't think my asking you to comply with a few reasonable suggestions is wrong. I deserve to know where you are. I want you to be safe. Doesn't my peace of mind count for anything?

5:00 Lobster is through the roof this morning. I shouldn't be diverting my attention with this stupid exercise. What am I supposed to learn? You probably aren't even up yet. . . .

5:15 I just called the house to see if you were up. Where the hell were you?

5:20 Come on, where are you?

5:45 You've got a nerve to yell at me on the phone like that. I asked a reasonable question. Where does a person go at five in the morning?

6:20 Artie and Cosmos making eyes at the new girl in the order department. You don't think I know what they have on their minds—what all men have on their minds? And she's an old bag.

6:45 New restaurant chain buyer just overbid on haddock. Incompetent jerk! And I have to pay for his stupidity by meeting the price. Making a living is tough. If I told you half of what goes on here.

7:00 Just bought and sold twenty-six hundred pounds of hard-shell lobster to a Korean outfit. Two pounders and up! They wanted it real bad. Treated the boys to doughnuts. Called you to share the news. No answer. You called back right after I hung up, angry at me for your being in the shower. How the hell was I supposed to know and why were you so angry? I just wanted you to know we made a dollar already today. I feel very unappreciated. Your brother will probably drop by tonight to hit me for some money and you'll plead with me to give it to him. Where the hell do you think it comes from? All I ask is a little give and take.

8:00 Feeling like I have an upset stomach. Too many cups of coffee. Maybe you're in a mood to talk.

8:15 Lucky me. You were feeling sympathetic. You can make me feel so good if you just try a little.

10:45 I've been thinking all morning, what is so wrong with asking you to go shopping with my sister instead of going alone? She can help you with the bundles. She's a good driver. What's such a big deal about shopping alone? I believe you that you don't meet anyone there. I trust you. I'm just trying to make things easier for you. So why do you always resist? What did I marry, a women's libber?

11:30 Called you and you were very cold. *Very* cold. I can tell that something is wrong. You seem real aloof. I hate that. What gets into you, turning like that?

11:45 Called you back and got a bad attitude from you. I deserve better than this crap.

11:55 You were out. I called five times!

2:00 P.M. I didn't put anything on this machine because I didn't want to run the risk of anyone finding it and hearing the language I would use, but I feel injured. Deeply wounded by your not caring. You knew how I felt. You knew my stomach was killing me. You could have called to see how I was. Not a word.

> 3:30 I am driving home. I don't want to fight. I just want my reward. A warm meal, a loving wife, and a happy home. Is that too much? I would sincerely like to know if you think I am asking too much of you? Tonight, if you don't want to go shopping with my sister I'll take you, just to show I'm not holding a grudge.

Notice how a little reassurance and warmth allowed Constantine to put his mind back on his work after the 8:15 call to Elena, but then he lapsed into his twisted logic, confusing his controlling Elena with protecting her. Then, probably because the mention of the stomach pain worked before to win her sympathy, he mentions it again, but this time to make her guilty. If she has the power to make him better, he also assumes she has the power to make him worse. His destiny is in her hands. He loves her so much that he complains that she is responsible for his feelings. His argument is that if she is a good person, she would not let him suffer.

Obviously, their relationship is headed for trouble. The only approach for Elena that would work here would be for her to be reassuring and warm and not confront Constantine, but he is so prejudiced and provocative that he wears her down, and it is not easy for her to remain calm. Constantine needs to see how his insecurity feeds his jealousy, how his suspicions and accusations hurt Elena and push her away, and how her withdrawal aggravates his insecurity even further. Both are caught in the jealously cycle, but a review of Constantine's diary made them aware of the problem and they were able to take constructive steps to solve it.

While the following will serve as a guide to completing your own jealousy diary, it's important that you capture your true feelings, so be as natural as possible. While Constantine did not bother to follow the guide, it can be of considerable help in understanding the causes of your anxiety and suspicion. For each entry in your diary, note when the feeling started, what made you aware of it, what made it worse, and what relieved it. Give specific details, comments you doubted, promises that were not kept, etc.

Be sure to identify and note the following:

Whenever you doubted your partner's love.

Whenever you felt your partner was paying too much attention to someone else.

Whenever you thought your partner was unfaithful.

After you have noted a jealous feeling, relate the following questions to the incident and answer them:

How realistic were your feelings? Were they triggered by an actual event, or by your own anxiety?

What was going on just before you felt jealous? What else might have provoked the suspicion? Hint: Consider anything that caused you to doubt yourself.

Did you share your feelings with anyone? With whom? Did it help or aggravate them? Sharing jealous feelings with envious friends is bound to make them worse, while sympathetic friends help you cope with your fears.

Did you share your jealous feelings with your partner? If not, why not? Did you fear you wouldn't be listened to or taken seriously? Or did you have an awareness that your feelings were unfounded and felt silly about expressing them? Important point: You can share even unfounded feelings of jealousy without damaging your relationship if you tell your partner that you know he is innocent and take all the responsibility for your doubt. Just say you would like some help sorting out your feelings. Any statement that does not accuse will reduce doubt and open communication.

If your partner's response increased your doubt, consider these questions: In what tone of voice and under what circumstances did you bring up your doubt to your partner? Did you assume he or she was guilty? Put yourself in his shoes. How would you have felt if he accused you of something you didn't do? Could your attitude and suspicion have created the response you got even if your partner were innocent? If you answered "no," you are probably fooling yourself.

As you review each incident in your diary, assume that your partner is without blame. If you assume your suspicious attitude had much to do with his negative reaction, you'll probably be right. If you are being betrayed as much as you believe you are, why are you there? The answer will probably be because you only *feel* betrayed, not because you have been betrayed.

Examine the entries in your diary again to see if you can uncover any similarities.

Do you tend to become jealous after certain events? Which?

When are you most likely to feel insecure?

When do you feel the most secure? If you have that feeling only when you are with your partner, you need to learn to be on your own more.

When you have done this, write a one-page note to your partner that starts off with: "I need your reassurance and help when . . ." Then indicate when you feel least sure of yourself and are, therefore, most likely to project your fears onto your partner. Also, indicate how you would like to be reassured, the doubts you have about yourself, and the responsibility you take for yourself. Finally, list the shortcomings that you need to correct.

Share your diary with your partner. Allow enough time to express all of your feelings about your mutual mistrust.

If you have problems with jealousy, it is useful to repeat this exercise at regular intervals. The object is to make it easier for you to talk about your insecurity and to make your partner aware of the problem. The worst damage jealousy can do to a relationship is to stop each partner from taking the other's emotions seriously. This is a natural adaptation to unreasonable accusations. Understanding and sharing the feelings beneath the accusations and your reactions to them can lead the way to the mutual compassion and comfort that is necessary to a lasting relationship.

Part Three

WORKING IT OUT

CHAPTER EIGHT

Kinds of People and How They Bond Together

P EOPLE ARE protective of the feelings they care about most and the issues most sensitive to them. What these issues are and how people guard themselves against painful feelings reflect their particular character type. There are three main character types: the dependent, the controlling, and the competitive. Each enters into a relationship to satisfy different emotional needs. Each deals with the important emotional issues in a relationship in a different way.

It will be easy to see yourself in all three of the descriptions that follow—everyone has dependent, controlling, and competitive traits, but one character type usually predominates under stress and people remain, for the most part, the same character type their entire lives. The object is not to change, but to become more honest in dealing with your emotions. By identifying your type, you can deal directly with the world without hiding behind your defenses. Understanding your style and that of your partner will help you have more meaningful interactions and allow you to accept and support each other more completely.

THE DEPENDENT TYPE

Dependent people need to be reassured that they are lovable. They need frequent contact with someone who expresses care for them. They need to be told repeatedly that they are good. They need physical stroking and quickly become attached to anyone who shows them affection. Affection is their gift and their quest. They bond closely and completely, sometimes before taking enough time to be sure that what they are doing is in their best interest. They seem hypnotized by the prospect of being close to a person, like a deer frozen by the headlights of an oncoming vehicle.

Dependent people are warm and loving, sometimes too much so. Their loving often seems motivated by their need to be loved in return. Dependent people have a blind spot created by this need and so are inclined to attach themselves to people indiscriminately. They misinterpret clinging for caring and control for involvement. Even when the quality of the relationship deteriorates, they tend to hold on because they feel having someone is better than being alone. This explains why some dependent people who should know better remain even in self-destructive relationships.

The dependent person's bond is as strong as their self-esteem is weak. Even so, dependent people can grow. However, when they discard an unhealthy relationship, they must overcome a great deal of guilt, since they have often bonded out of fear of being alone rather than love. Because the person they want to break away from is often just as dependent, breaking away can be traumatic, full of doubt, recriminations, panic, and remorse.

Because we are all dependent when we begin life, we have a natural inclination to bond to anyone who promises to take care of us. It is no surprise to learn that relationships entered into when we were young have the greatest dependency problems. Dependent people need to become more independent, but often such growth is seen by their partners, who count on their weakness to make them feel strong by comparison, as a betrayal.

Women are generally more dependent than men. To some extent this is the result of societal conditioning and family expectations, but it also reflects a biological reality. Even independent women become dependent when their children are young because they need another's support to carry out their mothering functions. In spite of all of the social and career gains they have achieved, women are still expected to adopt a dependent role to be homemakers, form the center of families, and socialize and humanize their men and children.

Society in general, and many men in particular, expect the woman to be the dependent partner in a relationship. In reality, however, it is often the man who is dependent. Ideally, the dependence in a relationship should be mutually recognized and satisfied. The dependent trait, when positively realized, is reflected in the person, whether man or woman, who nurtures others with care and love. At the negative extreme, dependent types tend to smother others with affection, to manipulate them by guilt, and to fail to recognize the legitimacy of anyone else's rights but their own. Extreme dependence can also become a burden on others.

Again, everyone has a dependent inclination. Even as we strive for independence, we still hope that someone will be there to see us through. This dependent wish defines our need for another person. But extreme or one-sided dependence makes it impossible to love freely without possessiveness or fear of abandonment.

THE CONTROLLING TYPE

Controlling people actually feel out of control of the most important forces in their lives—their own feelings—and so they want to control the way *other* people feel. They want other people to love them, but they don't want to give them the choice not to. Controlling people insist on being in charge and making all the decisions. When their partners disagree, controlling people try to intimidate them—taunting them, daring them to go—providing, of course, they feel confident their partners don't have the nerve. Gradually, the partner's affection wanes, for no matter how completely one's needs are met, no one loves his jailor. Any withdrawal of affection frightens controlling people deeply, for they secretly believe that if their partners were free, they would leave. Their fear of abandonment is the reason they try to control others in the first place.

Controlling people are too closed and proud to admit any weaknesses or that they depend on their partners to keep from being alone. Where the dependent person flaunts his need for others, the controlling person denies it but won't let others go free. When their partners resist them, they become irrational and unreasonable. They blame and punish. They don't really understand any feeling except loneliness and they frequently get depressed.

Understandably, many of those who bond with controlling people are dependent character types. The attraction between them is often born out of a need to rescue and be rescued. The dependent person perceives the controlling partner's gifts as a proof of love. Controlling people are frequently excellent earners but tend to confuse giving financial support with giving affection.

Controlling people insist on winning, being right, having the last word, making the other person wrong, and appearing blameless. They believe they know the way to do things best and ascribe all their mistakes to others not following their orders. They love to issue commands and edicts. They try to pass themselves off as perfect and so take criticism poorly. They tend to put others down, belittle their accomplishments, and devalue their feelings.

The great paradox is that controlling types are easily and deeply wounded. They cannot admit pain because it makes them seem weak, so they tend to bear grudges. They cannot risk rejection. Someone leaving them or their sphere of influence is a threat to the integrity of the system they believe in and to the logic that runs their world. They will actually sit down with a list of points and try to prove to you that you love them when, in fact, you are packing and leaving on the next flight to Reno. They refuse to take seriously those who disagree with them, especially when the person is the object of their affection. They will tell you that you really don't mean it when you threaten to leave. They will hide the car keys and tell you they are doing you a favor, and they will actually believe it. It's no wonder that their partners often stage outlandish displays to make their point and defy them.

Controlling people consider obedience the best proof of love. If you disagree with them, you prove you don't care. These same people are absolute pushovers when it comes to allowing their partners to control them sexually. This only brings out the worst in their partners, who retaliate by withholding sex, exercising the only power they have not completely given up.

Controlling people get their partners to yield their rights bit by

126

bit. They stage major confrontations over issues that do not seem worth fighting about and the weaker partner, who would rather have peace than fight, concedes. Over a period of time, vital inroads are made into the weaker partner's freedom. The rights that were once taken for granted are claimed by the controlling partner. It almost feels as if a master plan of invasion has been going on all along. This annexation of rights is a function of the controlling style. It reflects a weak person trying to get power anywhere he can. His desperation pushes him to cross every weak border. He misinterprets vulnerability as weakness and willingness to compromise as license to invade. At their worst, relationships with controlling people can be stifling and dehumanizing.

Understandably, controlling people frequently feel that their mates don't appreciate or encourage them. Why would a person want to help the person who controls him become even more powerful? In fact, partners of controlling people often harbor unspoken resentment, give joyless compliance, and have a secret wish that the controlling person not prosper.

Controlling people never feel close because they do not allow themselves to be vulnerable. If controlling people feel alone, it is because they have isolated themselves from their feelings in order not to be hurt and because they have ignored the feelings of others. They never get to hear what others really think except what is expressed in anger. One way their partners manage such difficult people is illustrated by one woman's advice on how to deal with controlling men: "I just tell them, 'I want to love you. I think you are wonderful, but something, I don't know what it is, stops me' and then I just wait for the presents to arrive."

These words may be crass and of no more merit than the tactics of the controlling person himself, but they show how values deteriorate in a relationship with a controlling person. Trying to control others always undermines the good and sincere feelings that are the building blocks of real trust.

THE COMPETITIVE TYPE

Competitive people like to come out on top, which may be their strength but is also their weakness. Competitive people are always trying to prove to the world that they are better than others. They are afraid of testing their self-worth, so they find an opponent they can easily beat rather than truly challenging themselves. As they become more secure, they may choose more worthy opponents, but they still fear confronting their own shortcomings. They need to learn to risk growing into their best, not just being better.

These people are often highly successful in the business world, where their powerful drive to win is rewarded with high salaries that, ironically, they feel they really do not deserve. So tentative is their self-esteem that they live stressful lives, for every new venture offers both the possibility of success and the discovery that they are not what they pretend to be.

The self-worth of competitive people is continually threatened from without. They can sometimes lose themselves by working exclusively for the esteem and adoration of others. Becoming so filled with praise, they lose their motivation and call it quits long before they reach their true potential. They tend to play for the effect more than the goal. This search for external proof of their value both inspires and limits them. Their life lesson is that they must learn to be their own critic, set their own standards and goals, and listen to the voice within that tells them whether they have done well or not.

This need for external reinforcement becomes an especially difficult problem in a relationship, for not only do these people want to be the star players, they want their partners to be their cheerleaders, which is all well and good so long as their partners do not have their own lives. Living with these people often resembles life in a performer's dressing room that is filled with an air of self-centered excitement. Their performance takes precedence over everything else. They always insist on having their way because they believe what they are doing is more important than anything else. This preoccupation can be understandable when the performance involves tomorrow's big negotiation, the upcoming trial, the difficult operation, or the sales presentation, but they are hardly less intense preparing for a driver's test or even dressing for a party where they think they will be noticed. They easily become preoccupied with themselves and put all else second.

Competitive people live in a world governed by what they imagine. They are the great dreamers, which is fine for Michelangelo looking at the blank ceiling of the Sistine Chapel. But unfortunately, in a relationship, the competitive person often uses his imagination to pretend something is of earth-shattering importance merely because he needs to feel worthwhile.

It is this characteristic of exaggerating the importance of trivial issues that makes a relationship with competitive people difficult. They so often demand center stage for minor matters that their partners soon lose the ability to discriminate between what is really important and what is imagined. As a result, competitive people lose their mates' support as their partners stop believing in them. This only reinforces the self-doubt that secretly eats at them. They tend to blame their failures on their partners' lack of appreciation and this becomes a source for conflict.

Competitive women tend to use their sexuality as a commodity. They demand that their partners shower them with approval and comment on their attractiveness. They expect attentiveness, act sweetly surprised, and pretend to put themselves down when such praise is given by saying, "Oh, you must be blind. I really look ugly today," as if begging for another compliment. And yet, when compliments are withheld the competitive woman is deeply wounded, and the offender has everything he can do to earn his forgiveness. If her partner doesn't give her attention, she will play on his jealousy and will tell him how much other people adore her or how beautiful others think she is.

Competitive women frequently use their sexual charms to get whatever they want. They know intuitively what excites their partner and often pretend to be sexually aroused, but then, when their partner responds, they often lose interest or try to pass off their seduction as harmless play. It is no wonder that these people have great difficulty achieving intimacy.

In addition to pretending to be sexually aroused, competitive people often role-play other feelings, for example, being hurt, angry, guilty, remorseful, or afraid. They do this to elicit from others the emotion they want to express without having to take responsibility for it. They can claim that they were only pretending. They often touch on sensitive issues that stir up their partner. Not surprisingly, competitive people have difficulty knowing whether the reaction they are seeing is real or just a response to their fantasy.

When questioned about their own sincerity, competitive people become deeply offended and easily fly out of control. They threaten to walk out, to do anything just to avoid being questioned and to keep the upper hand. Some of the most brutal scenes in a relationship take place during such confrontations, when the anger they provoke leads to physical violence.

As one might expect, competitive people are deeply sensitive to being embarrassed. Any public display of their shortcomings is a powerful source of hurt. Many ongoing battles with competitive people are "innocently" precipitated by their partners' public praise for another's looks or accomplishments, especially if they are in the same field as the competitive person. In the twisted logic of revenge, praising other people becomes their partners' secret weapon.

The competitive man brings his work with him, especially his emotional involvement with it. He talks incessantly about who he is and where his strengths lie. He puts down his competition. He divides his time between believing he is wonderful and doubting himself. Such men seem like overgrown schoolboys, and their preoccupation with their self-worth makes it impossible to love them. Love, in their terms, is praising them for their performance and supporting their weak egos. The only time they really pay attention to what others are saying is when it relates to them. This lack of self-value limits their caring for others.

HOW THESE TYPES
LIVE TOGETHER

No matter what sort of character type you or your partner happen to be, it is still possible to have a loving, lasting relationship. However, when dependent, controlling, or competitive people clash, their difficulties are predictable. Understanding these problems will help solve them.

Keep in mind that, in all of these conflicts, the solution is always reached by telling the truth about your feelings. Remember that you are a person before you are a partner—you must always do what you have to do to ensure that you can walk away from anything that is not good for you. Your first obligation is always to find and develop your strength and to point out what you see and feel to your partner in a loving way.

The Dependent-Dependent Relationship

When two dependent people bond they do so for safety, security, and permanence, but they want security so much they frequently do not permit each other to take the necessary risks to grow and truly feel comfortable together. The unwritten rule that governs these relationships is that each partner is the property of the other and is responsible for and to the other. Because there is so little room to reflect on one's independent needs or to fulfill them, the relationship soon becomes a prison. Since most of these dependent-dependent bonds are formed between two young people who still need to grow, there is an anxious quality to these relationships. Both partners still feel the need to grow but fear being abandoned.

When one partner does gain the strength to be more independent, the other becomes terrified. Nagging, smothering, checking up, forced affection, and demands for continuous reassurances and demonstrations of love prevail. This is guilt-provoking and alienating at the same time.

To the rest of the world, dependent-dependent relationships appear to be boring because they are vested in maintaining the status quo that existed when a couple first started going together. They may also appear to be the closest of all relationships, characterized by a mutual support system. In fact, however, they may be stifling, as both partners try to convince each other that they have nothing to fear, that they are both fine and live in the best of all possible worlds. They want to believe they are happy.

Barry and Julie married right after high school, where they were voted "Class Romance" in their yearbook. Barry went to work for his father and they lived in an apartment over Julie's parents' garage. Barry referred to himself as happily married and earning a solid living when he was only eighteen, but he was afraid of taking risks on his own and needed the protection of his father and the stability of a family to feel good about himself. Julie had two children by the time she was twenty-two and had put on fifty-five pounds. She was always home. Barry did not object because he always knew where she was and it made both of them feel secure to know they lived for each other.

Barry wanted them to have a home of their own, but Julie was reluctant to give up the convenient baby-sitting arrangement her mother provided. Barry was doing well as a salesman, his self-confidence had grown, and he felt that a move was in order. He persisted and they found a small house less than a mile away. It added to Barry's self-worth.

When his father died suddenly, Barry took over the business, and while he claimed to be feeling confident, he now needed more material signs to show people that he really was in charge. A bigger car was first on his list, and although they had been in their house only a year, Barry wanted a larger home in a better part of town. Julie complained, fearing that a larger home would totally over-whelm her. Barry against insisted, and before she could organize her objections they moved a second time.

When Barry made plans to expand the business and wanted Julie to travel with him, she began to have panic attacks, fearing something terrible would happen to the children if she left home. Barry was concerned at first, but as her symptoms increased he started to feel confined. He began to get angry at her and resentful of the problems with the children that, to his view at least, Julie seemed to invent. Julie began complaining that he no longer loved her. When he finally blurted out that she had gotten obese and wasn't as attractive as before, she was devastated.

Barry began to spend more time at work, and the more he withdrew the more clinging Julie became, continually demanding proof of his love and asking him to repeat that he would never leave her. He wanted to expand socially, but Julie practically refused to leave the house. Barry felt alone and abandoned by Julie.

When Barry discovered several empty wine bottles in the trash and Julie admitted that drinking was the only way she could feel comfortable staying alone, he became sick with guilt. Feeling that he had been responsible for all her problems, Barry felt torn and started to cry, explaining that while he still needed Julie, he wanted her to be a woman now and expand her horizons. Julie didn't understand. All she wanted was for him to love her as she was, as he always had done before. He had changed. It wasn't fair of him to ask her to be different.

In a moment of great courage Barry told the truth. He admitted

132

his anger at her confining symptoms and her failure to take care of herself. He told her that if she didn't want to get better she would lose him. He could feel his love fading. He also said he didn't want this to happen.

Outraged, Julie ran to her mother's, but the welcome soon wore thin and her mother sent her home saying that she belonged with her own family now. Julie feared divorce, but it took her several months of playing helpless and testing bottom before she realized that she was bringing on the very thing she dreaded most. Motivated at first by her desperation, she decided to try to change. Within a year she lost a great deal of weight and began to work in a friend's art poster shop. She did so well that when the friend expanded to a second shop, she took over as manager and began to organize shows, arranging the publicity and meeting with graphic artists. When she insisted on having full-time help to provide continuity of child care, Barry started to object—now *he* was beginning to feel threatened by Julie's growing independence. After all, they had only dated each other, and with Julie looking so attractive, Barry explained, she might want to experiment with other men. Julie reassured Barry that not only did she not want to experiment, she fully realized what he had gone through in trying to get her motivated. It was a wonderful moment for both of them.

Dependent people will sometimes risk changing only when disaster seems certain. If the partners in such a relationship can believe in their love for each other and risk being open about their fears, real strides toward independence can be made together.

DYNAMICS OF THE DEPENDENT–DEPENDENT RELATIONSHIP

Why they bond: Mutual need for support
Undermining forces: Any move toward independence
Conflicts: Withholding reassurance, support, or love
Why they break up: One finally outgrows the other
What each needs from the other: Reassurance when not growing
Direction for growth: To see each partner as independent

The Dependent-Controlling Relationship

More common than dependent-dependent relationships, the dependent-controlling relationship appears to be even more stable, but when it gets into trouble it is nightmarish. Dependent people often test their partners' love. But controlling people are so intellectualized that, for all the protection and security they offer, their dependent partners still don't feel loved. They feel something is missing in the relationship but lack the necessary courage or maturity to go it alone.

Some of the most frustrated and desperate people are the dependent partners in these relationships. They have limited their growth so much that they have lost their self-confidence, and when they feel abandoned, they may be completely helpless or threaten self-destruction. If they do manage to become self-sufficient, that, too, is seen as a threat to the controlling partner in the relationship. And if the dependent partner realizes that she is not getting the affection she needs and innocently turns elsewhere for support, usually to friends, then the controlling partner, who counted on the dependent partner needing and obeying him, tries to enforce ever tighter rules. The dependent partner again submits or the relationship quickly becomes a battlefield. Every attempt by the dependent partner to develop skills, work, or have a life of her own is seen as rebellion. The dependent-controlling relationship is trouble-free only when both partners accept their roles and have no desire to change.

Oddly, when love dies in such a relationship, both partners have great difficulty leaving it. The controlling partner can't give up what he controls and the dependent partner is overwhelmed by thoughts of starting again.

The following is an edited transcription of a call to my radio program, illustrating how a dependent partner will cling to a controlling partner, merely for the false sense of security that the controlling partner's rigidity creates. Dependent partners hold on even when they know doing so is not good for them. They feel that no matter how badly they are treated, it is not as fearful as the unknown. This fear is often the strongest force holding such a couple together.

M: My name is Marcia and I'm sixty. I wanted to ask you a question. Can my husband make me physically ill?

V: Why do you ask?

134

M: I have a severe bad back, but I notice that when he is around it's always worse.

V: Is he ever away?

M: Sometimes, for several weeks.

V: And then?

M: I'm symptom free.

V: Why is this so hard for you to figure out? How long have you had the problem?

M: Eighteen years.

V: Eighteen years! How long have you been married?

M: A little over eighteen years.

V: What's it like living with this man?

M: Well, he doesn't talk to me. He withholds money from me. I practically have to beg for money for food. Clothes money, forget it. He says I have enough clothes.

V: Do you tell him how you feel about the way he treats you?

M: (laughs) You think he would listen? He never listens.

V: Do you have a sexual relationship?

M: No, my back is always hurting when he is around.

V: How does he react when your back is hurting?

M: He just ignores me.

V: That's fine with you I take it?

M: Uh-huh.

V: Any children?

M: Not from this marriage. He dislikes my kids.

V: Mention some good points about this man.

M: (pause) Well, he's a good organizer. He always leaves me lists of what has to be done around the house when he's away, what plumber to call and the telephone number. But that's only when there's a bad leak. Things have to get pretty extreme for him to part with his money. He also takes care of all the finances and puts a roof over my head.

V: Do you love him?

M: I'd have to like him first.

V: I'm having difficulty understanding why you stay with him.

M: Where would I go?

V: What do you mean, where would you go? Ever hear of getting a job and supporting yourself?

M: I tried that, but my back is a problem.

V: When he's around. If you were on your own it sounds like your back would be better

M: I suppose.

V: What do you mean, suppose? Isn't what you told me the truth? Don't you know down deep that you're always better away from him?

M: I suppose.

V: You don't suppose, Marcia. You know.

M: I suppose I do.

V: How did you manage before you got married?

M: I worked, put my kids through school after my first husband died. I hated working and I felt pretty desperate. That's why I married him. He offered to take care of me.

V: Pretty irresistible huh?

M: (sighs)

V: So what are you going to do?

M: At my age?

V: At your age. How long have you been saying that to yourself? Ten, fifteen years?

M: (a knowing laugh) All my life.

V: You're not happy.

M: No, I'm not.

V: You deserve to be.

M: So why won't he treat me better?

V: That's how he is.

M: Do you think he can change?

V: Has he changed one bit in eighteen years?

M: You've got a point there.

V: Marcia, I can tell from your humor and from the way your voice sounds that you've got a lot of good years left and you deserve to live them happily. It's not your husband's restrictions that hold you in place, it's your own fears. You sold out your freedom to this man by avoiding taking responsibility for yourself. The pain you felt over the years should have prompted you to leave long ago, but instead you used your pain to keep your distance. You allowed yourself to become debilitated and to see yourself as handicapped.

M: That's true, I do. I'm always going to doctors. They even tell me I should leave.

V: You have to make a first step.

M: But I can't support myself.

V: Maybe not now, but there is a way somewhere. Did you ever tell your husband that you wanted to leave?

M: That's his threat.

V: It has to be your goal, even if it is just to prove to yourself that you feel better without him. You have been using pain as a weapon for so long you feel defenseless without it. You have to admit the pain of your own circumstances instead of focusing on your back. You've been holding on to your pain so tightly that you have forgotten that pain is a warning, an inspiration to risk. It's there to get you to move and see that you must make a better life for yourself.

Unfortunately, I don't know what Marcia did, but I hope she has come to realize that it's better to be a little afraid of the world than to feel helpless about your body and your life.

DYNAMICS OF THE DEPENDENT–CONTROLLING RELATIONSHIP

Why they bond: Mutual weakness, admitted by the dependent type, denied by the controlling person

Undermining forces: Anything that adds to the dependent person's strength; anything that diminishes the controlling person's power

Conflicts: The dependent person becomes a bigger burden or decides to grow up; the controlling person withholds material and emotional support

Why they break up: The dependent person develops self-esteem, the children grow up, and the controlling person can leave without feeling guilty

What each needs from the other: Dependent person needs room to grow; controlling person needs to grant more freedom

Direction for growth: To grant the right of personhood

The Dependent-Competitive Relationship

Dependent-competitive relationships are unstable because the two partners are at opposite ends of the growth spectrum. The dependent person doesn't want to take any risks while the competitive person appears to be taking too many. Understandably, the anxiety level of the dependent person in these relationships is high and jealousy is common. The competitive partner often feels held back by his mate.

Insecure competitive people are attracted to these relationships before they establish themselves in the world. They use their partners to provide them with an emotional foundation. Although they often quickly outgrow their partners, they pretend they cannot leave because their partners need them so much. In these dependent-competitive relationships, both partners are primed for infidelities, long-standing affairs on the part of the dependent partner and shorter, ego-building indiscretions on the part of the competitive partner. There is a delicate balance between stability and flamboyance in these relationships and, again, they only work when both partners are willing to play their assigned roles and feel no necessity to change.

Chet and Pauline had been married for fifteen years, during which time his acting career had blossomed. He had received major roles on the Broadway and London stage and in several feature films and mini-series on television. She originally worked as a photojournalist, but her shyness had prevented her from being aggressive enough to get the really telling pictures. Chet's financial success and Pauline's ability to manage their investments had made them rich. To all appearances they had a storybook life together, but there were problems. Over the years Pauline spent more and more time at home, working on a novel that never seemed to progress. Chet was very supportive of her artistic endeavors—when he took the time to think about her. At times, though, his attitude seemed a little patronizing and his compliments like a display of obligatory approval offered to ensure peace and allow him to talk about himself. Their life was largely about him, and to maintain her sense of independence Pauline often exaggerated the importance of what she was doing, spent hours dressing and delaying him, and once made him embarrassingly late for a dinner in his honor. He finally left without her.

Pauline was smart enough to know they were having difficulties. So one night, when Chet called her from the road, she taped their conversation without his knowing to illustrate the problems they were having. She had been trying to get him to listen to her complaints but could never get through to him.

C: Hi, honey.

P: Hi.

C: I was fantastic tonight. I was so open and free out there. I had that audience spellbound. I got right to the point where I almost became George without being George, if you know what I mean. I actually felt married to Martha. Some people think Albee is dated, but you can bring so much life to this part. It's a perfect vehicle for me and I'm always finding something new. The "hump the hostess" business was great tonight. I was great tonight. I just get so much good energy working on stage. I don't know why I even bother to do films.

P: So how did it go tonight?

C: What? . . . (pause, confusion) What's the matter?

P: Nothing.

C: Why did you just ask how it went?

P: Because I'm interested.

C: But I just told you.

P: You did?

C: You sound angry.

P: Do I?

C: Look, we're three thousand miles apart. I just called in for a little contact. A little love and support.

P: Sounds like you've got tons of love and support right where you are.

C: Come on, you know what I mean.

P: No, tell me what do you mean?

C: What kind of a question is this? What's with you tonight?

P: Are you aware that you get on the phone and don't ask about me, you just start talking about how wonderful you are.

C: I was good tonight. You would have been proud of me. I just wanted to share it.

P: I am proud of you. And you always share it. I do love you, but I am your wife, not your audience. You keep getting us confused.

C: Oh, come on, you're not going to start that.

P: Start what?

C: It's not important.

P: It's not important because it doesn't have to do with you.

C: I see I should just hang up and call later.

P: If you like.

C: I don't want to. I want to talk to you.

P: Let's pick a subject to talk about. Stop me when I mention your favorite.

C: Oh, for . . .

P: How about our quarterly taxes . . . hmm? I'm getting an estimate on replacing the spa. Am I getting warm? How about I've been feeling kind of down this last week. Not interested? Well, I've got a great idea. Let's talk about how wonderful you were tonight. You start talking and I'll go boil an egg. When it's done I'll pick up the phone again. Maybe you'll get it out of your system.

C: What did I do?

P: You didn't make me feel as if anything in your marvelous world mattered except you.

C: You matter.

P: Convincingly, now . . . start slowly, with restraint, and build to your need for me.

C: Cut it out. You'd think I didn't care.

P: You'd think that, wouldn't you?

C: This is going nowhere.

P: What "this"? This marriage or this conversation?

C: What the hell has happened to you since yesterday? You get so damn insecure and put it all on me. Okay, I admit it. I'm self-centered, egotistical, an egomaniac. Put me in a mental ward, give me a lobotomy, but I'm an actor and a terrific actor. I struggled for years and now I'm enjoying my success. Is that a crime?

P: I'll have our lawyer check the penal code in the morning.

C: Paulie, Paulie . . . (voice starting to crack)

P: You're right, you are a terrific actor.

C: What do you want from me?

P: To know that I'm missed. To know that you think of me.

C: I think of you. I placed this call, didn't I?

P: To brag to me, not to find out how I am. It's tiring. I need you to want to be with me because you feel better being with me. Once we were really close.

C: Sure, when you were so insecure you couldn't even go out of the house. We've grown up. You're more independent now. Look at all the great things you've done. The house. The novel.

P: Why doesn't this make me feel better?

C: (sigh of regret) Because I'm not being sincere and I'm not being kind. Paulie, I just lose touch sometimes. I love you and I am there for you and I want you to be there for me.

P: That's what I need to know. You know how easily I forget.

C: I'm sorry. I forget, too.

P: I'm glad you were wonderful tonight.

C: So am I. I thought I was going to fall on my face.

Pauline later played back their conversation for Chet and it was an eye-opener for both of them. Chet knew he was competitive but was unaware of the way he manipulated Pauline into giving his ego the support it needed. And Pauline knew she was dependent but was equally unaware of the way she manipulated Chet into giving her the support she needed. Both had been playing the same game for years and both were now able to admit to each other that they had secretly resented it. Once they were honest about their needs and their feelings, their relationship took a turn for the better.

So long as partners accept each other's vulnerability and are willing to be open, there is room to grow in dependent-competitive relationships. But when the dependent partner becomes too frightened or jealous of the competitive partner's success, or when the competitive partner becomes so self-preoccupied that he forgets the needs of the dependent partner, the relationship can be permanently undermined.

DYNAMICS OF THE DEPENDENT–COMPETITIVE RELATIONSHIP

Why they bond: Need for love and admiration on the part of the competitive person; the need for support and security on the part of the dependent person

Undermining forces: The competitive partner's need to be the center of attention causes the dependent partner to cling and test; the dependent partner's anxiety overwhelms the other

Conflicts: The dependent partner tends to play the emotional burden; the competitive partner is unable to give the dependent partner security and emotional support

Why they break up: Too much insecurity for the dependent person to manage; the competitive person becomes overburdened or bored and wants to move on

What each needs from the other: Dependent person needs to risk more and to be a more lively partner by becoming more of an independent person; competitive partner needs to temper his self-preoccupation

Direction for growth: Acceptance of each other's needs in an atmosphere of honesty in which the competitive person can admit his dependency on his partner's stability and the dependent person can admit manipulating the other by acting helpless.

The Controlling-Controlling Relationship

This kind of relationship requires a great deal of mutual respect to survive. The controlling posture is an unreasonable one that each can rationalize to himself. Both partners in this type of relationship must accept the fact that what they believe is true may have nothing to do with what is right for the other. Unfortunately, when a controlling person bonds with another controlling person, a power struggle is guaranteed. Under stress the partners project self-doubt onto each other and see betrayal and sinister motivation where it does not exist. They argue like two defense attorneys.

Sex tends to be rather mechanical in these relationships, but the partners, who both have a tendency to become obsessed, misconstrue frequency for intimacy and have the capacity for performing without deep feeling.

When such relationships work well, and there is understanding and acceptance, these couples can run businesses together, amass huge amounts of money, and not even notice that they are workaholics or aren't especially affectionate.

When the partners are not especially gifted or mature, these relationships deteriorate under stress. Each tries to control the other, setting up tests, making rules and manipulating, distorting gossip, fighting over power, creating conflict elsewhere.

Leonard and Myrna postponed their marriage plans three times to renegotiate their prenuptial agreement. Each kept discovering sinister intentions between the lines and they quarreled about the placement of commas. After they married, they quarreled about the placement of pictures, furniture, and anything else that required a decision. No matter how little they knew about a subject, each had an opinion, and when they had an opinion, they had a line of logic to back it up. Their life consisted of endless discussions, meetings with agendas, notes, and lists. Each always had to be right.

If their arguments sometimes got heated, it would usually be over some trivial point, for they rarely discussed anything personal. Their worst battles came over the checkbook. They could never agree on each others' accounting procedures. They carried on for years on an intellectual level, and although they were not especially close, they defended each other to the outside world and lived in relative peace. Their troubles began when their daughter Stephanie was born. Myrna did not like the idea of nursing. The thought of being a food source made her gag. Leonard felt nursing was essential for the baby's sense of security. They argued over everything that had to do with Stephanie. Leonard wanted Myrna to give up her management position and stay home. Myrna felt quality time was more important than quantity. The only reason she did not complain about Leonard being a workaholic was that she was too busy to notice whether he was home or not. They could agree on only one thing—Stephanie was brilliant—but each claimed primary responsibility for the genes that gave her intelligence and they argued over that.

They continually paraded every newly discovered sign of Stephanie's brilliance in front of the few friends they had. As if to document Stephanie's specialness—and her own exceptional parenting —for posterity, Myrna arranged for Stephanie to be a subject in a research program analyzing learning profiles of gifted children and actually manipulated the researchers into allowing her to assist in writing the thesis. For years Stephanie was their strongest bond. Although Myrna and Leonard had achieved all of their career goals, they were not happy together. The only reason they did not divorce is that neither wanted Stephanie to come from a broken home.

Two weeks before the ceremony in which she was to graduate as valedictorian of her high school class, Stephanie was arrested for selling marijuana. She was put on probation after claiming she had done it to get attention because her parents never talked or really listened to her. Leonard and Myrna were overwhelmed, embarrassed, and dismayed. Although each secretly felt responsible, they began to attack and blame the other right in the judge's chambers. This time the emotions they expressed were deep.

They were actually angry at Stephanie for letting them down, but because she had been their shining light they could not admit this or voice their disappointment directly to her. Realizing Stephanie was flawed cast doubts on their own sense of perfection. This so disturbed them that they could not unite to act in her interest. The couple that discussed everything could not talk about their most important problem at all, the kind of people and parents they were.

Stephanie finally confronted them and told how relieved she felt to be normal, that having them as parents was a burden and that she looked forward to college mostly to get away from them. Hearing this coming from their daughter they had to listen. It was the first time either had ever seriously considered the possibility that they might be wrong.

This case history shows the primary difficulty of a relationship between two controlling people. The partners each live in their own private world, walled off from the other. Their primary communication is to define the arrangements between them, not to live life openly. It often takes a calamity to break down these walls.

For two controlling partners to grow they must both risk being vulnerable. They need to make a commitment not to take advantage of the weaknesses they discover when they do so because their natural inclination is to blame their partner for their own shortcomings. In order to grow closer, they have to risk being manipulated. This is their greatest fear. Understandably, they are slow to change, except in the face of tragedy.

DYNAMICS OF THE CONTROLLING–CONTROLLING RELATIONSHIP

Why they bond: Similar ambitions, goals, and intellectual style

Undermining forces: Dissimilar opinions about how to achieve their goals and any change that alters the balance of power between them

Conflicts: Money, control, permission, autonomy

Why they break up: One or the other can't stand being controlled or the state of low self-esteem that manipulation creates

What each needs from the other: Greater freedom and autonomy

Direction for growth: To accept one's own imperfections and allow the other person their own room to be imperfect

The Controlling-Competitive Relationship

When these relationships work, each partner offers the other what seems to be missing in his or her life. The controlling partner, usually older, more wealthy or influential, gives the competitive partner the opportunity to have his big chance. The competitive partner brings passion and excitement to the relationship. This is the relationship of the patron and his protégé. They can be stunning matches!

When life gets rough—when the controlling person's power wanes or the competitive person fails to win success—this relationship can become tumultuous and unsatisfying. When the competitive person's career falters he generally accuses the controlling partner of withholding support, not doing enough for him, or trying to limit his success. On the other hand, too much career success may threaten the controlling partner, who may withhold his support to reassert control over the competitive partner. The competitive partner quickly retaliates by reaching out to someone who truly appreciates and is willing to replace what was withheld.

Whenever the controlling partner doesn't deliver as promised, the competitive partner tends to fall out of love, creating panic in the controlling partner. There is considerable barter in this relationship: passion and money are the two main commodities traded. The pain of withholding can become excruciating. Just as the controlling partner can become rigid and manipulative, the competitive partner can also become manipulative or indifferent. These people can bring out the best and the worst in each other.

Eva had been in the United States on a student's visa for only a few weeks when she met Dennis at the opening of an Impressionist exhibit at the museum. Eva was in her early thirties and professed to be from a titled German family. Dennis was almost fifty, the heir to a large fortune and a family whose roots went back before the American Revolution. He did not work but he was well educated, active in the arts, and prominent in society. In spite of his portly frame, he was charming and possessed an inbred social ease. Eva immediately found him attractive, and when she discovered that two of the Monets, one Cézanne, and a small van Gogh displayed in the exhibition were on loan from his family's private collection, he seemed almost irresistible. A few discreet questions revealed that Dennis was just divorced and living in a beautiful town house without a single piece of furniture. He needed a woman's touch, and badly, Eva decided. She worked her way into a conversation with the curator and quickly pronounced Dennis's paintings as the best in show, making sure Dennis overheard her. His eye caught her striking figure and he pointed out with typical graciousness that the works on loan from the Art Institute of Chicago were far better than his own.

Within the week Eva had moved into Dennis's house.

Dennis had never known passion like this. Eva was totally uninhibited sexually and made Dennis feel alive. She flattered him by telling him that making love with him "was like heaven on earth." He was not difficult to convince. He began to lose weight without realizing that she had put him on a diet. She started choosing his clothes and buying furniture with his money, managing to wheedle little trifles for herself by hinting unabashedly as they shopped together and then lavishing love and affection on him afterward, manipulative reinforcements he recognized but to which he did not object. Had his former wife acted this way, he would have refused her flatly, but he regarded Eva's antics as adorable.

By nature, Dennis was a tightwad. He had been taught from childhood that although the family holdings were extensive, they were established before income taxes existed. If they were squandered they could never be reacquired. He learned to live on interest and never touch principal, never sell assets. Eva found his soft spot. He was bored. She was the personification of his sexual fantasies. She could reassure him at the core of his being and therefore had the power to threaten him as well. While Dennis could be rigid and intimidating with his business associates, he became a complete pushover with Eva.

Eva was ambitious, bright, and highly competitive, although when feeling unsure she could range from being a little scattered to uncontrollably hysterical. Her flaw was that she had always relied on others and so never developed the confidence that she was special or the belief that she could make it on her own. Not surprisingly, rather than look to herself for the strength to succeed, she found it easier to use Dennis. For his part, Dennis was proud of her beauty, her taste, and her style, all of which reflected favorably on him. But when he complained mildly that Eva was spending too much money, or dragging him to parties that he didn't particularly enjoy just to show off a new gown or a new piece of jewelry, she became deeply wounded and overreacted, creating a hysterical scene that made him forget his point. He was always glad to settle for a truce. And Eva knew how to seal the bargain so he would feel good about his acquiescence.

Dennis was not a weak man, but he had no control over Eva, a feeling he could not bear. For that reason alone he postponed the decision to marry Eva but continued to allow her to spend his money lavishly. She had him wound completely around her little finger and he did what he had to do to keep her love.

Then one afternoon his attorneys informed Dennis that imprudent overdrafts from his trust fund had depleted his capital and reduced his income. He was placed on a frugal budget. He hoped Eva's love would compensate for the deprivation they would have to undergo. After all, they still had each other.

Not entirely sure of his position, he took Eva to lunch at a fashionable restaurant to explain his new financial situation in the hope that the public atmosphere would temper her reaction. Before he could say a word, Eva said she needed a new gown for a charity ball. When Dennis suggested that she wear one of her other dresses, Eva was crushed and pleaded that she couldn't go to such an important function with a dress that had been seen before. She would rather stay home, she said. Dennis said he would go alone. Eva stood up and threw a glass of water in his face and stormed out of the restaurant. When he reached the street he saw her running toward his car, but when he caught up with her she acted as if he were attacking her. Tears and insults flowed as they drove away. She accused Dennis of abusing her and worked herself into such an excited state that she jumped out of the car at the next traffic light and ran blindly across the busy street, causing cars to screech to a stop around her. Once home she blamed Dennis for nearly being run over.

When Eva understood that Dennis was only on an allowance and had no real control over his money, their relationship deteriorated. While protesting she loved him, any financial stress they endured somehow managed to precipitate an argument. However, Dennis's name still meant power and plenty of invitations. Eva used his influence to cut a wide swath in social circles, dropping Dennis's name and praising him in public while abusing him viciously in private. She would belittle him until he was ready to explode and then placate him with her sexual magic. He began to hate himself for his need for her, but he still believed he could not function without her.

In the middle of all this, a member of Dennis's family died and he found himself flush with money again. His confidence returned, and with it, his suspiciousness. He knew he could not hold his own against Eva and so he kept the amount of his windfall a secret from her. Thus Eva was unaware of the shift in the balance of power between them.

With his new sense of power, Dennis became more cautious and began to pull away from Eva. When she saw Dennis talking with a younger woman at a yacht club dance, Eva immediately got a headache and insisted he take her home. Dennis quietly suggested that she was jealous. She was horrified, practically shouted "How could you say such a thing?" and haughtily strutted out, being careful to give him time to catch up.

Dennis turned and looked at the young woman to whom he'd been talking, whose face projected the sympathetic warmth and courtly attention that people usually had lavished on him, the respect that had recently been missing in his life. He decided to finish his drink and lost track of the time. When he arrived home Eva was packing to leave, but instead of going upstairs to confront her, he poured himself a nightcap and, feeling completely in control again for the first time in months, he sat patiently in the living room waiting for Eva to make her frenzied exit. Anticipating her needs, Dennis called a cab and sent the driver upstairs to help with her bags.

Eva had miscalculated how much humiliation and manipulation Dennis would tolerate. He needed a woman's love and support and was desperately afraid of being alone. What Eva did not comprehend was that controlling people like Dennis are capable of falling out of love as precipitously as they fall in love. When Eva called Dennis two weeks later, ready to resume their old relationship on what she thought would be her terms, a young woman answered the phone. Burning with curiosity, Eva asked the woman to identify herself. She replied that she was Dennis's new wife.

The capacity of the controlling partner to show strength is usually damaged in a relationship with a competitive partner; were it not for his unsuspected good fortune Dennis might never have regained his courage. Dennis's money was his real source of power, for he had never really distinguished himself in his own right. Many controlling people have no personal power apart from their financial leverage. Once he was financially liquid again, Dennis was able to distance himself from his involvement and see himself as separate from Eva. He embraced his regained power and the good feeling it gave him. His sudden marriage was just another maneuver demonstrating his freedom to himself. As for Eva, she miscalculated by assuming that Dennis's sexual needs were greater than his need to control.

DYNAMICS OF THE CONTROLLING–COMPETITIVE RELATIONSHIP

Why they bond: They feel incomplete without the other

Undermining forces: Changes in the marketplace in the value of love or power

Conflicts: Each withholds whatever the other wants

Why they break up: Supplies not delivered as contracted

What each needs from the other: A greater understanding of and a willingness to satisfy mutual needs

Direction for growth: To learn to go it alone and still be together.

The Competitive-Competitive Relationship

If their schedules can be worked out and the tendency for self-involvement can be overcome, people in a competitive-competitive relationship can have highly interesting and challenging lives together. The problems here are predictable. If there are two careers and one is going better than the other, envy and its companion, self-doubt, cast long shadows over the relationship. Sharing the spotlight is the continual problem. Love has to bridge the difference and change "Why not me?" to "Good for him/her"—a difficult transition for two people who tend to be insecure and base their well-being on how strongly they are applauded. If two competitive people can overcome their mutual insecurity and use their shared vulnerability to understand each other, their relationship can be among the strongest and most vibrant of all.

150

Erik and his wife, Martina, were two highly competitive people on the way up. Erik worked in the aerospace industry as a cost analyst. On the day of his fifth wedding anniversary, his company was submitting a bid for a new launch system and his department had a deadline to meet. Martina had just been promoted to head of marketing of a large medical services corporation. The company was developing a new marketing strategy and that very same day she was in charge of the presentation.

The following is a re-creation of their communications with each other during the day:

10:20 A.M. To Erik: (telephone note) "Your wife called and said she loves you. Is looking forward to tonight."

11:00 To Martina: (telephone note) "Erik called to say he loves you, too. He'll try to reach you before lunch."

12:00 To Martina: (telephone note) "Erik called. I told him your lunch plans had been changed and you were brown bagging it to a meeting.

1:45 P.M. To Erik: (secretary on intercom) "Your wife called and said she would keep trying to reach you, but they have run into some snags and it looks like they'll be tied up till four. I told her you are booked on the mainframe then to review models. She suggested to call at five, but she thinks she might be late, so she's changing dinner reservations to eight-thirty to be sure."

5:00 To Erik: (telephone note) "Martina said it still looks good for eight-thirty, but they are running late. She told me how cute she thought you looked this morning."

6:00 To Erik: (message on his office answering machine) "Pretty busy day, honey. We're still going over some final details. It looks like the guy I replaced was asleep at the wheel. I'm just looking at some papers we found. I don't think he ever understood the problem he was supposed to solve. Why am I bothering you with this? I hope you haven't forgotten what today is. I can hardly wait to see you. Looks like I'll be here till seven now, but not any later. Sounds like you're having a busy day, too."

7:30 Erik calls Martina's office. No answer.

7:31 To Martina: (home answering machine) "Real complicated problem. Will try again, later."

7:50 To Martina: (home answering machine) "Maybe you're still at the office. Will try there."

7:55 To Martina: (message to an associate who happened to pick up her phone) "Tell her to reach me on the 5505 extension to get past the switchboard. I'm in a mess, tell her."

8:30 They make contact.

Martina: "Honey, I'm just finishing up."

Erik: "I've got real problems."

Martina: "Don't talk about them for a second. I love you, baby. I've been missing you terribly all day."

Erik: "Me, too. I'm beat."

Martina: "I'll bet. What's wrong?"

Erik: "The worst. Some of the data had been entered using an old program, so we had to re-enter it and the results are pretty scary. Our real costs look eleven percent higher. If I sent the original figures in, we'd be in a marginal profit position. I still don't have the right numbers."

Martina: "Why don't you just increase your costs across the board by fifteen percent and go home."

Erik: (laughs) "Very funny. Nice sense of humor you got there."

Martina: "How long will it take?"

Erik: "I won't even know till nine. Probably another hour, . . . hour and a half."

Martina: "Hmmm. . . ."

Erik: "Disappointed?"

Martina: "It's your anniversary, too. Look, I'll cancel Giardino's and make reservations at that Greek place we used to go to when we were dating. It's open till three in the morning."

Erik: "Sophie's! Great idea."

Martina: "I'll go home and take a bath and get ready and you come in whenever you can and I'll have a surprise that will make you crazy."

Erik: "Do you suppose anyone would notice if I programmed the computer to erase all the data?"

Martina: "Everyone would notice."

Erik: "You're sure?"

Martina: "Just take your time. Don't rush. I'll be there . . . and Erik?"

Erik: "Hmmm?"
Martina: "Maybe you'll get lucky."
Erik: "I'm already lucky."

When both partners in a relationship are intensely competitive and work, the importance of being equals in managing the stresses of their relationship cannot be overestimated. Any one of Erik and Martina's communications could have been used as seeds of disappointment that might have flowered into arguments or misunderstandings. Instead, they stayed aware of each other's reality. They trusted each other's love and good intentions and they remembered their own.

DYNAMICS OF THE COMPETITIVE–COMPETITIVE RELATIONSHIP

Why they bond: They believe they have found the kind of person they have always wanted to be with

Undermining forces: Failure or too much success creates an imbalance in the equality they once shared

Conflicts: Withholding one's attention and time due to intense preoccupation with one's self and career especially when the partner's career is stagnant

Why they break up: Insecurity becomes so great that the support and appreciation they get falls short so they seek another person to fill their needs

What each needs from the other: Applause, mutual respect, tolerance of moodiness during periods of self-doubt, patience

Direction for growth: To trust one's self and the other's love and to forgive comments and actions made under stress

Whatever your own or your partner's dominant character type, it was your mutual attraction, your hope to satisfy your own needs, and your willingness to satisfy your partner's needs that drew you together in the first place. But when that balance tips, when only one partner's needs become paramount, or when the needs of either partner are totally unrealistic and cannot possibly be met, the relationship can never be a completely happy one.

CHAPTER NINE

Couple Styles and How They Solve Problems

A HAPPY couple and an unhappy couple have the same kinds of problems, they just solve them differently. An open approach to solving problems reflects a commitment to work out differences together, communicating openly and honestly, sharing feelings, getting closer, giving support, and learning to trust. The closed approach ignores the problem, allows negative feelings to accumulate, and leads the partners to blame each other and become isolated.

Dominant dependent or controlling or competitive character traits are accentuated in a relationship that is under stress. When partners revert to their characteristic defensive patterns rather than being open, they become rigid, tend to aggravate the problem, and make it seem unsolvable. It is easy to become trapped in these rigid responses.

There are times in a relationship when two people who once loved each other very much cannot remember a recent day without a fight or a talk that did not end in an argument. There are times when every problem seems to reawaken the unresolved remnants of the last disagreement. A simple mention of an in-law's name, a child's failure in school, or an unpaid bill seems to trigger, full-blown, the previous argument. The past intrudes on the present and we become lost in our feelings, unable to tell what is real and what is simply resentment for not feeling loved.

Take heart; we've all been there. Everyone has stared out a lonely window on a rainy day feeling hopeless and overwhelmed, wondering what the world has in store for him, questioning if the pain of the present relationship is all there is, speculating on whether or not he should leave. After all, when things are going wrong, wouldn't we all be better off alone?

Then again, there are those fears of loneliness, the sadness of leaving the other person, the fear that maybe we'd be doing the wrong thing. And there is always the gnawing doubt that another person might rediscover the wonderful person we once knew and rekindle the intimate closeness we once shared. So we stay, but we don't always work it out.

WHY DON'T WE WORK IT OUT?

Sometimes we wait for the situation to be made better in some magical way. Our eyes look to the future, to the day when we will have more money, when our career problems will be straightened out, when we lose thirty pounds and are more sexually attractive, when our partner is over his depression, when our parents finally accept us as we are. And we wait . . . and wait. But no matter what we do, as one problem seems to fade another rises to take its place. The milestones of our expectations are met but somehow we are still the same together, still waiting vainly for something to happen to make it possible for us to be happy.

Any couple can be happy when their problems have all been worked out. The real mark of a good relationship is being happy while solving problems together, by living in the knowledge that you are committed to a solution. A happy couple measures its happiness by its willingness to share the burden of living together and openly meeting whatever problems occur. Everything is discussable. All feelings are important. No issue is considered minor if it can diminish the flow of love between the partners. Happy partners take each other's feelings seriously. Happy partners do not withhold their love or question whether they are getting enough. If they feel a lack, their first response is to give more love to fill the void—it is the nature of love to fill all spaces and to give.

Happy partners accept each other. Love is expressed for the way the partners are right this minute, not for the way one hopes they will become. The partners do not feel that they are on trial, that if they make a mistake or fail they will be rejected. There is nothing tentative about real happiness. If you are ever to be happy in your relationship, you have to be happy with your partner right now, just the way he or she is, just the way you are together. If you are staying together only in the hope that it will get better when it never was much to begin with, you are sure to be disappointed. Your hope has more to do with your fear of being alone than with the realistic appraisal of your situation.

The words "if only" have no business in the sentence "I love you." The conditions for being loved have either already been met or will never be met. You must accept this before you go any further. The only change that occurs in people is that they become more or less of their best. To give up your negative and defensive ways of being, you need to develop faith in yourself as lovable. Doubting yourself is negative; so is blaming others for not getting what you think you deserve.

With few exceptions, you get what you deserve in life. If you don't believe this, you have not yet taken responsibility for your life. Real change will not be possible until you see that it was largely your doing that brought you to this time and this place with this other person.

When you join in a relationship with another person, you are still the same two people, but you are also a couple. And each couple has its own style in dealing with problems. That style reflects the way the couple functions together, and it can either enhance or destroy the relationship.

Closed Couples

A closed couple rarely discusses problems directly. The partners tend to react to situations after they have become fact rather than intervene in the problem as it is evolving. Because the partners wish to avoid problems, there is a silent hope that things will get better if they are just left alone. Each partner has some general knowledge of what the other partner is feeling. The specifics, however, are often vague. An example is the husband who comes home in angry silence collapsing in a heap in front of the television while his wife instructs the children, "Daddy had a rough day so be quiet," while making it her business to get out of his way. In a closed relationship, each partner sees him or herself as playing a specific role and carries out that role without much comment. Food is prepared. The children are marshaled to homework and bed. The husband is "serviced" to take the edge off his anxiety so he can get a good night's sleep and go back out into the thankless world. Such partners show a sense of gratitude toward each other that mystifies outsiders who think "How can they put up with this?" The joy of these couples is in their mere survival.

In a closed relationship, feelings are not expressed and the only issues that get discussed regularly have to do with the mechanics of survival. The prevailing attitude is that they all should be grateful for not being worse off than they are. The term "bad times" is used to refer to economic struggles, not emotional disagreements. There is little room for enjoyment, just temporary moments of peace in the struggle. To bring up problems at these "happy" times, such as the infrequent weekend away, would seem unfair. Long-suffering and stoic, these partners tend to let their lives pass by without questioning their pain or stopping to enjoy the pleasure of being together every day. Although placid on the surface, these relationships may teem with unexpressed anger, anxiety, or resentment, and they are especially prone to crises in midlife when sudden dissatisfaction and doubt lead one or the other partner to question if he really has all life has to offer.

Open Couples

The most open couple is never completely open, but openness is always its goal. If closed couples never bring important issues up, open couples discuss everything they care about.

Open partners rely on each other to point out what they are missing, cannot see, or will not look at. Their commitment to honesty and openness is what attracted them to each other in the first place. If one partner in an open relationship becomes closed, the other feels a loss and immediately expresses discomfort and disillusionment. Conflicts run high as the closed partner is confronted. The couple works on this until the closed partner is finally willing to discuss his feelings. The turning point usually comes when the closed partner trusts that his mate is willing to love him and so he risks admitting what was hidden.

When both partners in an open relationship become closed, it is seldom for long. The scene is set for explosion and the resulting fireworks either clear the air or end the relationship. The commitment to being open is not a couple's decision, but a partner's individual way of being. To remain locked in a closed relationship is unthinkable for an open person, and sooner or later he will open up the unsolved conflict.

Open relationships, when they are working, are everyone's envy, for the partners are free to be themselves, to say what they think, and do what they want. Less open people view such relationships with mixed feelings of envy and fear thinking, "I know I would like to be free, but would I want my partner to have that much freedom?" This ambivalent viewpoint reflects the feelings that motivate people to find an open partner when they are not really that open themselves.

The following case illustrates how disrupting it can be when one partner in a closed relationship suddenly becomes dissatisfied and tries to make the relationship more open. The closed relationship provided both partners with a false sense of comfort and security. Change is seen as a violation of trust.

Andy and Susan fought all the time, but always over trivial things. They had an unspoken pact to avoid serious matters. Andy was a modestly successful businessman whose success frightened Susan because it caused him to grow while she remained the same. She put him down, and he exaggerated his success both to impress and threaten her, a kind of punishment for Susan's lack of support. It was difficult for her to tell what was real and what Andy imagined. She found it simpler to insist that his success was completely made up and to ignore it.

Susan disliked change. While she enjoyed their income and lifestyle, she never really felt comfortable with Andy's risk-taking. When he built himself up by bragging, she continually put him down, belittled his accomplishments, and was quick to point out how much money he owed. She refused to listen to his complicated explanations of how his finances worked and paraded her doubt in front of friends and relatives.

While some of what Andy said was grossly exaggerated, there

was a core of real inventiveness and high energy that won the support of business associates. Unfortunately, his forces were becoming increasingly scattered as his life with Susan grew less tranquil. The quiet predictable life they originally had led was changing.

Andy's pride was the condominium he bought at a ski resort, and he loved to invite friends to see what a happy family he had and how athletic his two sons had become. In many ways he was more of a homebody than Susan, but because Susan feared risking, he was always made to feel as if he were threatening the integrity of his family—just by being the person he was. She often corrected and chastised him in front of others, using his earlier behavior as a standard.

Although Andy was never unfaithful, he was an adventurer in his fantasies. He would meet young girls while skiing and more and more he would imagine what his life would be like with them. He would fantasize during the day and return to Susan highly energized. When he redirected his newly awakened sexual feelings toward her, she resisted. She saw him as crazy. He saw her as cold and closed to new experiences. He was living in a fantasy that he wanted to become his life. She wanted reality to stay as it was, stable and familiar. Of course, Susan kept denying that the situation had changed. But Andy *was* different.

One day while skiing Andy met a young woman who was deeply involved teaching a course designed to help people transform their lives. They spent only a few minutes together. She had trouble with her bindings and Andy, always willing to come to the rescue, took several minutes to get her equipment in order. Their eyes met and she told him that she saw in him someone who had great potential for growth and a rich feeling for life, but added that she sensed he was blocked. She got up, thanked him, and skied down the mountain. Andy was stunned by the powerful response he felt to her comments and could only stand motionless and stare as she skied out of sight. He could not put his finger on it, but he had the sense that this woman had verbalized all his inner desires. All he wanted was to be open with Susan, to have a life where they could share feelings and discuss anything.

He skied to their condominium brimming with revelation and disclosure only to find Susan preoccupied with their eight-year-old, who had just twisted an ankle in a fall. As he walked through the door, Susan greeted him by shouting, "If you had stayed with him this wouldn't have happened." Andy wanted to talk. Susan wanted to blame. Andy was ready to walk into the sunset with her to a new life. Susan was resentful that he had added to her anxiety. All the way to the emergency room Andy tried to tell Susan that he saw great things for them. Susan would hear none of it. She had been let down. This dreaming, scheming, indebted man only cared about crazy ideas and had allowed her son to become injured. It was *his* idea to buy the condominium. It was *his* responsibility to watch the kids. She wanted someone who really cared and who wasn't afraid to be attached to a family. Someone she could count on. Andy grew silent and for the first time realized how alone he was. He had invented the togetherness in his marriage just to have something to believe in. Susan merely felt betrayed.

Andy became involved in various self-improvement programs, at first looking for the woman he had met on the ski slopes but later looking for himself. Susan was now more convinced than ever that what she wanted was a solid relationship without continual testing and discussing of every feeling. She methodically alienated Andy from his children, friends, and family by portraying him as a reckless loser. By staging fights in front of others she created the embarrassment that she used as an excuse to leave him. Andy felt highly manipulated, but his relief was so great that he welcomed his freedom gladly.

After they divorced, Susan married a sedate professional man. Andy met Amy at a business lunch at which he was planning to sell his company's services to her firm. In the middle of his opening greeting Amy remarked that he looked preoccupied; without another prompt from Amy, Andy told her the story of his marriage —his hurt and his feelings of being manipulated and unappreciated. Amy responded by telling him that she felt he was wonderfully vulnerable and spontaneously hugged him in the restaurant. They were instantly bonded. Andy had never felt so encouraged or acknowledged. To Amy he could admit all the faults about which Susan had badgered him. He stopped exaggerating, and in his newfound honesty began to channel his creativity into business. Amy joined forces with him and together they formed a new company and made a fortune. What seemed like a continual struggle with

Susan was natural and easy with Amy. She wanted to know his feelings, his ideas, and his hopes. It was as if his entire world had changed, and he had been reborn. In fact, finally he was being allowed to be the person he had long since evolved into.

Andy and Susan were like most closed couples, stable till one of them changed. Unless both partners change together, these relationships survive on borrowed time. With Amy, Andy found an echo and a support to his deepest needs and desires. He was finally free to grow without apologizing for the way he was.

Analytical Couples

Analytical couples pride themselves on their rational approach to problem solving. They are very good at it. They can decide with ease where to spend vacations and what automobile deal is the best. They are equally adept at choosing the color of the carpet, criticizing a young violinist's approach to Tchaikovski, pointing out the inconsistencies in the secretary of state's account of the summit talks, and deciding which of the candidates for advanced study is most qualified.

They love discussions about any proper subject, and they fight over what is proper. But any discussion about emotions is *not* proper. And so when the need to express hurt or anger occurs, these partners are out of their element. They either intellectualize their feelings or brush them under the carpet. They have an obvious weakness in dealing with their emotions, which for the most part goes untested until some external event overwhelms them.

While this may sound like an unfair appraisal, covering one's emotional response to life by assuming that life is always logical and understandable is simply a defensive position. It is a view held by people who are afraid to feel, who never want to be reduced to equality with anyone. Questions of dignity, appropriateness, and respect are what they focus on rather than such more important issues as honesty, fairness, and caring.

The intellect is always a little distancing. While it is a good practice to use one's analytical skills to stand back in the middle of an argument and gain perspective, using one's intellectual functions to deal with people you love and who love you is a sign of weakness.

161

Analytical types may object, but the intellect is always flawed in dealing with the feelings of a relationship. Using your intellect to manage feelings is a bit like trying to swim while wearing ice skates. You can do it, but it's not very satisfying, effective, or real.

Most of the important understanding between people in a relationship is purely emotional. You *sense* that your partner is angry. You *feel* that your partner is sad. You may be able to explain away a feeling to your partner, but without empathy your intellectual understanding is just another problem for your partner to overcome. If you understand everything about the psychodynamics of your partner's feelings, but are not touched, what is your understanding worth?

Analytical couples tend to be snobs who need to put others down in order to feel secure about their tenuous emotional posture. They describe the world as "interesting" rather than commit themselves emotionally. These analytical couples get in trouble when one of the partners suffers a severe career or social setback or becomes involved in a love affair and consumed by unfamiliar emotions. These affairs often end ruinously, especially if the alliance is with someone outside their socioeconomic class—for example, the college professor and the show girl. But when an affair takes place within their circle of friends, arrangements are made with surgical precision. As long as it is not messy, any amorous adventure can be dealt with in a civilized fashion.

I know of one situation in an academic community where two professors, next-door neighbors, had long-standing affairs with each other's wives. The affairs, while discreetly conducted, were nonetheless obvious to all concerned. At a lunch the two professors decided to bring the matter into the open. Each was concerned about wasting valuable time in his present situation. Moreover, making special arrangements was sometimes inconvenient and embarrassing. The need to be secretive was an undignified annoyance as well, and the potential for damage to their reputations was both high and unnecessary. They decided to divorce. Their children could stay in their own bedrooms and the two professors would simply switch houses. They did so without disturbing so much as a plate of chopped liver in the refrigerator. They remained friends exactly as before and each moved into a carbon copy of the relationship he had left. Both prided themselves on their painless handling of the situation. Of course, it was all pointless—there was no real passion involved.

The intellect is the observer, but the emotions are the force of life.

The need for ventilating feelings often becomes an unsolvable problem in analytical relationships. In order to find peace of mind, the troubled partner must, in effect, go against the very foundation of the relationship and a way of life. The loneliness and isolation of seeking a feeling response in such an analytical world can lead a person to the depths of despair, questioning the value of the relationship and of life itself.

Emotional Couples

Couples that are consumed by emotion have their own special problems, most of which remain unresolved because of the nature of their relationship. Emotional relationships tend to be primitive. What is felt is expressed and feelings are translated into action before they are considered, questioned, or reviewed for their reasonableness or appropriateness. There is very little sorting in highly emotional relationships. Everything becomes a crisis of crippling preoccupation—from an ambiguous message on the answering machine to a social slight. Worry consumes such couples. The partners are so concerned with every emotional detail, see so much potential danger everywhere, and assume the worst possible outcome that they are not able to concentrate and work effectively. There are so many emotions in the air that it is difficult to put a value on the importance of a particular feeling. Emotions are rarely resolved; instead, they are simply flung out at random. Expressing one hurt just leads to expressing another. The victim becomes the villain. And the real issues behind the feelings get lost.

Each of the highly emotional partners in this kind of relationship gives the other a peculiar acceptance that he gets nowhere else. Expressing *all* emotions, no matter how farfetched or exaggerated, is understandable to the other. After all, they do the same thing.

While it is almost the rule to find two intellectual types together, validating each other, it is rare to see a relationship between two highly emotional types. They would wear each other out. More typical is a situation with one emotional partner and one control-

163

ling or dependent partner. While this person appears to be the stronger part of the couple, the *style* of the couple is emotional— the outbursts and preoccupation of the emotional partner take up all the couple's psychic room and energy.

Telling the truth in such a relationship is an unforgivable act. When a painful truth is revealed, there is much overreacting, crying, threats of self-destruction and cruel retaliation, and demands for an apology. The underlying issue is never as important as the hurt suffered in bringing it up. While expressing feelings is their style, these people do not really want to hear what hurts or why.

While living like this all the time would be draining for most people, from time to time many relationships slip into emotional disarray. Relationships in which the couple's reality sense has been distorted by alcohol or drugs, or where chronic low self-esteem, unfaithfulness, or sociopathic behavior have predominated, are especially prone to such emotional deterioration. In fact, under the stress of overwhelming losses or reversals, people who are usually controlled and unemotional can become emotionally brittle. Much domestic violence occurs when couples lose their perspective and focus relentlessly on their hurt. They see only betrayal, feel only pain and helplessness, and erupt in a frenzy of blame usually followed by a siege of self-hatred.

I have seen people who have lost their confidence and immersed themselves in emotional and highly destructive relationships in order to embrace the punishment of being together rather than risk taking responsibility for themselves. It is easy to lose yourself in a relationship where it is hard to tell where you leave off and the other person begins.

In order to solve problems in any relationship, it is necessary to become distanced from the fray. In a highly emotional relationship, however, feelings can be so intense on both sides that the only way to solve problems is to end the relationship.

There is a balance between the intellect and the emotions in all lasting relationships. The rule is that neither should be a defense against the other. Where there is a tendency to be intellectual, you need to remember what it is you feel. Where there is a tendency to be emotional, you need to ask yourself what it is you think.

Sexual Couples

Relationships that are based on a powerful sexual or physical attraction are a blessing and a burden at the same time. When two people have strong chemistry between them and are easily aroused by the other, they tend to make sexuality more important than anything else. Their intense sexuality may conceal the fact that the rest of the relationship is not really working. Or the partners may become so involved in the compulsion to be together that they do not notice each other's shortcomings. Often, these exclusively sexual relationships are formed by partners who have felt deprived in other relationships. When they find each other, it seems like magic, but each merely projects the image of the person they want onto the other and falls in love with their illusion.

When couples are highly sexually attracted to each other there is a danger of neglecting other needs, especially if they believe they can solve every problem by making love. It may work for a while, but unaddressed problems tend to build up and eventually undermine sexual spontaneity. So when their feelings catch up with them, these couples are often overwhelmed and unable to cope.

When the relationship gets rough and the partners discover that they cannot work it out, it is common for them to lament "But I'm still *in love* with him/her." The sexual attraction still pulses, still pushes them toward the wrong solution. While couples with a lower sexual drive may envy couples who are more sexual, an intense sexual attraction can interfere with sorting out feelings and letting go of a relationship that may not be a good one.

Because one partner is often more affected than the other, many of these relationships are obsessional, and rejection and abuse are typical. Replays in fantasy of the most torrid times together fill the voids when the partners are not getting along and lead them to desire what is not in their best interest. Often these "good times" were an illusion in the first place, a flight from reality in which they used sex as a universal antidote for their pain and loneliness. Such sex is highly addictive and, again, the need for it can be stronger in one partner than in the other. In that case, the very foundation of their relationship—sex—becomes a problem that, if unresolved, destroys the relationship. If the couple is lucky, the sexual bond between them becomes less intense with time, and the partners are able to find the emotional distance necessary to evaluate their other needs. Usually, however, they must leave the relationship to gain this clarity.

Sexual attraction alone is not enough to sustain a relationship. When there is sex everywhere, there may not be much room for love.

Affectionate Couples

Affectionate couples can be of any age, but typically they have been together a long time and each has become the other's friend. Whether or not there is much sexual activity is not nearly as important as each being there for the other. This is what everyone secretly yearns for: an affectionate, attentive partner who is loving and understanding, gives the benefit of the doubt, and is forgiving and accepting. There is no need for sexual activity to make these feelings of affection complete. Yet the total absence of sex in a relationship can also be a problem that must be resolved. It is especially difficult for many men to understand that the warmth and friendship of just being together is as important as sex in a relationship. Without this closeness, most women feel cheated, unloved, and unwilling to be sexually involved, although they may have sex in the hope that there will be a tender moment afterward. Unfortunately, if the tender moment is not there before, it is unlikely that it will be there later.

Affection is diminished when it is misread as an invitation for sex. Mostly it is men who misinterpret affectionate approaches. The woman, usually wanting closeness, with sex far removed from her mind, reaches out to be affectionate to her mate and finds him suddenly sexually aroused, thinking she wants to make love. This disappoints and hurts her and she pulls back. He accuses her of starting something she won't finish. They may fight; she may give in reluctantly, but the moment has been ruined. Such experiences cause women to become guarded and hold back their natural inclination to touch and simply be close. They repress expressing the needs they want most to be fulfilled. They do not want to arouse a mate and risk disappointing him when they are merely in the mood to be tender. They do not want the moment to change from acceptance to rejection.

166

The couple whose relationship is formed around a solid core of friendship, mutual affection, and trust can usually solve this and any other problem in their lives together. It is that very affection that allows them the freedom to express their true feelings and to explore the ways in which they can fulfill their needs.

Romantic Couples

Truly romantic relationships seem to be made in heaven, but they are probably less rare than we think. Many partners in a relationship are able to achieve a healthy and nourishing balance between love and sex, dependency and freedom. There are great romances that make the headlines, but there are also quiet loves that no one hears about. Romantic couples suffer the same problems as other relationships, but they can, and do, work them out despite their fears of losing each other or becoming consumed by the depth of involvement that they risk. Romantic relationships demand time. They are worth it, but such a union becomes your entire life, because both partners must be dedicated to each other's careers and evolving selves.

The passion of these relationships extends into every aspect of the couple's life together. Discussions about all subjects that matter run deep. Unlike closed couples, who hide problems to keep peace, these passionate relationships demand openness. They invite and insist upon disclosure. Their discussions are natural, born of curiosity and a wish to understand. The loving acceptance that makes this possible is assumed, for both partners know that there is nothing they can discover about the other that will change the way they feel. They are committed to talk about everything that can be in the way of their love.

In every great romance, there is a great friendship.

The key to keeping romance alive is acceptance. When lovers are late, schedules overwhelm, or careers distract, their time together is used to celebrate the relief of being together again and not to blame the other for being absent. The need is to be together, and once together, the couple is free to be themselves. They do not need to make love. They do not need to hug or kiss. They do not need to light candles or sip wine. They may do all of this, but it is icing on the cake. Romantic couples are willing to take risks. Every

moment together is an adventure, offering the possibility of something new. Their romance keeps them young.

Great romances continually celebrate being in each other's presence.

Keeping a relationship like this alive is worth everything, but it
is not always easy. It requires work and complete commitment.
While you may be lucky to find each other, it takes more than luck
to keep romance alive. Romance is a living thing, it grows, and
these guidelines will go a long way toward making your relationship more romantic.

The Rules

Create an atmosphere in which you and your partner can always
be yourselves:

Remind yourself and your partner of your love. Take nothing
for granted.
Treat each other with honesty and respect.
Be totally open with everything you feel.
Be completely vulnerable in admitting your shortcomings.
Listen to and be present for each other.
Accept each other just as you are.
Remember how lucky you are to be together.
Allow your partner to be free.

A CYCLE OF COUPLE FAILURE

The Low-Risk Couple: Low-risk couples always seem old before
their time. The partners seem to assume a role beyond their years
the moment they get together. At twenty-one, the woman in such
a relationship adopts matronly attitudes toward her friends and
partner. The man tends to become rigid, taking the role of head of
household too seriously. These new identities are so fully embraced
that it is difficult to imagine either partner ever having been a child.

In spite of appearances, these partners are usually immature, desperately searching for an identity together that each feels lacking by himself. Their need, like everyone, is to grow, but since they meet this need by acting grown-up and only playing an adult role, their union is often static. Although they may be running away from a difficult home, a boring job, or the fear of being alone, these couples often work hard to establish a relationship just to create an identity and bolster their self-esteem. They assume that the survival of their relationship is the most important commitment for both of them.

Resistance to change is implied and is the limiting factor in these relationships. Change is the source of their most threatening conflicts. To get out of this trap, the partners need to remind each other of their love and support and to realize that if they cannot grow, their relationship eventually dies. The risk of change is a necessary part of growing for both partners. But there is often a natural resistance to change by the partner who wants life to go on as it always has. Both partners need to bear in mind that staying young is expecting to grow.

The Pessimistic Couple: When the challenge to grow goes unmet, the partners in a low-risk relationship become entrenched in their roles and more serious difficulties develop. Usually, one partner yields to the other and abandons plans for him or herself. Resentment grows but is often unexpressed because admitting anger goes against this couple's unspoken agreement to avoid conflict and change at all costs. Both partners know something is wrong, but they cannot put their fingers on it. What is wrong is their original notion of what living with another person is all about.

Pessimism is the prevailing mood when a couple's relationship reaches this stage. They may try to convince themselves that they are happy, but their inner knowledge that somehow, somewhere, they have let themselves down adds to their feeling of being lost. Still they lack the courage to ask what it is that is wrong with them.

What *is* wrong with them?

They have not found their real purpose or meaning in life; they have instead assumed an identity by following a recipe, dictated by social pressures and career demands. More is not the answer. They need fewer restraints and more time for themselves and the courage to pursue whatever dreams give them pleasure even though they seem impractical or silly. If they do not know what their dreams are, they need to be reassured that it is all right not to know as long as they are searching. It may take some years to find a direction that is right.

The pessimism such partners feel reflects their loneliness in not finding a self they really like. Choosing a relationship as one's primary role may provide a temporary identity and shelter from the storms of life, but real growth only continues when a person risks full exposure to his own potential. A relationship without growing pains is a dying relationship.

Burned-out Couples: Those couples who have given up hope of living happily together or of pursuing a life that fulfills them are in the final phase of a dying relationship. They are burned out. Each resents the other for his own failure. Blame and accusation are the most common forms of conversation. Years of fighting have taken their toll here. Their arguments have mostly been shouting matches and have resolved little. Those feelings that have been ventilated have either been ignored or have provoked another explosive episode in the cycle of hurt and anger. In time the fighting may seem to tone down, but in reality the couple has adopted a shorthand form of arguing in which a negative feeling is expressed by a sarcastic comment or look and bitter silence.

Such couples stay together only because the partners feel trapped, often by their guilt over wanting to leave or their fear of surviving alone. In some perverse way they sink to punishing each other by their bad moods and negativity, as if hoping the other will go away. Nevertheless, they often stay together because both partners are insecure and neither has a life without the other.

There is little hope for a relationship when it reaches this final phase. That is why it is imperative to identify the symptoms of trouble in a relationship as soon as possible and take the necessary steps to relieve them. There are problems in all relationships. The greatest sign of love is being willing to work them out.

CHAPTER TEN

How You Settle Disputes

T HERE IS conflict in every relationship, but *how* you fight is almost always more important to the survival of a relationship than what you fight about.

Everyone hates fighting, and for good reason. During fights the complaints of the past are presented with the heat of renewed resentment. Negative comments are expressed more to relieve past injury and hurt than to reach peace. If you can learn to be patient and allow this ventilation to occur without defending or vindicating yourself, you stand the best chance of finding peace. If you choose to retaliate when long held-in pain is expressed, you only create new pain and even more resentment. You do not need to prove you're right. You only need to allow your partner to get it all off his or her chest. Do not take it personally.

HOW TO AVOID TAKING IT PERSONALLY

Listen.
Observe.

Try to understand.

Avoid retaliating in any way.

Remind yourself that everything negative that is being expressed is one thing less to get in the way of feeling good.

See the expression of feelings as relieving pressure.

Be glad for the discussion, even if it makes you uneasy.

And when your partner is finished, be still and allow room for more to be expressed. Don't jump right in. Keep listening.

A Disagreement Diary

To help you define what you and your partner fight about—and *how* you fight—keep a diary of your disagreements over a one- to two-week period. It should be kept individually by both partners according to the following guide.

Use a separate page of your diary for each disagreement, argument, or fight. The word "disagreement" stands for all conflicts, no matter how civilized or out of control. The object is to determine what you disagree about, when, and why, in an effort to understand all of the unsettled issues between you. If you have any doubts about including a particular subject, include it. Issues of doubt and confusion are also sources of conflict. Also, include everything between you that doesn't feel the way you'd like it to feel. For example, if you feel wonderful about an issue and it hurts your partner to discuss it, include it.

It is important to make your entry as soon after the argument as possible. It is also important to note the date and time of the argument, indicating when you decided to raise the issue and why you chose the time you did. Then answer the following questions after each disagreement. Again, these should be individual responses that you put down without discussion between you and your partner. Some of it is for sharing later, but much of it is to help you sort out your feelings and develop some objectivity.

What was the disagreement about?

Who brought it up?

How did the disagreement start? You said: Your partner said:

What questions were asked?

How were they responded to?

What did you want to say but couldn't?

What didn't you want to hear?

What did your partner wish to avoid?

Did anyone blame or accuse?

Did anyone make excuses?

Did the conversation expand to other issues? List them.

Are these other issues ever discussed by themselves?

Were there any past problems involved in the present conflict? List them, too.

Are these questions ever discussed by themselves?

Are any subjects taboo between you and your partner? What are they? Why?

Indicate whenever you wanted to bring a point up but didn't and why.

How long did the disagreement last?

How did you finally resolve the problem?

Did you both agree? Are you sure? Was the understanding spelled out in detail?

Could you have settled the disagreement more easily? How?

If you allowed the disagreement to ruin your day, indicate how you let it get the best of you (building revenge fantasies, nurturing a bad mood that in turn caused other arguments, allowing it to affect your energy or ability to concentrate).

If you completely ignored the argument, how did you accomplish that?

What was your main point?

What was your partner's main point?

How many times have you had this discussion?

If you could do anything you wanted about the matter in question, what would you do? Give a brief, unemotional, clear response.

What keeps you from doing what you want?

Now that you have a moment to think more clearly, what would you have said differently or retracted? Write that down.

What do you suppose your partner is going through right now as a result of this conflict? Put that down.

This inventory will give you the distance to observe what goes wrong between you and your partner. You deserve to have the best relationship possible, so you need to grasp what stands in your way. If you are unwilling to work on your problems you can't be happy together. If you are afraid of what you might find, take courage and complete the exercise step by step anyway.

If you decide to share your entries with your partner, do so within a day to keep the material fresh in your mind. Hold your comments until you have both shared. Listen quietly as your partner reads his diary entries. Do not interrupt or correct each other's entries even if they are grossly distorted or self-serving. Just notice the differences in your point of view. Try to hear your partner's side without defending your position.

If your partner refuses to keep a diary, you can still keep one yourself and share it with him. You've got to start somewhere to keep your relationship alive.

Reviewing Your Diary

Gather a number of diary entries, but it is best to accumulate several weeks' or a months' worth of disagreements for the purpose of this exercise. Now review them by yourself or with your partner and answer the following questions:

How many arguments have you had?

How frequently do you argue?

When are you most likely to fight?

Who brings up painful subjects the most often? Why? What problem is not being addressed?

What subjects cause the most trouble? List these in order of occurrence.

Is there any pattern to your arguing? How does it start? Where does it go?

Are you logical or emotional? Heated or coolheaded?

How completely do you discuss issues?

What is usually left unspoken?

What issues still persist?

Who isn't taking responsibility? For what?

What disagreements did you resolve successfully?

Why were these easier than the others? Is there anything to learn from solving them that you could apply to those problems that still remain?

When did the arguments get out of control? Why?

Is there anything one of you could have said that would have prevented the blow-up?

ANALYZING YOUR STYLE OF FIGHTING

Now that you have an understanding of what you and your partner argue about, it is also important to understand what really goes on in your arguments. To examine your style of fighting, I am going to ask you to do something that both of you may initially wish to resist; however, it is such a powerful tool in getting to see yourself that I urge you to try it. It will repay you many times over with clarity and understanding.

I would like you to tape record your next disagreement.

You need to agree beforehand that the next time you argue, you will record your interchange. If you do not, taking out the tape recorder will become what you fight about.

Recording your argument will help you see your blind spots, your knee-jerk responses, your bullying and cowering, your repetition and thickheadedness, probably all the reasons why you'd rather not look at yourself. Then again, they are exactly the things

175

of which you must become aware, for they define a style of arguing that may be hurtful.

Once you have agreed to make the recording, the next time you argue, fight, or disagree turn on the tape recorder and continue talking. When the argument is over, allow sufficient time to pass so that you have cooled down and then replay the tape either by yourself or with your partner.

Be silent. Pay attention. Listen. Observe your partner. Remember, the object is to understand and make things better between you.

As you listen, consider the dynamics of your argument:

THE INJURY
What are you really fighting about?

Who felt hurt, when and why?

DEFENDING
When did you interrupt?

When were you interrupted?

When did you refuse to listen?

What caused voices to be raised?

When did you ignore what was said?

What editing of your comments did you make because of the tape recorder? Why?

When did you feel trapped and most like running away?

DISTORTING
How logical did you sound?

How unreasonable did you seem?

When did you sound selfish?

When were you unfair?

When did you bully?

When did you insist on being right?

TELLING THE TRUTH
What would you like to take back?

Why did you say it to begin with?

When were you lying?

What feelings or facts did you omit? Why?

When could you have been more direct?

When did you have trouble understanding?

When did you feel misunderstood?

ATTACKING

Who blamed whom and when?

At what specific point did you get drawn into fighting?

Why did you lose your distance?

What tender spots were touched and when?

How did you provoke your partner?

When were you hurtful?

What led up to your attack?

RETREATING

When did you become silent?

What were you feeling and thinking during the silence?

When were you not really listening?

What was it that shut you off?

When did you feel let down?

What compromises did you make to keep the peace?

What positive feelings did you have for your partner during the argument?

Honest answers to these questions will give you new insight into how you argue. Once you have actually heard yourself arguing you will become much more aware of the tactics you use, tactics that may very well aggravate the problems between you and your partner rather than solve them.

HOW TO HAVE A GOOD ARGUMENT

Don't wait for feelings to build up.

Express your hurt as soon as you are aware of it. Indicate what hurts and why.

Be direct and simple.

If you mention your discomfort soon enough, you will be able to resolve the issue in a few moments. If you wait, it will take much longer.

Do not attribute sinister motives or suggest that your partner is bad.

Don't try to make your partner feel guilty.

Don't say things for effect.

Don't attack sensitive areas as a way of retaliating. Remember, confronting someone with their weakness always produces a negative response that is difficult to manage. It may precipitate a heated argument fought from rigid positions, one that is unlikely to result in anything profitable.

Don't look for a fight. You'll find it.

The correct attitude is to expect a positive result.

Let unimportant negative remarks pass without comment. If you lie or say something you do not mean, stop immediately and take it back. A statement like "I misspoke; I really meant to say . . ." is needed. If your partner is still dwelling on the mis-statement, indicate that you are sorry and allow yourself to get past it and move on without commenting.

Don't walk out just because you disagree. Just indicate that you disagree.

Don't pout or become sullen. This is only an attempt to make your partner feel sorry for you. It is childish and diminishes your partner's respect for you and increases his anger because you are not taking the argument seriously.

Do not issue an ultimatum during an argument. If you want to give your partner an ultimatum, be sure that you mean what you say and plan to stick with it and make the comment at another, less heated moment. An ultimatum delivered during an argument is insincere and provocative. It diminishes your credibility, causes more harm than good, and should be avoided.

Again, and this cannot be expressed too strongly, if during the argument you feel warm feelings for your partner, be encouraged; it means you are on the right track and your relationship is already improving. Express these feelings as well and share your newfound hope.

Don't allow any argument to precipitate a crisis. If you feel that you are being pushed to the limits of your reasonableness and acceptance, indicate that you don't want to make any rash comments or decisions and would like to take a break to cool down.

STATEMENTS OF
SELF-AWARENESS

It would be wonderful if each of us could admit our faults freely without fear of recrimination. Letting your partner know you were at fault and can admit you were wrong has great power to end arguments and restore the trust between you. Statements like "When you hurt me, I become silent and act more hurt than I am to try to make you feel guilty" may sound like a humbling self-revelation, but it has a marvelous way of relieving stress and lowering defensiveness. Try to risk being this open in admitting your faults. It can work wonders.

Some sample statements to help you on your way:

"I was wrong."
"I was trying to control you because I felt powerless."
"I was just being spiteful."
"I was trying to hurt you."
"I was being a spoiled brat."
"I was just acting like an idiot."
"I didn't feel good about myself and I took it out on you."

With a little practice you can make these statements at the time of your disagreement and save yourself a lot of pain and suffering.

There's nothing like admitting you were wrong to get a crisis behind you, but don't admit to things you don't believe in merely to end a fight. It's okay to disagree. And once you have made an honest and sincere attempt to solve the problem between you, it's even better to make up.

BREAKING A VICIOUS CYCLE

Sometimes partners find themselves continually drawn into the same hopeless fight. Even when talking about safe issues they can sense the destructive subject just waiting to surface. Their old hurt is easily fanned into resentment by the slightest innuendo and can be explosively brought out into the open. Dismayed to be fighting again, the discouraged partners blame each other, make terrible accusations, draw unflattering comparisons, and deliver devastating assessments of character and motive. Once more feelings are hurt over the old problem. Voices rise and both partners are reduced to their worst. How could they have permitted this to happen again? How could they have done this to themselves? Why couldn't they have stopped themselves? Why is this painful issue still part of their life? Why can't it be settled once and for all?

Such a deteriorating spiral almost always reflects incompletely expressed negative feelings. Some of these destructive feelings may have been trapped years before you and your partner met. The reason that you are dealing with them now may be that your relationship offers the first safe opportunity to examine and settle them honestly. So this may actually be an advantage if you approach it with the right attitude. For example, if during an argument a partner is allowed to express unrealistic anger at her mate without being contradicted, and her mate merely points out that the anger she is expressing seems out of proportion to whatever he has said or done, she may come to realize that she is not angry at him but, say, at her father. Whereas if her partner defended himself and retaliated, he would probably reinforce her belief that he had done something wrong and the spiral of accusation would continue. She would still have the old untested anger to deal with and it would present itself at another time. So even if you think it is unfair that you should have to pick up the messy baggage of your partner's past, just permit these old feelings to be expressed. You may discover that you can solve some of these lingering problems by proxy.

That's what a healthy relationship is all about: allowing all feelings to be expressed openly to someone you trust, put in proper perspective, and resolved directly.

There is a natural inclination in all relationships both to bury and uncover painful subjects, but not always to resolve them completely. In order for a relationship to grow beyond such an impasse, the partners have to be willing to risk the consequences of facing issues directly together. If you value your love, you must find the courage to deal with what hurts each of you. Allow yourselves to express everything that's bothering you without interruption.

Again, to be good fighters you must understand that your partner's comments will often be exaggerated, unfair, misconstrued, vicious, intentional, and undermining. They will also be purposefully constructed to hurt you in your most vulnerable place. Keep in mind that although they are purposely hurtful, they may only be directed at you because you happen to be around. Let them all be spoken without refuting them. Just observe them and try to imagine the pain your partner feels.

Don't respond when attacked. Don't get into a frame of mind where you say "No one talks to me like that." Merely identify the feeling and say something like "You really seem hurt. Is all of this anger just for me?" Be prepared to be attacked for attempting to play therapist, but still, do not respond.

Listen, but don't just be a stone wall. Indicate that you are sorry your partner hurts but that you still don't fully understand. Encouraging your partner to explain his hurt in detail is always the best direction. Should your partner blame you, do not defend your actions. Admit whatever you did wrong and say that you are sorry your partner was injured and allow the feelings to flow.

It may not be entirely possible for you to remain uninvolved during your partner's attack. You may well be hurt again and you will probably regret being present while all this is going on. Still, do not retaliate. Just remember your love and trust it. Venting the negative emotions that plague your relationship is a necessary readjustment from concealment to openness.

A good argument provides a direction. Many differences cannot and need not be resolved, but they still need to be expressed. A good argument begins in trust and gives both partners a choice to do what each thinks is best. No matter what else is decided, if the partners have not expressed their pain, they will return to the same point over and over again. No decision has any value unless both partners desire it. A good argument starts with the benefit of the doubt and ends with the possibility of reconciliation. When the partners settle an issue, the matter should become part of their past.

When the pain is gone, the promise of loving is reborn again.

CHAPTER ELEVEN

The Growing Edge

ANY TIME people grow, they have done so by stretching themselves, taking risks, trying the unknown, and testing their strengths and talents. Growing pains are part of a happy productive life. At these times you are especially vulnerable, for you are giving up your security to explore new territory. Although the risking partner requires support more than ever, it is precisely at such moments that their emerging strength threatens their mate.

When one partner grows, the other must also grow.

Here are the problems people fight over and the underlying issues that complicate them.

HOW PEOPLE ARGUE

People argue in the same defensive style they use to handle their emotions. While dependent people tend to deny an injury or painful event, controlling people make excuses for it, and competitive people pretend not to care about it. But remember that while one style may predominate, everyone uses all three of these defenses from time to time. The following charts show the three defensive styles of addressing problems and contrast them with the ideal approach of a mature person. They should make it easier to understand your partner and yourself.

Bear in mind that a problem often takes processing in all three defensive styles before you arrive at the ideal approach. Even though you may not be a controlling type, you may behave in a controlling way over a particular issue. On other issues you may be dependent, or competitive, or act as a mature person. The object is to know yourself, your characteristic reactions under particular circumstances and with certain issues, and to understand your partner as well.

The mature approach is not necessarily a perfect solution to every problem, but rather the most reasonable approach considering the circumstances. For example, there are certain conditions that lead even well-balanced, integrated people to cheat on their partners, but still, cheating is not a defensible action. I have tried to show the conditions under which well-adjusted people become involved in negative behavior and to reveal the dynamics of their actions.

WHAT PEOPLE ARGUE ABOUT

Money

Both partners should have an equal voice in finances that are involved in maintaining their relationship whether or not they are equal contributors. There are no set rules, but each partner also has the right to have his or her own private financial resources. In the best circumstances this is not to hide transactions from the other, but to enable each partner to maintain a base of control over his or her own life.

Each partner should have the same control over finances they enjoyed before they met. Budget compromises should be made mutually without pressure. Openness and trust should prevail. Innocence of intention is presumed. Money becomes an issue of conflict when there is not enough to meet basic needs, when partners are poor planners, when only one partner holds the purse strings

DEFENSIVE STRUCTURES

	Dependent Type	Controlling Type	Competitive Type	Mature Type
MAJOR DEFENSE	Denial	Excuses self, blames others	Pretends not to care	Accepts reality honestly
DEFENSE RANGES	From refusal to look at a problem to being overwhelmed by everything	From controlling and punishing behavior to irresponsible, compulsive risk-taking	From acting above it all to hysterical overreacting	From protecting self from potential hurt to defending self from injury
DEFENSIVE POSITION	Helplessness and panic	All powerful, all knowing	So what? It doesn't matter	Tries to understand
SELF-DOUBT	I'm unlovable	I'm no good	I'm a failure	I made a mistake
LIES ABOUT	Whatever may decrease partner's love	Strength, wealth, knowledge, influence	Caring, age, confidence, talent	Tells the truth
DAYDREAMS ABOUT	Being together	Sex, money, revenge	Old conquests, what's missing	Solving problems, goals, creating
THREATENS WITH	Injuring self	Withdrawing support	Another person	Tries not to threaten

IMPORTANT CONSIDERATIONS

	Dependent Type	Controlling Type	Competitive Type	Mature Type
WHAT THEY MEASURE	Others' affections	Compliance with their demands	How others esteem them	How they feel
WHAT STARTS FIGHT	The threat of abandonment	Disputing their judgment	Embarrassing them	Hurting their feelings
THEY FEAR	Losing love	Losing influence	Losing impact	Losing self
THEY FIGHT TO SHOW	They are not helpless	They are still in control	They are still the best	They won't be mistreated
STRENGTH	Loyalty	Organization	Ambition	Flexibility
WEAKNESS	Clings	Manipulates	Brags	No fatal flaw
TALKS ABOUT	Us, being together	What I'm doing for you	My life, career, myself	The matter at hand
BEST OCCASION	Golden anniversary	Gold stock increases	Wins solid gold award	Finds golden moments everywhere
STRENGTH OF COMMITMENT	Too willing to form union	Afraid to lose self, belongings	Commits for now and if it stays good	Appropriate to need
REACTION TO PARTNER'S DISTANCE FROM THEM	Closes	Keeps	Measures	Understands

HOW THEY FIGHT

	Dependent Type	Controlling Type	Competitive Type	Mature Type
TACTICS	Flaunts weakness, hides strength	Hides weakness, bullies	Exaggerates strength, teases	Seeks truth everywhere
STYLE OF ARGUING	Abused child	Grand inquisitor	Wounded celebrity	Lets the hurt speak
GAME PLAN	To make partner feel sorry for them	To make partner feel helpless without them	To make partner worry about losing them	To define and solve problem
ACKNOWLEDGES THAT PROBLEM EXISTS	Reluctantly, is afraid of what it means	Sees it first, tries to get alibi straight	"It doesn't matter, and I'm busy right now."	"We're not us lately. Let's talk."
ADMITS TO BEING AT FAULT	Too easily, passive manipulator	Incompletely and only after proving partner wrong	"How could you even suggest such a thing?"	Matter-of-factly
ACCUSES PARTNER OF	Wishing to leave	Undermining best efforts	Preferring another	Gives benefit of doubt
COMPLAINS PARTNER IS	Ungiving, cruel, unfeeling	Disobedient, ruins the good times	Disrespectful, unappreciative	Not being open and honest
RESPONSIBILITY	Blames self excessively	Blames partner	Blames circumstances	Accepts role in problem
CONTROLS BY	Guilt, self-denial	Money, threats of punishment	Threatening to leave	Tells the truth
FIGHTING WORDS	You're unlovable	You're all wrong	You're a failure	You don't matter
SOLVES PROBLEM	Wants everything the way it was, without working	Too rigidly, doesn't allow room to grow	Discouraged by effort required, quits	Gives best effort, draws others out
WHEN OUT OF CONTROL	Panics, creates confusion, acts helpless	Gets lost trying to control the smallest details	Goes public with hysterical feelings, runs	Admits feeling overwhelmed
REASSURING WORDS	We're fine, but we have to talk. I love you	There's still room for improvement. I love you	Let's create the best solution. I love you	I believe in us. I love you

WHEN THEY LEAVE

	Dependent Type	Controlling Type	Competitive Type	Mature Type
WHY THEY LEAVE	For safety	Rarely leave if still in control	Loss of partner's respect, esteem	Can't be their best together
WHAT IT TAKES TO PUSH THEM OUT	Undeniable danger	Can't be pushed out, you must leave them	Putting them down again	Unable to be self or little freedom to grow
WHAT THEY WON'T FORGIVE	Abandonment	Disobedience	Being embarrassed	Psychopathic or evil behavior
PARTING SHOTS	You let me down	I'm still right, you're still wrong	I'm better off without you	I'm sorry
WALKS OUT WHEN	It's almost too late	Other person is about to leave	It will hurt the most	Staying doesn't make sense
WHEN PARTNER LEAVES	Mourns at length or soon remarries	Retreats into routine	Looks elsewhere, quickly	Takes it on the chin, recovers

WHEN THEY MAKE UP

	Dependent Type	Controlling Type	Competitive Type	Mature Type
THEY NEED	Security	Their rules, order	Recognition	To be themselves
WILL STAY IF THEY FEEL	Protected	In charge	Acknowledged	Free to leave
THEY WANT PARTNER TO	Express need for them	Show dependence on them	Express appreciation	Be yourself
TO REPAIR BROKEN TRUST, YOU MUST AGREE NOT TO	Play on their weaknesses	Defy them out of spite	Ridicule or demean them	Lie or cheat
BASIS OF SECOND CHANCE	Unqualified love and support	Let them control what is theirs	Accept them, support risks	Total freedom, total honesty
THEY NEED TO REMEMBER	Count on yourself more, you can do it	Allow your mate to make decisions and to be free	Be your own best critic and support	You cannot compromise honesty
THEY NEED TO HEAR	You're irreplaceable	You're smart, strong, and good	You're the best	Your feelings matter to me

and uses money to control the other, and when a breadwinner wishes to conceal expenditures.

Sex

Ideally, sex is a natural extension of the love that flows between partners. The magic of sex is in its free bestowal—both partners are glad to give as well as receive. The thrill of sex comes as much from arousing your partner and sensing your sensual impact on another as in being satisfied. Responding to your partner also validates his or her sexual identity. However, sex loses its spontaneity and excitement when it is used as a reward or as a punishment. When sex is routinely used as a sedative to calm agitated partners, arousal is dampened by the expectation of sleep. Our sexual drive is affected by the events in our lives. Illness, career reversals, losses, and family conflicts easily distract us. Understanding and patience help the most in restoring sexual passion. Remember your love for each other during the times of sexual drought and keep the faith of your love even when evidence seems skimpy. To maintain spontaneity, try to act on the feelings of the moment.

Family and Children

Ideally, children should be born into a family that wants them. The right reasons for having children are to create a physical manifestation of your love and pass along what that love has taught you. The wrong reasons for having children include wanting a child to prove to the world that you are gifted and had you been given the advantages that you give to your children you, too, would have succeeded; to establish a tradition in which your personal goals are carried on by your child; or to make your relationship better by finally having a common interest. Children who are expected to carry on the family business or uphold the family reputation often sense that their feelings don't really matter. They usually resent their parents' high expectations and retaliate by failing, sometimes doing great damage to the family.

A parent who lives through his or her children lives by proxy and is usually resented no matter how great his sacrifice. The parent who needs his child's success to feel good is less tolerant and offers

	Dependent Type	Controlling Type	Competitive Type	Mature Type
WHAT MONEY MEANS	Security	Power	Reward	Means to an end
ATTITUDE TOWARD MONEY	Take care of me and I'll love you	Buys allegiance and resents it	I earned it, it's mine	What do we need and want
BOTTOM LINE	As long as I'm provided for, everything's okay	I earn the money, I make the big decisions, serve me	I'm the star, I can do what I want	Let's decide how to live our lives
UNDERLYING ISSUES	Afraid of being on his own	Fear of others being out of his debt	Successful rival is a threat	Losing personal income is like losing freedom
TYPICAL CONFLICT	The family is always first	I'm in control, care to test me?	Wants praise for giving	Supply and demand
TO RESOLVE CONFLICT	Take risks to fulfill self	Broaden rules, share burdens and chores	Appreciate partner's talents	Review priorities
CORRECTIVE ACTION	Contribute to self-support	Give money without conditions	Accept self	Continue growing

	Dependent Type	Controlling Type	Competitive Type	Mature Type
QUALITY OF LOVEMAKING	Hugging, often cloying	Gives the minimum affection needed	Display of prowess	Spontaneous intimacy
IT OFTEN FEELS	Smothering	Cold, mechanical	Like an act	Special
ITS IMPORTANCE	Family first	Only when I need it	Tends to overvalue	Sometimes too busy, but makes the time
FANTASY LIFE	Rescue by powerful type	Obsessed with certain acts	The world's a stage	All three, but reality is best
FREQUENCY	To keep partner happy	Prefers as often as possible	When partner is deserving	When the mood moves us
AFTERWARD	Clings	Sleeps, watches TV, works	Awaits praise	Love goes on
SEX IS USED	To demonstrate closeness	As a nightcap, tension relief	Sex is everything	To enhance the good
WHAT SEX MEANS	Belonging	Exercise of privilege	Proof of attractiveness	We're great together
WITHHOLDS SEX WHEN	Frightened	Resentful	Negotiating	Doesn't feel sexy
UNDERLYING ISSUES	Any threat to security	Expects mate to apologize: "After all, you started it."	Reconsiders available options: "Can I do any better?"	Unexpressed hurt: "We have to talk."
TYPICAL CONFLICT	Conceals doubt by clinging even tighter	Expects love: "I work hard, I'm entitled to it."	Not sure if still in love, bored	Not enough available time
TO RESOLVE CONFLICT	Show genuine concern for partner's fears	Explore partner's hurt, don't take it personally	Don't play the game, but be friendly	Be patient, listen, understand

little room for the child to make mistakes. Children need to make, discover, and correct their own mistakes and live up to their own standards of success. Working for a parent's approval is always a handicap.

Parents and In-Laws

If you do not separate from your parents, your growth is incomplete and your self-esteem suffers. Failure to break away from your parents when the time is right creates power struggles in which your parents and your partner vie for your allegiance. You can avoid making a choice between the people you love by being for yourself and doing what you want most. The person who really loves you wants you to be happy on your own terms. So decide what you want and pursue it.

Powerful parents often continue to exact proof of obedience long after their children have left home and have children of their own. "Good" children are held up as examples to "bad" children even when they are in their forties. The parents who control in this way need their children even more than their children need them. Once a "child" realizes this and lets go he is often surprised to discover, after the accusations and manipulations have been played out, that it is the parent who has been holding on all this time.

Risk being your strongest self, forgive your parents' shortcomings, and depend on yourself for what you need.

Careers

There is always a danger that the single breadwinner will be given more rights than other family members. In fact, he may come to expect that other family members be grateful and silent.

It takes a special effort to make a two-career relationship work. The partners need to divide their chores so that neither partner feels used. Leisure time needs to be carefully planned to ensure that two busy schedules do not overshadow the limited opportunities to be together. The demands of work, the preoccupation of moving up the ladder of success, and the need for additional training and education can all intrude on family time. It is almost too easy to justify these demands as more important than family responsibilities be-

	Dependent Type	**Controlling Type**	**Competitive Type**	**Mature Type**
FAMILY MEANS	A real home	A dynasty	Source of pride	A tradition of love
DYNAMICS OF CONFLICT	Kids grow up, parents lose their identity	When kids resist manipulation, they tighten controls	Kids surpass parents and create anxiety	Tries to set correct goal
UNDERLYING ISSUES	Sees danger lurking everywhere	Doesn't trust kids' judgment	Wants kids to make him look good	To provide opportunities as deserved
PARENTING ATTITUDE	Main reason for living, overprotective	Resents kids' imperfections, overcritical	At times too self-involved to be helpful	Seeks the emerging adult
STYLE OF DISCIPLINE	A softie, afraid to deprive kids	Unrealistic, tough, punitive	Inconsistent, over/underinvolved	Appropriate
TYPICAL CONFLICT	Babies kids and undermines risking	Inhibits kids' freedom, doesn't trust	Compares self to kids, wishes to relive life	What is a reasonable risk?
TO RESOLVE, REMEMBER	There's more to life than being a parent	If you don't trust your kids, who should?	Accept yourself and your kids as you are	Support growth with love

	Dependent Type	**Controlling Type**	**Competitive Type**	**Mature Type**
NATURE OF RELATIONSHIP TO OWN PARENTS	Still a kid to them, needs them	Harbors old resentment, but won't express it directly	Still "Look, Ma, no hands" or rebellious	Accepts them as they are
TO MATE'S PARENTS	Tries to be like their kid	Creates power struggles, criticizes	Tries to impress	Follows mate's lead, yet supports mate's independence
SOURCE OF CONFLICT WITH PARENTS	One holds on, one tries to break away	Still angry over manipulation, old or recent	Lack of praise or acceptance still hurts	When they try to limit freedom
WHEN IN-LAWS INTERFERE	Placates with self-denial: "It's okay, no trouble."	Punitive, rigid limit setting: "You can't see the kids."	Gets too busy to deal with their nonsense	Restates limits, intentions
UNDERLYING ISSUES	Wants/needs their love, approval	Still proving they can do it themselves	Parents' praise still shapes behavior, mood	All three issues, but appropriately
TO RESOLVE CONFLICT	Say "no" firmly with love	Accept their shortcomings, forgive	Follow your own standards and pleasure	Trust your own instincts and feelings

cause they make a pleasant life-style possible. Children and family need to feel that they are at least as important as co-workers or customers.

A relationship should serve as a launching pad for both partners whether in a career or community service. It is easier to succeed alone than with a partner who does not wish you well.

Substance Abuse and Addiction

Ideally, there is no room for substance abuse in a relationship. Any substance that distorts reality always creates a barrier between the couple and limits the ability to recognize and deal with the truth. Most abused substances have the effect of putting the brain's centers of higher sensibility to sleep. The net result is that the person who abuses a substance or relies on compulsive behavior has cut off some of his humanness from the relationship. These abused substances and addictive behaviors act as a buffer against a painful feeling and serve as a kind of defense. An addiction blocks growth by blocking the resolution of pain. As a result, there is less of the real person to love.

People become addicted when they are afraid to be themselves. An addiction may offer so much relief from anxiety that giving it up seems both impossible and unreasonable. Understandably, substance abuse is accompanied by lying, manipulation, and distortion.

When a partner denies being addicted, the only course of action is to get the partner to admit it. After all, everyone else knows the truth, even though they may not feel free to talk about it. Addictions make friends and family members deeply resentful. They see changes in the person they love, but feel powerless to correct them. The confusion, irritability, mood swings, sloppiness, and forgetfulness are constant intruders that undermine love. The unaddicted partner often pretends to himself that the problem is not so bad or attributes it to stress or some fantasy situation rather than facing the matter honestly.

Someone needs to be brave and responsible, and that usually means the unaddicted partner. If your partner is addicted, you have to risk creating a conflict by bringing up the subject each and every time the abuse occurs. You need your partner to admit his problem

	Dependent Type	Controlling Type	Competitive Type	Mature Type
THEY NEED A CAREER	As a place to call their own	As a power base	To prove they're special	To do life work
ATTITUDE TOWARD MATE'S CAREER	Grateful for the support	Okay, as long as they don't forget who's boss	My career is what really matters	Two views make a fuller life
CONFLICT ARISES WHEN PARTNER	Risks	Becomes independent	Succeeds in a big way	Work expands into play, family time
UNDERLYING OBSTACLES	Fear of risking	Doubts value of work, self, worships the rules	Pursues lesser goals to ensure a win	Limited by talents and efforts alone
ACHILLES HEEL	Rejection	Criticism	Bad reviews	Changes as they grow
BEST CAREER	Healer, helper, team player	Manager, agent, comptroller	Artist, entrepreneur	All three at times
CAREER INTRUDES WHEN THEY	Work overtime to please boss	Become obsessed with details of the work	Invent a crisis to motivate self	Lose perspective
BEST CAREER ADVICE	Be your own person	You don't need to be perfect	Just give your best	Follow your instincts
INTERPRETS CRITICISM TO MEAN	You're unworthy	You're stupid, weak, and bad	You're a failure	Motive for improvement

to gain his cooperation. Without this admission nothing will happen. Be assured of this: If your relationship has an abuse problem, this is where your relationship will break apart.

There may be some discussion of whether the amount of abuse is significant or the criticism unreasonable. After all, everyone has a drink or two, and what's an occasional bet on a horse, puff of marijuana, or one five-milligram Valium? If a substance is used to insulate you from the pain of life, it also keeps you from solving your problems and fulfilling your real needs. If you think the substance is being abused, it probably is.

Life-styles

The happiest couples feel the same way about the life they share. This may seem obvious, but many partners resent being stuck in a town one of them hates, near a family one is afraid of leaving, or with friends one has outgrown. If one partner cannot be happy in a certain situation, the relationship cannot be happy there either.

All life-style decisions are mutual or else they imply that one partner is better than the other.

It does not matter where you live, but how you live there. It does not matter who your friends are as long as you can be open with them. It does not matter what you do for entertainment as long as it amuses or refreshes both of you. The key to being happy is to allow your life-style to evolve naturally and to follow the growing needs of both parties. From time to time everyone's tastes and needs change. You are together to enhance your pleasure, so be open and seek new experiences together.

Cheating

Cheating can mean many things in a relationship. It can be an act of spite, a momentary loss of control under the influence of alcohol or drugs, a long-standing passion for another person, a way to make up for what is perceived as missing in a relationship, a compulsion, a reflection of insecurity or great unhappiness with one's life or partner. It can also mean that a relationship is wrong, is over, or is inadequate to the partners' needs. It can also mean that the right person has finally been found. It can be a response to lone-

197

	Dependent Type	Controlling Type	Competitive Type	Mature Type
WHY ADDICTED	Relieves anxiety	Feels powerless	Gets the rush life lacks	Seeks self naturally
SUBSTANCE MOST ABUSED (VARIES)	Alcohol, depressants, marijuana, tranquilizers	Cocaine, stimulants, alcohol, marijuana	Cocaine, hallucinogens, diet pills, marijuana	Doesn't abuse
ALTERNATIVE behavior	Belonging, family slave	Gambling, laxatives, any obsession, power trips, work, eating disorders	Pursuing the impossible dream, sex, plastic surgery	Sports, possessions, collecting, being an enthusiast
DRUG USE FUELED BY	Self-pity	Self-doubt	Low self-esteem	Curiosity
STYLE OF ABUSE	Addictive	Compulsive	Dramatic	Mixed
DESIRED DRUG EFFECT	To heighten denial	To give a sense of power and control	To improve low self-esteem	To be self/enhance creativity
SUBSTANCE PROVIDES	Sleep through the pain	Mastery by proxy	The thrill is back	Can take or leave it
DRUG-INDUCED CONFLICT	Not present for partner	Self-absorbed, compulsively driven	Mate excluded, private rapture	Overdoes it, acts stupid
TO HELP BREAK HABIT	Resolve fear directly	Find self-acceptance	Define realistic goals	Get high on self

	Dependent Type	Controlling Type	Competitive Type	Mature Type
WHERE THEY LIVE	Near family	Where network is established	Where career flourishes	Where we can best grow
PURPOSE OF LIFE	The home	Maintain power lines	Find place in the sun	Discover gifts
IDEAL LIFE GOALS	We are family	Master of all I survey	A star is born	Make a difference
FAVORITE NIGHT OUT	Disneyland with the kids	With an associate, customer; working	With "friend" who has contacts	Celebration
FRIENDS' ROLE	Support	Reinforcement	Applause	Sharing
RULING INFLUENCE	Wants to be together	Wants to be productive	Wants to be seen	Wants to be happy
UNDERLYING OBSTACLES	Afraid to try something new	Can't leave work in the office	Always trying to upgrade the situation	Makes the most of the present
RECREATIONAL PREFERENCE	Family vacation	Organized events, taking a course	New faces, new places	All three
CORRECTIVE MOTTO	Be a little braver	Forget the trees, look at the forest	Be your best	Steady, you've already won

liness, boredom, anxiety, or reflect overwhelming doubt about where you are in life or whether you have found all life has to offer.

The motives for cheating are so complex, and its destructive potential in a relationship so great, that I will discuss the problem fully in the following chapter. However, cheating can also be related to the character type that dominates in the partners in a relationship.

	Dependent Type	Controlling Type	Competitive Type	Mature Type
WHY THEY CHEAT	They think someone finally loves them	Urge overwhelms	Spite, or they doubt their attractiveness	Reawakened passion, comfort
THEY CHEAT WITH	Old friend, nurturing person, neighbor	Superficial acquaintance or co-worker	Someone "better" than mate	Embodiment of unmet need
WHEN THEY CHEAT	After long rejection	When fantasy and reality meet, on a business trip	To prove themselves; acting out an impulse	Relationship feels over
WHY THEY GET CAUGHT	Anxious confession	Leaves clues everywhere, guilt	They plan it to get even	To help make decision to leave
WHAT AFFAIR MEANS OR REFLECTS	Long-standing deprivation	Often purely physical	Insecurity, lack of attention	"We're on the rocks if it's come to this."
HOW THEY THINK ABOUT IT	Preoccupied with hurting others: "How can I do this?"	Can't think of anything else, guilt: "Am I bad?"	Consumed by it: "Why can't my partner be like this?"	"Can I save my relationship? Do I want to?"
DYNAMICS OF CONFLICT	Feels abandoned, needs more love	Feels cheated, deserves more sex	Feels ignored, demands more attention	Feels trapped, wants freedom
UNDERLYING ISSUES	Take care of me	Satisfy me	Worship me	Relate to me

CHAPTER TWELVE

Cheating

THERE ARE as many reasons why people cheat as there are unhappy relationships. Cheating is always a symptom of something more serious. Open couples are the least likely to cheat while closed couples invite cheating. Partners often resort to cheating when they wish to avoid confronting a problem but still need some way to lower tension. Cheating is also a way partners seek to bolster their self-esteem when they do not feel loved or to bring to a head a hidden conflict that cannot be openly discussed. Cheating is sometimes used to force a partner to take an issue or a feeling seriously. When partners cheat, they reach beyond their relationship for solutions they could have found if only they had risked being open and shared.

Frequently, the reason a person cheats is more complicated than it looks. For example, a person may be motivated to cheat because he is angry, but comes to discover that he really cheated to resolve his doubt over being sexually attractive. The nature of cheating is that it simplifies matters and complicates them at the same time. You ask yourself: "Would I feel more fulfilled with another person?" So you cheat to find the answer and discover that someone else *can* satisfy you more completely. Another question immediately comes to mind: "Am I in love with this person to feel this way?" Now you're even more confused. Remorse and excitement occupy the same stage. When you are apart, all you can think about is being together. After you've been together, you're anxious to leave. You feel like a kid again. The lyrics of popular songs are suddenly full of meaning. You feel wonderful about it. Reborn! You feel like the worst heel in the world, positively rotten. How can something so wonderful feel so bad?

What is cheating?

Cheating is investing in another person the emotional and sexual energy that should properly be focused on your partner. You do not need to have intercourse to cheat. A passionate kiss with abandon and desire is cheating even if it goes no further. If that is difficult for you to accept, you have created a definition of cheating that is designed to allow you to cheat without feeling guilty. Ask yourself why you don't go all the way. It's not because you don't have the desire, but because you are afraid. Cheating is a matter of desire and intent. Cheating begins once the idea has been placed into action, no matter how simple it is. Someone who intends to cheat often begins with a simple kiss and permits things to become more involved.

It is not the point at which you stop that determines whether you have cheated. Kissing a partner's close friend on the lips at a Christmas party when you both have had one too many may be cheating for one of you and not for the other. It is the intention, the waiting to see what will happen, and the willingness to follow through that makes all the difference.

The following case histories illustrate several underlying issues and conflicts in a relationship that were brought to light by an affair.

CASE I: MARRIED TO THE WRONG PERSON—LIVING THE WRONG LIFE

Candy had been a child of the sexual revolution and sexually active from the age of fourteen. A beautiful and brilliant student but with no particular direction in life, she decided to settle down in college, and during her junior year moved in with her boyfriend. It was a convenient arrangement created to give her a sense of stability, but even so she had several affairs while living with him, including one with a married man. Although they loved each other passionately, her lover was not inclined to leave his wife and children. Off and on she entertained the thought of becoming a physician, but lacked the discipline to follow through. She graduated with honors, moved out of her boyfriend's apartment, and became an executive secretary. As a single working woman she had many affairs, one with a professional baseball player, one with a writer for the local paper. In all of them she was searching for someone with an established identity as if she could borrow it and release some of her concern over not finding herself.

When Candy was twenty-two she met George, a slightly obese investment banker with a tendency to be chronically depressed, which she misread as being sensitive. Tired of all the running around and her boring job, Candy married George and did a credible job convincing herself that she was happy and talked her friends and relatives into agreeing with her. She threw herself into the role of housewife, eventually expanding her gourmet cooking into a small catering business, but it did not please her. Two sons gave her a new role to play, but although she was a Cub Scout den leader and put on a baseball glove to teach her boys to catch and throw—a vestige of the relationship with her old shortstop lover —she felt empty and unfulfilled.

George was always more interested in what his neighbors thought about their relationship than the relationship itself. He would sit on the porch getting fatter each year, watching Candy play with the children. Every time Candy tried to bring up her concerns, George had an excuse not to talk. Financial matters were always pressing on him. He seemed increasingly more depressed and more desperate. He wanted Candy to be the sex kitten he had married as well as a model mother. Her pain was an unwelcome intrusion as incomprehensible as his own depression.

Candy fantasized about other men almost from the first year she married George. At first she was embarrassed by her thoughts— not because the feelings were unacceptable to her but because they represented a flaw in her game plan. She wanted to be happy married to George. It wasn't working.

"This is the dumbest thing you ever did," she said aloud to

herself in the bathroom mirror of a motel room. She had called a former friend to meet her and they had sex. It seemed stupid and she suddenly felt unclean, whereas before she never felt bad about being with any man. She knew she didn't feel bad about cheating on George. "It had to be the guy," she thought as she drove home. She resolved to find someone who would make having an affair worthwhile.

At first Candy felt sorry for George when she was with other men, but she soon began to resent having to take his feelings into consideration when making her elusive plans. She was now more promiscuous than she had ever been in her teens. Just as she had talked herself into believing she was happy as a housewife, she convinced herself that she was in love, but the older she grew, the shorter these self-deceptions lasted.

One day en route to an assignation, Candy stopped at a convenience store to complete the errand she had used as an excuse to get out of the house, but when she returned to her car she found she had locked herself out. Although she hadn't done anything wrong, she started to panic and created a scene in front of the market. One of the customers offered to help, discovered that the window on the opposite side was open and let her in. With a knowing look the stranger said, "You're unhappy, huh?"

Candy did not know how to respond, but then she laughed, shook her head, and surprised herself as she said, "I'm miserable as hell."

They spent an hour talking. Jeff was a food broker, married, full of humor in spite of his unhappy marriage, the father of three great kids whom he felt he would someday have to leave. Jeff and Candy were instant soul mates. They exchanged telephone numbers and safe access times and Candy went home. Although Candy had slept with dozens of men since her marriage, George had never suspected, but this evening when Candy returned, he cross-examined her relentlessly. For the first time Candy had given herself away, even though she had done nothing but think about having an affair. She defended herself self-righteously and fought with George. All night long she couldn't sleep. Thoughts of this kind man ran through her head. "It doesn't work," she said to herself, and for the first time was sure her relationship with George was over.

Candy and Jeff were pulled to each other, but leaving their families seemed impossible. Jeff had great doubts. "My relationship isn't good enough to stay and it isn't bad enough to leave," he said with a sigh. And yet Jeff loved Candy as much as she loved him. It had been a long time since Candy felt loved like this. Her old dreams of becoming a physician started to return as her self-esteem rose. She knew she could never love Jeff as fully as she wanted to until she fulfilled herself. It was not Candy's marriage that didn't work, it was her life. She had to take the risks she'd been avoiding and find and build an identity of which she could be proud— something she could not acquire by leaning on a man or sleeping around.

Strengthened by her new sense of herself and also feeling that she had little to lose, Candy pressured George to seek professional help to relieve his depression and to prepare him for the inevitable. Candy was surprised at how honestly she could now talk to George and not be inhibited by his hurt feelings. It was not that her feelings for him had changed. It was just that she was now open enough to admit the distance between them for the first time. She realized that what she felt for George now was what she had felt for him all along, but that she had convinced herself she was loved because she needed to be loved and George's desperation had filled her needs.

Candy enrolled in medical school determined to fulfill her dream and not sacrifice herself for the illusion of safety again. Of course she still had doubts, mostly about hurting her family: "How can I justify doing all this to these innocent people?" she reflected. "How could I have been so stupid to have done this to myself?" She resolved never to let herself become dependent again. Eventually, she and Jeff drifted apart—he was not willing to take the same risk she was taking—but at least she had found herself.

Untested fears always grow. Undeveloped talents always seem more distant and less real when you don't try them out. We all want to avoid seeing how we fall short. When the pain of not being what we want becomes greater than our fears, we finally take risks.

Cheating is often the first open sign that one's life is not working. Unfortunately, cheating partners get so caught up in their intrigues that they do not have the clarity to assess their unhappiness or find solutions that address their real problems. Sometimes it seems one's whole world has to collapse before people can admit the truth and take the right steps. It is always difficult to admit that your partner is wrong for you and make a change when you are not sure who you are or if you can really do any better on your own. The longer you wait, the weaker you feel and the less likely you are to take any risks. It is in a situation like this that partners flirt with disaster, hoping that they will find it easier to walk away from a relationship in ruins than confront their weakness and grow.

CASE II: INCOMPATIBILITY— SEXUAL OBSESSION IN A CONVENTIONAL MARRIAGE

Len and Robin grew up in the late fifties. Robin was arguably the prettiest girl in high school, if a bit aloof and overprotected. She came from a well-to-do family whose high expectations of her she could not meet and against which she never had the courage to rebel. So when her parents encouraged her to date Len, a handsome track star on the way to dental school, she went along, in no small way supported by her upwardly mobile friends who felt she had landed the best catch in town. Len's parents were conservative people. His father, a prominent orthodontist, always planned that Len would go into practice with him. Len did not resist his father's wishes even though secretly he felt confined by them. Robin had no special plans beyond finishing college. Bright, attractive, and twenty-one, hardly knowing what life was all about, they had plans for a storybook life together. Although they had been dating for years, they were practically strangers, never speaking about anything intimate or deep. Everyone felt their marriage was made in heaven. After all, it was the fifties.

To the outside world their marriage was indeed ideal: three beautiful daughters exactly three years apart, a lovely home in a fashionable suburb, a growing dental practice, and a supportive group of friends. But in private there were great difficulties. Robin wanted her family life to be precisely as advertised: always happy, conflict free, no raised voices or arguing—and she did not want to be obliged to work at it. Len went along with the façade. Even though he was often angry at Robin, he never showed it. Understandably, Len was troubled by guilt. He also wanted to be practicing on his own, away from his father, but every time the thought came into his mind he repressed it. He felt discouraged, so he buried his resentment and became depressed.

Len went into therapy to discuss his wish to separate from his father, but in fact his real concern was deeper. He was frustrated sexually. Robin was cold and participated in sex out of a sense of duty, occasionally faking orgasm and showering after making love because she felt unclean. Len was secretly obsessed with sex. Afraid to be involved with another person outside his marriage, he masturbated daily, collected pornography, and lived in fear that someone would uncover his dark secret. While working on patients, all he could think of was sex. The smell of a woman's perfume would practically put him into a trance. In traffic he would sometimes follow a pretty girl for miles out of his way, timidly exchanging a smile when they came to a light; for weeks after he would think about her as a sexual object, even returning daily to the intersection where he met her. On the rare occasions that he tentatively suggested a variation in lovemaking to Robin, she either treated the suggestion like a sick joke or called him perverted. Inexperienced in these matters, Len came to believe that something was really wrong with him. The conflict between his sexual needs and Robin's inhibition grew inside him.

In the sixties, the sexual revolution produced disorganizing effects in Len's life. Books encouraging adventurous experimentation were being written about the very sexual acts Robin was denying him. Len felt cheated and began to examine his relationship. Their communication seemed contrived and superficial. Their love felt perfunctory and obligatory. Yet in spite of Len's rationalizations that his marriage was wrong for him, he could not find the courage to go against the social pressures that shaped him. Len and Robin's parents were close. They had shared the same friends since childhood. Len feared rejection and isolation for acting on his impulses. Even though getting a divorce might appear normal in the context of the upheaval of the sixties, such behavior was still foreign to his friends and family.

After much tortured thought, Len opened an office of his own, deeply hurting his father and incurring his family's disapproval. His mother sent him a note asking him to reconsider his decision and closed with the remark, "How can you abandon the person who has loved and supported you at the very moment his health is deteriorating?" In spite of the added pressures, Len began to feel freer, more his own person. He hired his own staff, including Sylvia, a free-spirited divorcee with a seven-year-old son who had a learning disability and a need for special education that was beyond her financial capability. Sylvia saw an opportunity and seized it.

It took only one night together for Sylvia to throw Len completely off balance. Sylvia's finely tuned sexual instincts immediately brought Len to and beyond the limits of his fantasy life as she demanded he perform the very sexual acts Robin would not even discuss. His sexual drive and potency, now reinforced by reality and augmented by ample amounts of cocaine and marijuana, rose to heights beyond his imagination. He found himself staying away from home for increasingly longer periods of time. Sylvia used Len as a sexual toy. When Len traveled to dental conventions he abandoned caution; he left Robin home and brought Sylvia, showing her off to old friends who asked after his wife. As he watched other men becoming aroused by Sylvia, his excitement grew. Their life was sex—in the car, in elevators, in the office, on the beach, in little out-out-the-way motels. Sylvia had an inventive spirit and Len was totally submerged in her sexual energy.

The boundary between what was real and what was fantasy began to fade for Len. He started to support Sylvia's child. He hung around Sylvia's house and spent more time with her son than with his own girls. When he was home, Len seemed disjointed and preoccupied. Robin assumed that he was working too hard. When he bought her lavish presents, Robin did not even notice he was acting guilty. The idea that anyone could have a sexual need like Len's was beyond her comprehension. She suspected nothing because, even with all the evidence staring her in the face, she did not want to know.

Sylvia, feeling her talons deeply set, began to make greater demands on Len, spurring him to new sexual experiences, buying each and every new sex manual, circling pages with red crayon and leaving them open on his desk at the office where patients could see. Len found himself covering up in reality for the same feelings he used to cover up in fantasy. Finally, he sought the help of a therapist, but told him none of this, insisting instead that his peculiar behavior was his guilt over abandoning his father and his mother's pressure on him. His uncertainty deepened as his conflict between wanting to abandon himself completely to Sylvia and maintaining a home with Robin grew; his increasing drug dependency and his inability to admit his obsession began to overwhelm him. He could not pull away from Sylvia. He could not leave his "perfect home" and wife because he could not allow himself to see his own or Robin's imperfections. He became impotent, taking the responsibility away from himself.

Sylvia saw Len's impotence as a challenge and put her best efforts toward resolving his problem. Len was unmoved. Robin, who had been seemingly uninterested in sex all those years, now took Len's impotence personally and as a great loss. She asked herself what was wrong with her. She began to get more seductive and to adopt an adventurous new attitude toward sex. Strangely, although Len's impotence improved dramatically with Robin, he saw her efforts as staged and insincere. With Sylvia he had tasted of the real thing and he felt contempt for his wife's newly awakened sexuality. He used sex now to vent his deep and long-unexpressed anger for Robin. Although his potency had never been as great, his enjoyment was blunted, for his vigorous lovemaking was the expression of a grudge. Robin could not tell the difference. She now enjoyed sex, but not because she was having sex with Len; it was the sex itself she wanted. It was a challenge. Len resented her increased pleasure and indifference toward him more than anything.

Wanting sex with Sylvia, but afraid to give in, he remained impotent with her. Having sex with his wife and resenting it and using cocaine continually, his sense of reality blurred. For his wedding anniversary he bought a dream house in Aspen and flew all his friends in to celebrate his perfect marriage. Everyone believed it and envied them.

The week after the anniversary, Len found himself behind the wheel of his car in a strange town, having driven there automatically. Disorganized and terrified, he somehow got to a phone booth and called to tell Sylvia how much he loved her, that he needed her, and that he had never really loved his wife. He went on for ten minutes in a fragmented monologue, filled with detailed references to their sexual involvement, and then he broke down and cried. When the voice on the other end finally responded, Len felt his world drift away, for in his confusion he had called his wife who had been listening in silent astonishment.

Too shattered to gain his composure and too exposed to pretend it was a joke, Len encouraged his already disorganized thought processes to deteriorate further in the hope it would intervene between him and Robin, that his craziness would act as a buffer and gain sympathy for him. Unfortunately, the craziness was not entirely under his control. When Robin reacted without the slightest shred of compassion, but instead played on his guilt and supported her story with references to his hurting his father and abandoning his family, Len felt overwhelmed and let reality slip away. Somehow he arrived at Sylvia's house, retelling the story, floridly disconnected.

I saw Len in therapy. Over the course of his treatment he finally confronted the issues of his life and regained the distance he needed to accept that he was never happily married. He came to see that his affair with Sylvia served to bring his obsession to the surface, which helped him resolve his guilt. He separated from Robin and they eventually divorced.

When cheating is a symptom of a serious unresolved emotional conflict, the relationship either gets better or dissolves when the conflict is finally uncovered. The underlying problems, once expressed, require that the relationship change and adapt to resolve them. However, in a relationship like Len and Robin's, in which roles are rigidly set and behavior measured against unrealistic standards, cheating is regarded with great dismay and the underlying reasons are never taken seriously. The injured party focuses on his hurt. In its decline, the relationship takes on the appearance of an armed camp, both sides justifying their failure to bend because of what has been done to them: one has not felt loved; the other has been betrayed. Len's problems became important to Robin only when he became impotent. She was only concerned that he was no longer attracted to her. Whatever his real needs, she preferred not to deal with them.

Many partners in a relationship have a rich and pervasive sexual fantasy life. This becomes a problem only when the partner is forced to keep his needs secret. Such hidden desires expand to capture all of a person's attention and in time nearly all of the person's thoughts tend to focus on sexual matters. The belief that these repressed sexual feelings are bad causes the problem to get worse. To conceal a sexual obsession requires the use of defenses, just as concealing any other kind of feeling does. The stronger the defense, the greater the distance the person feels from reality. Partners who cheat obsessionally often exhibit behavior that borders on being crazy. Indeed, they feel that way. They become preoccupied with being caught, being apart, being together, calling their spouse by the wrong name and getting their alibi confused. Their mates often explain away such actions as the result of stress, which is present in abundance, but shy away from probing deeply enough to understand, for they are hesitant to prove that what they suspect is true.

Allowing all feelings in a relationship to be expressed and greeted with sympathy and understanding is the best way to prevent a situation like Robin and Len's from developing. Unfortunately, Len's real problem was that he never wanted to be married to Robin in the first place, but could not resist the social pressure or admit it to himself. If Robin was portrayed as perfect, what must he be to feel reluctant about marrying her? His low self-worth did not permit him to reject her. His sexual preoccupation was the only safe form his protest could take. When Len's wish to leave became fueled with sexual energy, it pushed his conflict to the breaking point. If he could have admitted his reluctance to get married, his obsession would probably never have developed, for at the heart of the obsession was an anger he did not feel safe expressing.

If you get married before you come to terms with your need to be free, you struggle with freedom throughout your relationship. You use the relationship to help cover what you do not wish to discover about yourself. You blame the relationship for your unhappiness, and your partner for not responding to or fulfilling your needs, when the truth is that you were probably unclear or unwilling to admit your needs in the first place. On the one hand you need to ask yourself some questions, but on the other you're afraid to hear the answers. What are these questions? "Am I good?" "Am I sexually worthy and normal to feel this way?" "Does anyone else have these feelings?" When these questions persist they cause doubt and a certain brittleness of spirit; you feel as if anything can tip you over.

Exploring sex instead of one's feelings is always a misdirection.

Often, as part of his coverup, the cheating partner is so successful in isolating his emotions that he loses contact with his mate's feelings. In time the relationship grows cold. The partners suspect each other for what they can't admit to themselves. They'd do better to tell the truth and deal with real matters in the open.

There is no one more generous in forgiving than a person who does not want to see.

CASE III: THE CHRONICALLY ILL PARTNER

Charles grew up in the shadow of his successful businessman father, a high roller in the stock brokerage business. Chuck Sr. was brusque and intimidating, often close to rich, and just as often dead broke. A creative financier, he failed to appreciate fully that his son was gifted in mathematics and electronics. Resenting his father for this and for the way he cheated on his mother, Charles resolved never to be like him.

At MIT Charles excelled, but never developed the self-confidence his talent should have earned him. Unsure of himself, he sometimes became blustery like his father to impress people that he was good. The difference was that, unlike his father, Charles actually had an outstanding mind, but because of the undermining he had suffered at his father's hands he felt too insecure to believe in himself. So when he doubted himself Charles acted just like his father, and at those times it was hard to believe that he was in reality a warm and loving man of subtle taste and educated style.

Charles discovered Edith playing second flute at a college orchestra concert. He couldn't take his eyes off her and thought she was beautiful. She was, however, a severe asthmatic and had taken up the flute on the advice of her family doctor to help with her breathing; however, her allergies were so severe she could not play at all during the ragweed season. Edith was frail and looked up to Charles. She was less secure than he and Charles felt strong just being with her. Her delicate bearing brought out feelings of protectiveness, the furthest thing he ever felt from his own father. It was a perfect match.

They married. Charles joined a hi-tech company and after a year left to form his own computer company. All through the seventies he struggled with modest success. His profits were spent on his family. Edith required a lot of medical assistance. The home they built cost a quarter of a million dollars because countless extras were included to protect Edith. An elaborate dust precipitation system built into the air-conditioning and heating system made certain that the house they had constructed out of hypoallergenic materials would remain free of irritants.

Edith's health was a constant preoccupation, and she gave up her dream of playing flute. Charles was fond of telling people exaggerated tales of her earlier musical promise, especially at those times when his affection for her waned. He made protecting her his life concern and when doubt about her affection for him entered his mind, he pushed the thought away and rallied to her side.

As the eighties approached, Charles's company became successful beyond their wildest dreams. Suddenly they were worth millions. Strangely, Edith felt envious of Charles's success. She became more reclusive and her withdrawal from Charles made him more insecure and caused him to be more boastful and socially obnoxious. Overflowing with success, he now wanted to take great financial risks to prove to the world that he was good, where his father had just been a pretender. Still, his outward display of love for Edith continued undiminished. When she refused sex because she felt too weak or when she stopped in the middle— occasionally feigning shortness of breath—he was always understanding.

It was easy for Charles to be understanding. He had a vested interest in perceiving Edith as loving him and gave her an endless benefit of the doubt. Charles *was* right—Edith was sick. She did have asthma, but her most symptomatic illness was depression. Her lagging self-esteem could no longer be denied. She started to withdraw more into the house. Edith didn't feel capable of having a life of her own and found it especially painful to be living with a man who was continually compensating for living in his father's shadow. Moreover, Charles showed it was possible to overcome weakness and succeed. His success challenged the logic Edith used when she claimed that her asthma limited her life. And Charles did achieve great success. Unlike his father, he was the real thing, but Edith's withholding made him feel emotionally poor. Worse, un-

Cheating

able to discuss his feelings openly with her, he also felt alone in his sadness and unable to admit to himself that they had grown apart.

Charles decided that he wanted to build an estate. "Not to prove to my father, but to do something for us and to reward myself for a job well done," he pleaded to Edith.

"What about the air-filter system? It took years to get this place right. I don't want to go through any more adjustments. You remember how sick I was when we first moved in."

Charles remembered. "Of course," he said.

Edith picked up her knitting and smiled.

Charles looked over to Edith and thought about his life. He felt something was missing, but wasn't sure exactly what. Edith has become controlling over the years, he reflected, but it's understandable. She misses her career. She's put on weight, probably from water retention from all those steroids. She's been through a lot. I wish we could live in a bigger place; not to show off, but just to have more room. Finally, he suggested, "What if we started construction on a new home now and moved into it when all the adjustments were worked out. Let me do it for you. We can afford it. I'll computerize the entire ventilation system. You'll see, it'll be state of the art. I'm really good at that."

Edith turned and looked coldly at Charles. "I don't want another house."

"If you don't like it, we'll just sell it."

"I'm happy here."

"But I can afford it. It'll be all in cash I don't need. Besides it's my money."

"Always 'I.' What happened to 'we'?" Edith said and started to wheeze.

Charles felt put down and trapped. He stood up automatically to get Edith's inhaler and stopped to look at himself in the medicine cabinet mirror. I'm forty-five. I look ten years older, he mused. I still have my best years ahead of me. My success is just starting to take off. I can afford anything I want. I should look the part. I should have everything I want. He patted his tummy with an unfamiliar sense of resolve.

The next day Charles enrolled in a health club.

Although he was successful, Charles's business was meeting stiff competition. While Edith needed Charles to provide for her, she was afraid to encourage his desire to acquire the trappings of success. She feared that the new house would make him more arrogant and obnoxious, a trait she seldom spoke about directly. She tried to control him by putting him down. Edith was also genuinely afraid of being uprooted and used her fear to manage Charles. When competition caused profits to dwindle and Charles's stress to increase, his renewed struggle gave Edith a perverse sense of relief, somehow she didn't feel so bad about herself. And yet when he needily came to her for support and intimacy her asthma worsened.

Charles still did not permit himself to feel resentment toward Edith, for he sensed that his actions made her anxious. Instead, as his company teetered, he allowed his plans for the house to progress, partially to prove to himself that he was still sound financially and, though he would never have admitted it, partially to torment Edith. Edith continually undermined his efforts on the house, and whenever he put the architectural plans in front of her for her approval, she stated repeatedly that they couldn't afford it and that she had no intention of ever moving in.

"Don't you understand, I want to build it. This is just a passing phase, a technical adjustment in the market. There will be a shake-out. The weaker companies will fail, but I'm certain I'll come out on top. I'm the best—young, tough, and lean. Everyone knows it."

"I don't want that house," Edith said, looking pained.

"But I *need* that house." Charles's eyes were glistening with tears.

"That's just what your father would have said," Edith taunted.

Charles was stunned by the comment and after a few moments quietly admitted, "I know."

There was nothing special about the secretary Charles spent two hours with in a suburban motel several days later. Most of the time he told her how wonderful Edith was and all about her flute playing. Although he sent the secretary flowers the next day and a valentine several months later, they only had sex once. Still, Charles thought about her all the time.

He tried to make sex work with Edith, sometimes imagining the secretary in her place, but Edith wasn't very interested, and when she was she only wanted to get it over with quickly. Although sex was no different from what it had ever been, Charles now felt chilled by Edith's response to his demands.

216

He walked along the birch-lined stream at the back of the new house lot looking from the woods to the road, surveying his dream. It was spring and the flowering trees scented the air. It was a lovely moment, but Charles was in it all by himself. He wanted something else. He wasn't sure what. He decided to let Edith have her way and not bother her with his needs. I'll just make the best of it, he thought. There's no need to throw my life into turmoil and destroy my marriage. It's not Edith's fault she's sick. I have to make a mature decision. I have to be grown up and get what I'm missing. This isn't an impulsive act. No more falling in love. Everything will be superficial and physical, but nice women. Maybe married women who have as much to lose as I do. Charles walked to his car as a spring rain annointed the moment. It felt wonderful, full of promise. He felt young again.

He searched for sexual companions and, on occasion, found them.

A Chicago investment group recognized the hidden worth in Charles's company's depressed stock and Charles found himself in the center of a hostile takeover fight. His father would have been more suited to handle the situation, and although he did the best he could, Charles lost the company and it was disposed of with great prejudice and damaging tax disadvantages. What seemed like so many secure millions evaporated almost overnight. Charles sadly bailed out of the new house. Edith was very understanding of his failure and comforted him. She reminded him how fortunate they were to have a home they really loved and that they still had each other.

What had been carefully measured cheating when Charles was wealthy became uncontrollable when his financial worth was diminishing. Charles's need to prove himself was displaced from the boardroom to the bedroom. The door of sexuality had been opened and now he found a growing need where before he had only had an unanswered question. Charles reached out to women. He still tried to be indifferent and cool about it. He wanted to keep his relationships uncomplicated, just sex. "Gotta go back to work now," was his standard farewell. Charles began to feel bad about himself because his greatest need was for intimacy and having sex for its own sake really didn't make sense to him. While he continued to talk lovingly about Edith to his sexual partners, any sympathy he gained from them had a strong pull on him. In spite of his best intentions, he permitted himself to fall in love and got carried away once more. He started to come home late and to drink to cope with his anxiety.

Edith had a built-in need to accept his excuses. She never suspected his extramarital activities, but attributed his strange behavior to his cash flow problems. There was one close call when Edith found a Polaroid picture of his girlfriend in his briefcase, but Charles made a brilliant excuse that the woman was an applicant for a new job and nothing more was ever mentioned about it. The encounter, however, terrified Charles. He thought about it continually and decided that although he would try to be more discreet it would only be a matter of time before he got caught. If Edith ever found out, he was sure it would kill her. With all of his repressed anger, the threat came too close to home. He broke off the relationship, but still looked outside to fulfill his needs.

Edith's asthma created many problems for Charles. As much as he loved her, he was hurt by her physical decline. He felt he could not blame her for being sick and yet Edith was so manipulative that when she used her illness to control him he could not help but take her illness personally. No matter how he tried, he could never find a point from which to begin an open discussion of his needs and their relationship. He insisted to the world that they were the same loving couple he had always portrayed them as being. He rationalized his cowardice in not confronting her by telling himself that she was already beleaguered by her physical problems and he did not want to add to them. The truth was that he felt so insecure that his fear of risking rejection would have kept him from testing his love even if Edith's health had been perfect. While he had pretended to adjust to her illness, he still had unanswered physical needs. Because he was too afraid to express them openly, these needs took control unopposed.

It takes a special understanding of one's self to venture into the world for sexual gratification and not be pulled off center. Charles managed well enough until his business failed. Then the critical balance between sex to replace what he was missing and sex to bolster his self-esteem was upset. He needed increasingly more sex to feel good about himself, but in the outside world he did not get the support he needed in order to remain stable. Understandably, his boastfulness grew with his insecurity. He found himself trapped in many stupid situations with women he did not even like, let alone respect. He found himself becoming fragmented. Am I becoming like my father? he asked himself after leaving his twenty-year-old girlfriend's apartment at three in the morning. He suspected that he already had. Filled with guilt and sadness, he resolved to change his life.

Charles decided that he needed to have a long-standing relationship that did not threaten his marriage. At a church supper he let his heart out to Cybel, an old and trusted friend whose husband had severe arthritis. Cybel listened to him for a moment and smiled, "I've known you've been unhappy for years," she said.

Their arrangement was perfect. Cybel had as much to lose as he did. Neither of them wanted to break up their marriages. They were both afraid of venturing into the world alone and needed a friend. This arrangement has worked for them for years. Committing to stay with their partners allows them to be free to express their love. However, times of stress at home also create stress in their relationship, for when Edith or Cybel's husband becomes difficult, Charles or Cybel can plead for marriage. While they may fight over this, each is secretly glad the other refuses. Their relationship allows them to express feelings that would normally have been held in while at the same time they're supporting each other during the crisis. They both feel answered without feeling guilty. Cybel often helps Edith and Charles is currently exploring starting up a new company with Cybel's husband.

This long-suffering couple—Edith with her manipulative withholding and Charles with his denial—is more typical than couples whose relationships are torn apart by affairs. Most people stay in place, and the longer they do, the more likely they are to remain there. It was Charles's affair with Cybel that finally allowed him to admit that sex was just part of what was missing in his relationship with Edith. While he continues to insist that Edith is noble and well-meaning, he now recognizes that her ability to give is limited and his dependency on her frailness to give him strength contributed much of the so-called stability to their bond.

Cheating when a partner is chronically ill may be understandable, but it is never entirely free of guilt. No matter how the guilt is handled—either by rationalizing that in reducing sexual needs the affair makes it easier to be a better partner, or by insisting that this is the only way the relationship can remain intact—it intrudes upon the mental life of the couple.

Sometimes, through illness, a partner no longer resembles his former self. Sometimes the traits on which the original love was founded are no longer in evidence. The need to take care of each other that once was the basis of the relationship becomes one-sided. When one person only gives and the other only takes, the energy for loving understanding is consumed by the illness. Real understanding and giving are needed to make the relationship work. It takes maturity and the love born of self-acceptance. There is no greater test of love than this. When indiscretions do occur in such relationships, there is a long history of internal debate behind them.

Unlike short-term illnesses, in which the healthy partner has a recent memory of an active exchange of love, in long-term illness, especially where depression is involved, it is easy to forget that love ever existed.

When the ill partner continually uses failing health as an excuse, the situation becomes clouded with resentment, denial, and guilt. Charles would have found it practically impossible to have an open discussion with Edith about the way she used her illness to control him because he tried so hard not to admit this to himself.

There is a great deal more that Charles could have done. Edith could have been encouraged to play the flute for her own enjoyment. Charles needed to learn to present his needs more openly so that Edith could have an opportunity to learn other ways of being sexually giving and to make their relationship stronger. Charles needed to become more assertive and learn to reduce his vulnerability to her controlling so he could help her venture out more and extend herself in the areas that gave her satisfaction and recognition. This would have increased her self-esteem and in turn allowed her to give more to him.

When a person uses illness for gain, giving up the illness can seem like a serious loss of power over one's environment. After a person has been ill for some time, to risk being whole again can be as great a threat as coping with the illness itself. Learning to expand one's world from the narrow confines of an illness, to accept what cannot change, to feel lovable in spite of limitations or decline requires the support of love that exists only when a couple is open with each other, trusts the love between them, and is dedicated to cherishing and celebrating whatever good they find in the relation-ship.

The love that is found in small places can fill the entire world.

CASE IV: SWINGING COUPLES—
PROVING ONE'S SEXUAL WORTH

Arnold was fifty when he married LuAnn, a twenty-five-year-old secretary he'd hired for his design business. Although they worked hard together and business prospered, their life-style exceeded their income and they were constantly in debt. When LuAnn expressed her concerns about the business and pointed out Arnold's account-ing errors, instead of thanking her for preventing further problems, he would attack and belittle her. His ego prevented him from hear-ing any criticism. She was usually right, but instead of confronting Arnold she silently corrected his mistakes and tried to keep the books in balance.

LuAnn was far brighter than Arnold had suspected when they first married. He had misinterpreted her passivity for slowness. As she became more confident, she probed Arnold's books and dis-covered that he had been selling reproduction furniture as originals. Her dismay and her feeling of responsibility depressed her. She no longer felt the compelling sexual attraction for Arnold that origi-nally led her into the marriage. The attractive, debonair Arnold was just a sleaze at heart. LuAnn felt like his accomplice—too weak to confront him, too afraid to leave.

Arnold was the kind of man who used the bed to make every-thing better. LuAnn always enjoyed sex, and although she would eagerly consent whenever Arnold approached her, she never initi-ated it. Arnold craved sex continually and when his advances for sex were occasionally averted by LuAnn he grew agitated. He be-came obsessed with the age difference between them and asked LuAnn repeatedly what was causing the problem. LuAnn denied a problem existed, but allowed Arnold to buy her elaborate jewelry to win her over. She knew full well the kind of dishonesty that was needed to support this giving, so her self-esteem eroded and her depression deepened further. She hated herself for being so needy.

LuAnn surprised herself by agreeing to participate when Arnold suggested that they go to a party with several couples to engage in group sex. She did not understand it at the time, but she seemed to welcome the degradation. It was as if she could punish herself and atone for selling out.

They went to such parties every week and Arnold made it a point to be with every woman there, always insisting on ending with LuAnn as if to recommit symbolically to her and make it all better. He never asked LuAnn how she felt about her participation because he was completely absorbed in proving his own prowess, but he always kept his eye on her when she was with another man, as if to make sure she was not really enjoying herself.

One evening a new couple joined the group and when LuAnn was with the man Arnold noticed that she was highly aroused and involved. Suddenly threatened, he pushed his partner away and reached over to touch her. LuAnn did not respond.

He was crushed and felt she had cheated on him!

Arnold sought out my psychiatric services the next day, dragging a reluctant LuAnn along with him.

"Can you imagine the nerve of this woman! Here I was reaching out to make contact and show her love and affection when she was with this young punk. I started stroking her leg, touching her hair and she just brushed me aside. I couldn't believe it. My own wife making me look like a fool in front of all these caring people." Arnold made a fist and punched his palm.

LuAnn stared out the office window, tears welling in her eyes, embarrassed to be talked about, to admit her participation in all of Arnold's sordid activities.

"What does she want? Our marriage feels like it is going down the drain. Look at her jewels. Look at her clothes. She gets taken care of beautifully. I give her everything she wants. And sex, too, I give her whatever she needs." Arnold reached over and pushed his index finger into my chest. "How many fifty-four-year-old men do you know can be with eight different women in one night?"

"Or need to?" I answered wryly.

LuAnn looked stunned as if struck by lightning. "That's right," she said. "He needs to prove himself and uses me to do it."

The revelation freed LuAnn and she suddenly realized how much she had given up by permitting a weaker, less intelligent person to rule her life. She had become all the things she'd hated most about Arnold. She resolved on the spot to change and risk being on her own again so she could hold her head up and live a life that was under her own control. Arnold's powerful personality and Lu-Ann's weakness permitted her to accept his corrupt ways. She realized that none of this had anything to do with her and that Arnold would always be cheating. She was only able to change when she realized that she was also corruptible and that she had to assume responsibility for her own weakness.

CASE V: COERCING A SPOUSE TO CHEAT

Angela and Marvin were married after a tempestuous courtship and prolonged engagement that was broken six times according to her count, five according to his. They fought about that as well as everything else. Angela went through with the marriage to resolve her ambivalence. At least the indecision was over. She continued working and decided to go to graduate school instead of having children. Marvin moved up the company ladder and became regional sales manager for a large office supply firm.

Their marriage was emotionally closed. Angela realized that the relationship was wrong but had no idea how to go about changing it. Marvin was unwilling to admit his unhappiness and protested that he loved Angela and that he wanted her to love him. Angela knew better: Marvin ignored her feelings, permitted work concerns to dominate their conversations, used money to control her, and put her down all the time. She felt disdain for him and withheld affection and support, but she still played the role of the sweet, mistreated wife.

Then Angela met Robert, who was equally unhappy with his wife, Charlene, and who also lacked the courage to end what was obviously not working for him. The two schemed about getting out of their marriages. Since neither couple was having satisfactory sexual relations, Robert and Angela focused their discussions with their mates on improving their sexual life. While the logistics may seem impossible and the likelihood improbable, they managed to get their spouses to participate in a strange religious cult's sexual awakening course. In this bizarre setting couples were asked to exchange partners and allow themselves to sense the newness of sex with another person. The stated object was to return home with reawakened sexual energy and redirect it to their partner.

It was entirely fraudulent, but served the two perpetrators.

Robert and Angela immediately paired up at the door leaving Marvin and Charlene to fend for themselves. Charlene pretended to be horrified, but came to every meeting. Marvin felt the experience was beneficial and relished having sex with whomever he wanted, but after seeing Angela and Robert together, he became jealous. After the meetings, when he tried to get Angela to share her "newly awakened sexuality" and show that she still loved him, she was always too tired.

After several meetings Angela announced that she had formed a serious attachment to Robert and felt that for the time being she and Robert should nurture their feelings together without outside interference. The group leader concurred. Charlene did not seem to care, but Marvin, who initially had played distant and uninvolved, began to panic and threatened to start legal proceedings against the group leader for alienation of affection. It was too late. Angela and Robert declared their "newfound" love, rationalized to their partners that they had all gone into this with their eyes open and that they were all adults. What happened, they explained, happened. The rest was all history.

It was the con job of the century.

This form of cheating is really nothing more than manipulating a partner to have sex in order to justify one's own infidelity. In part, this serves to lower guilt, but it is nothing more than doubly injuring another person, first by cheating on him and then by taking away his dignity and right to criticize by lowering him to your level. Setting up your partner to reduce your ambivalence or mitigate your guilt is only adding insult to injury. If you are going to cheat, don't compound the problem by insisting that your partner keep you company. If you are doing this to gain your partner's cooperation in ending a relationship that you feel powerless to leave on our own, you will never feel right about it.

CASE VI: LOVE AS GRIEF'S PROXY

Irene's father owned an empire—mills, chemical plants, forests, mines, oil, shipping, manufacturing, and distribution. When he died on Irene's fifteenth birthday, his company was doing business in seventy-one countries. Irene loved him very much. She was his favorite.

The business was split among three brothers and Irene. Although Irene was extremely bright, she was unable to concentrate and seemed to drift after her father's death. She had many brief affairs, all of them in the context of a spoiled rich girl, willfully doing whatever she wanted. She always seemed preoccupied by romance and when the affairs ended she never seemed to care. Another romance was always around the corner. She attended a junior college, flunked out in her first year, and married Thomas when she was eighteen to the great relief of her mother. The marriage was a society event, covered by three newspapers and mentioned in two national magazines. The family neither approved nor disapproved of Thomas. They were just pleased that Irene had settled down.

Thomas and Irene prospered and had four children. Irene had no profession and no desire or need to work. She enjoyed sports and filled her week with riding, tennis, water skiing, and swimming. Although she was never involved in more than one extramarital relationship at a time, she had affairs with virtually every man she was attracted to. Her rules were simple: She controlled the relationship. When she had all she wanted, she ended it. Having all she wanted meant loving and breaking it off at the point of getting close. Over the years, Irene had dozens of such affairs, playing each one until the wave crested and then abandoning it just as it threatened to break. Irene did not know if Thomas was aware of her activity, but remained discreet and never inquired about how he spent his free time.

On the day her own daughter turned fifteen Irene became agitated, and after a small family party she got in her car, saying she needed some air, and drove to the apartment of an old lover demanding to be held and loved. Afterward when the old lover jokingly predicted that she would now dress and bolt out the door,

Irene collapsed into deep sobs and refused to leave, making a scene that was entirely uncharacteristic of her.

Irene saw a psychiatrist, unfortunately an older lonely man who had needs that matched hers. Her girlish charm and fragile vulnerability overwhelmed him. She played right into it and seduced him during the second session. The idea came into her head when he started asking about her father. She terminated therapy after the next visit when he offered to return his fee and carry on their relationship as equals outside the office. The psychiatrist called her for weeks before he could accept that she had rejected him. He felt used and manipulated into abandoning his ethical standards, something he had never done before. His self-esteem had fallen and he was at wits' end. The psychiatrist's phone calls made Irene despondent. She had hurt him deeply. Although she had remained in control, as she always insisted on doing, her caring for this man kept her from pushing the event out of her mind. He had been so kind to her that she had allowed him to matter. Irene realized for the first time that there was something wrong with her cheating. She had always been able to break it off before feelings were involved, but now she felt terrible and did not think she could go on.

When I saw Irene in my office she seemed like a fragile child, but she was armed with a socialite's grace and easy manner that covered her inner uncertainty. I helped her understand that she had never dealt with the death of her father and had been using these affairs to get close to men and have the feeling of control over them that was missing when her own father died. We discovered that she feared abandonment, but by abandoning all these men in her life she felt as if she were identifying with her father abandoning her. It was only after she had permitted herself to feel close to the other psychiatrist and experience his hurt that she came to realize how much she must have suffered when her father died.

Inhibited grief is responsible for much self-destructive, sexually impulsive, or hurtful behavior. A happy person knows how to mourn. An unhappy person is filled with the unresolved grief of his past. Life is full of losses. If you do not express the hurt and anger of each loss as it occurs, it lives within you and sensitizes you toward future losses, causing you to anticipate them with dread, to rush through your painful experiences or or avoid them entirely. This only creates more unresolved grief and so the burden of emotional debt increases.

Mourning is expressing the anger over the hurt of a loss.

Each of Irene's affairs became a dress rehearsal for giving up her father. But she was so socially facile, she could easily manipulate men and keep the loss under her control; in that way she kept the mourning at a distance.

You cannot mourn successfully unless you have good self-esteem. This is why children have such a difficult time with losses. They, like Irene, often depend on their parents for their self-esteem, and when a parent dies, their ability to handle the loss is diminished. Irene actually remarked, "If only my dad were here to see me through the pain of his death."

It had been the story of her life.

WHY PEOPLE CHEAT

There are as many reasons for cheating as there are for avoiding pain. Cheating always points to a weakness in your relationship. There is no such thing as an innocent, harmless affair. If an affair is considered meaningless, what is the worth of the partner who can be cheated on with impunity?

Many married businesspeople engage in one-night stands on the road, but then so do skiers away for a holiday, girls out on the town, and boys out with the boys. In some cultures such behavior is passed off as normal, but this is a self-deception. If every trespass against a relationship's exclusivity can be pardoned by citing excuses, drugs, or circumstances, the relationship cannot really matter to either party. When all is said and done, excuses given to lessen the pain of the injury of cheating are just that—excuses. The facts remain simple and clear: Your partner has been unfaithful and you are hurt because you are no longer regarded as special.

It has become the vogue these days to label infidelity by thirty- or forty-year-old partners as "a mid-life crisis." In the typical case, a partner reaches mid-life and begins to acknowledge his or her unfulfillment and to question whether the life he or she is leading is the best it could be. The people most likely to suffer a mid-life crisis are those who have never questioned the values they live by, who lack the courage to follow what they feel or to discuss what really matters to them.

We all need to grow up. We all need to become honest about our needs and our situations, to realize that this is the only chance we get at life. Living life to the fullest is our first imperative and deepest need. Partners must understand that expressing this wish is not a betrayal of loyalty, but a growing realization that life is unfolding and happiness living together only comes to those who are still free to pursue it.

Cheating is often the safety valve to vent frustrations that build as people realize they are unhappy and desperately grope around trying to find fulfillment. Even if you do not get caught, someone always gets hurt whenever you cheat. You cannot cheat and feel totally good about yourself because cheating is a dishonest act. You may rationalize your behavior, claim that you are unloved, deprived, or deserving of better treatment. But even if that is true, why waste your energy in an affair, especially if your relationship is worth saving? Why not risk being open before your cheat, when you still have nothing to hide?

If by chance the person you are cheating with is right for you, it is difficult to enjoy the love between you. You cannot love freely because you cannot totally be yourself and cheat at the same time. If you are using the other person to explore a life without your partner or determine your value as a sexual commodity, the act of cheating may provide answers, but it makes the affair into an experiment.

There are exceptions to this in which someone finds their true love outside their current relationship and leaves to fulfill themselves by starting a new life, but this is not as much cheating as it is starting over. Cheating while expecting to stay in the original relationship almost always makes matters worse. Couples can recover, but only to the extent that they can be honest with each other. Start being honest before you cheat.

THE PROBLEM WITH CHEATING

If you become involved in cheating to catch up with the experiences you feel you have been denied, you run the risk of living a fantasy and becoming disheartened. You can never go home again, they say. You certainly can never return to the past. Probably a good thing, too, because no matter how palmy those days appear to you, you attribute to them what you feel is lacking in your life now. Testing out the life of a single may also discourage you and intimidate you so that you stay in a relationship that is bad for you. Having tested the life you have fantasized from the restricted point of view of a married person, you may draw the wrong conclusions and feel that you can never do better.

For all its excitement and intrigue—the release and sharing of passion so long held in, the rediscovery of one's sexual self, the orgasmic delight of sexual congress with someone who knows nothing about taking the garbage out, the bounced check, the sick child, or the mother-in-law crazed with bitterness—cheating diminishes you in some way. It is an anesthetic to the pain of life and therefore it also limits its joy.

Further, cheating complicates your life. You become preoccupied with infatuations that linger in your consciousness. You debase your credibility by making excuses for every trip outside the house even when you aren't using the errand to make a secret telephone call. You risk losing your believability as an honest person.

The worst part about cheating is that it makes a liar out of you. It causes you to shelter parts of your consciousness both from your mate and from yourself. If you are afraid to be open with your partner out of fear of what you might say, you have already betrayed yourself by limiting the freedom of your intimate expression at home.

When you cheat, you are also the one being cheated on. Cheating limits your freedom by providing the illusion that you are free to cheat. If you are free, why do you have to cheat? Perhaps because you recognize that you have come to the end of your relationship and acknowledge that you no longer belong there. Your cheating is a sign that you have not as yet completed the work of separation.

Should you discover that your partner has cheated on you, it is very easy to attack your partner, bask in self-pity, and indulge in guilt-producing behavior. Such reactions are common initially, but it makes little sense to stay hurt. You need to listen to your partner and to understand why he or she cheated. If you find this difficult to do, then your partner's reason for cheating is that you are not easy to communicate with intimately and that you are controlling or punitive. Unless you decide to become more open about this, the problem is likely to continue and get worse.

Cheating is a signal. In the long run, partners get caught on purpose to allow their deeds to speak for the feelings they are afraid to express. Accepting the cheating as a desperate attempt to communicate is the best attitude and the one most likely to achieve a successful resolution.

SHOULD YOU TELL?

If you are cheating on your partner, should you tell?

Because cheating is a deception, at first people always say, "Are you crazy? Of course not." But there are those instances where you would like your partner to meet the other person and become friends, understand that you love them both, and accept that your relationship has changed and you want it to be open now. You toy with the idea. You want to be accepted. You really don't want to hurt anyone. You just want to have your cake and eat it, too. Is that really so bad? Deep in your heart you know if you told your partner he or she would be devastated. You dread the reaction. You hate the problems in your relationship for making you reach outside for such an uncomfortable and compromising solution. You'd be perfectly happy if your partner were more like this other person: open, excited, happy, interested in and aroused by you. You start comparing the two, and where before you were loving, you are now impatient.

So unless you decide to confess everything and declare your desire to recommit to your partner at a new level of honesty and mean it, don't tell.

It is not a good idea to tell your partner to relieve your guilt without any intention of changing your behavior or to repay your partner for hurting you. You only bring yourself down to the level of a villain and lose your self-respect.

The problem with cheating is that it is always a perverted form of communication. Instead, it would be better to think about what you would like to say and say it. Cheating only confuses communication. Instead of making a quiet statement, indicating something is wrong, when you cheat you blast your partner into a state of shock, self-doubt, disbelief, and disorganization. Your message is totally lost and you have made it more difficult to get through in the future.

BEFORE YOU CHEAT

I realize that none of this is going to stop someone from cheating when the discomfort of feeling unloved is greater than the courage of speaking directly. But as a guide, try to remember this: When you create an unstable situation to express your unhappiness, the unhappiness you create also obscures your communication.

Again, before you cheat, express what is in your heart. Risk being rejected, disapproved of, and not taken seriously. Speak everything you feel honestly. Remember, if cheating is in your heart, you have nothing to lose by giving honesty another try. Who knows? If you say what you really mean for a change, this time you may be listened to. If you are ignored or told that your feelings do not matter, you may find new courage to act on your own behalf and to do so in a way that preserves your self-esteem and dignity.

You may not have to live with your partner, but you always have to live with yourself.

CHAPTER THIRTEEN

Forgiving

F ORGIVING IS telling the person who injured you that you no longer hurt. Perhaps the greatest pain in a relationship is caused by cheating, but even smaller injuries can be a threat unless they are forgiven.

To forgive another you need to be vulnerable and admit you have been injured. You also need to take responsibility for exposing yourself to injury, especially if that person has hurt you before. When you allow someone to hurt you, you feel angry for not protecting yourself. You need to realize that people usually hurt each other unintentionally and, therefore, deserve a second chance. People hurt others on purpose when they have been hurt. They also deserve a second chance. People hurt others when they are weak, afraid to tell the truth, are addicted or thoughtless. They may not deserve a second chance, but you still need to forgive them.

You can't forgive another person if you are unwilling to let go of your pain. When you refuse to forgive, your prolonged expression of hurt becomes an annoyance because it is an attempt to make the other person feel guilty.

Consider how you've felt when you hurt someone. Even if you had good reason to be angry and to hurt back, hurting another never feels good. When you seek revenge, you become an injuring party in your own right. Acting in anger always lowers your self-esteem.

It is universally common to have angry fantasies before expressing hurt. However, when these fantasies are allowed to build we can become so enraged that we fear we will lose control and do harm to the other person if we express ourselves. This traps us in our anger, a dangerous position, because withheld anger always ends up hurting us. It's difficult to think well of yourself if you are preoccupied with doing someone in. Still, when we cannot express ourselves directly, we humiliate our tormentors in fantasy and bring them to their knees. It is a perverse victory.

If you attempt to act on these angry feelings, you have to put your love aside and change your attitude from caring to hurtful. You have to wallow in hatred, a terrible place to rest your consciousness. From such a place the whole world appears evil. You look all around you to build a case that justifies being nasty and it drains your energy to do so. You have to shut out the good in your relationship, deny that you love the other person, that he is lovable or loves you.

Learn to say "That hurts." It will do more to keep your relationship open to love than anything else.

For your own sake, you need to let go of your hurt. You need to forgive your partner, not to free him from guilt, but to free yourself from anger. You need to live in the present. Holding on to pain always ties you to the past. This is especially true when your partner has hurt you deeply enough to destroy your relationship. Even if the relationship seems beyond hope, you need to set the emotional accounts straight. It's one thing to lose a relationship. You can get over that. It's quite another matter to get lost in self-pity, to refuse to recover from an injury in order to make your partner appear the villain. As much as others may sympathize with you, no one really cares when you feel sorry for yourself. Eventually you lose self-esteem and come to believe that you deserve to be treated the way you were.

A GUIDE TO FORGIVING

Prepare your partner by telling him that he hurt you and that you want to tell him how. Explain that your intention is to forgive him. Tell him you just need him to listen.

Accept the situation for what it is. Don't bargain with reality.

Don't forgive superficially or rush the process just to get it over with. Take the time to be complete. Your partner needs to know how he has hurt you. You need to know why you're forgiving your partner.

Don't complain. Don't point to broken promises. If you have discussed this same injury many times before and nothing has changed, you need to accept that nothing is likely to change. Don't fight over it. You need to decide what you want to do about this problem independent of any promises you hope your partner will make and keep.

Stay focused. Tell your partner you feel hurt and exactly why. Follow your natural expression without censoring your feelings.

If you have to wait before sharing, make a note of your hurt feelings and read them to your partner the next time you see him. This allows you to get those feelings out and greatly lowers your stress. Stress is the pressure caused by a withheld feeling. Just getting the feeling out will do wonders for your anxiety because you won't have to use your defenses to contain it. You won't feel like exploding. You will be better able to concentrate. Blaming your partner for a bad day is a mistake. Your partner may be responsible for injuring you, but you are responsible for repressing your feelings.

Let your partner's response be free and spontaneous. You have to risk discovering that the other person doesn't care about having hurt you or your feelings and, therefore, doesn't care about you. This also means that you risk discovering that you are not loved.

Try to avoid accusations or sinister insinuations. Again, remember most injuries are just thoughtless and insensitive. They are not planned. Your object is to educate your partner to your particular sensitivities, to make him aware of his own hurtfulness, and so make his behavior less automatic, more discriminating. You do this by lowering his defenses. Yelling or attacking his weaknesses will only close him down.

234

If your partner starts making excuses or cutting you off, repeat that you are hurting and you need to get the hurt out so you can feel good about being together again. Remind him that holding in these negative feelings devalues the relationship and undermines your love.

Once you have expressed your feelings, ask your partner for his side of the story. Listen silently. He is likely to present hurts of his own. Show him the consideration you would like to receive when you share your feelings. When he is through, comment on his pain and express what remains of yours. Remember, opening up the hurt will relieve the stress, but more hurt may rise to the surface, especially if you have held it in for some time. Express this as well.

When you are done say, "I feel better. The hurt is gone. I forgive you."

Now you are free to stay or go as you choose.

You can avoid a confrontation with the person who injured you if you choose. But living in your hurt and displaying your wounds to friends to gather sympathy does little good if your friends encourage you to stay angry and unforgiving. Sympathy is not release if it prolongs your misery.

Your object is to be free of your pain, not to nurture it to fortify your anger. The object of surviving is not to live in anger but in contentment, with peace of mind. Forgiving is the only way this is possible.

If you are planning to stay with your partner, forgive. Even if you never want to see the person who hurt you again, it is especially important that you forgive him, for the hurts that you do not forgive will fuel angry recollections that will intrude on the good times to come.

You are responsible for your own suffering. No matter how badly you were hurt it is *your* responsibility to get over it. The reason that you have pain is to make you aware that something is wrong and needs to be corrected. You are the only person who can make that correction.

If your partner is unwilling to admit that he hurt you, it is impossible to trust him. There is no middle ground here. If a person is willing to admit he injured you, there is hope. If the other person does not admit he hurt you, your love cannot mean much to him and his love is not worth having.

Expressions of hurt often become fighting matches because partners focus on their anger instead of the hurt. Stay with the hurt. The anger is implied in the injury and will dissipate when the hurt is out. Focusing on anger is merely retaliating, and this works against forgiving.

You are responsible for expressing your hurt in a nonhurtful way. If you believe that the other person deserves to be injured, you are really saying that he is not a good person. If that is true, what are you doing living together?

Acts of forgiveness are quiet, tender things. They are the expression of the trust in your love and in each others' goodness. You need to give the other person the benefit of the doubt again, but you can only do this if you are willing to be vulnerable.

A deep love permits partners to accept each others' weaknesses. It reveals how to injure and how to blame. Instead of taking unfair advantage of the closeness and intimacy their love generates, loving partners seek evidence of their affection and build on it by clearing away the negative feelings that block the expression of love.

Be honest about expressing your hurt and your love will keep you whole.

CHAPTER FOURTEEN

Planning a Separation

SOMETIMES IT just doesn't work out. The fighting, the unresolvable differences, the failure to consider the value of each others' feelings, and the continual conflict make it impossible for partners to be their best together or apart. When this happens, people become disheartened about living together and about themselves. As a relationship starts to deteriorate, partners fight to get to high ground and save themselves, often putting the other down as the first step in climbing back to safety.

It is difficult to live with an enemy who knows your weak points, who views you with suspicion and is building a case against you. You cannot be yourself in such a situation. You have to measure your comments out of fear that they will be distorted and used against you. You have to hide your vulnerable feelings and your needs lest they be used to manipulate you. In the end stage of relationships this demoralizing situation is more typical than not.

You always need to preserve your independent identity, especially when your relationship is troubled. You are a person first, in a troubled or happy relationship second. Insisting on being your own person is not a sign of disloyalty or lack of commitment. It is a sign of strength.

If you can still be yourself in a relationship, even if it doesn't always support you, you are at least free. Unfortunately, being able to be oneself is often the first casualty of a declining relationship. Although the issues that bring relationships to an end may vary, losing one's freedom is the real reason people leave. The best reason to leave a relationship is to regain the part of yourself that no longer appears when you are together.

There is always great resentment when you lose the freedom to be yourself. We all yearn to become something better, to give up the false views of ourselves, and develop our potential so we can make a meaningful contribution. But your ability to give your best depends on your freedom to be yourself. Perhaps you feel you have only minor talents, limited education, paltry gifts. It is no matter. You have a unique life. If you can identify and develop your uniqueness, you become a source of strength to those around you. Just imagine what the world would be like if everyone evolved as their best.

What does all this have to do with separation?

When your relationship is torn by conflict and continual hurt, it is easy to lose sight of your value as a person. At such times the effort needed to start over again can seem overwhelming. When you have used your relationship to hide from the world, giving it up feels doubly risky. You can never escape your own destiny. Whether you abandoned a career for your marriage or took on a more secure job for the sake of your family, the dormant embers of a life that could truly fulfill you remain deep within you.

Unfortunately, when people finally admit that they are unhappy or that something is missing, they often take the wrong risks and look to a lover to spark them back into life or to an addiction to lower their discomfort. This only confuses and distracts them. The real solution is to risk testing yourself and to feel the excitement of being fully alive again.

TAKING TIME ALONE

When living together unhappily has made you lose sight of your worth and your direction, it is helpful to take some time alone to sense what you are like by yourself. This need not be a long or hostile separation, but one that allows you to think things over so you can decide what you want to do without your partner's inhibiting influence.

Some years ago, when my first marriage was failing, I took my wife to Norway on a vacation where we talked about our unhappy situation and what we should do about it. Norway that summer was a land of exaggerated contrasts to our dark mood. We drove past lakes, by meadows dotted with wildflowers, snow-capped mountains, waterfalls, and upland pastures where the herds are driven for the summer. Just in time for dinner, we arrived at the town of Balestrand on the Søgne Fjørd shimmering in the gold saturated light of the midnight sun. It was not a happy arrival. We had been arguing angrily against this beautiful backdrop all day. By the time dinner was served we were not speaking.

An older woman at another table had been observing us and was inspired to send us a bottle of wine with her compliments. I smiled and thanked her. After dinner my wife retired and the innkeeper and the lady asked me to join them for some homemade cherry brandy on the shore of the fjord. The sun had gone to the edge of the horizon to make its circle and reappear in an hour or two. "To the magic of the North," the lady pledged. "I come here every year for two weeks in the summer. I come here alone. It was an agreement I made with my husband when we got married on my birthday twenty-five years ago. I'm fifty tomorrow."

"Congratulations," I said and added some more wood to the fire that the innkeeper had built. The mountains cradling the little town were in deep shadows, but although it was almost eleven the fjord's glassy surface still reflected the decaying gold and silver sky.

"The agreement I made with my husband," the lady began to explain, "was that I would go away each year to reconsider whether or not I wanted to come back. He was upset this year for the first time because he wanted to give a special party. People are funny about dates and years. What does fifty or twenty-five mean really? It's all what you feel now. Isn't that true?"

"Yes," I said and wondered where in the world this woman had come from.

She poked at the fire and smiled at me. She seemed so free and open. I felt immediately drawn to her.

"You can't make promises forever," she said. "I tell that to my

239

husband each year before I leave. He still doesn't know whether I'll come back to Oslo next week."

"Will you?" I was genuinely curious. The uncertainties in my own marriage flashed through my mind.

"Ask me at the end of my two weeks," she laughed. "Maybe I am just kidding myself and always intend to return, but just knowing that once a year I have an opportunity to reconsider my life and am free to leave and start all over gives my soul room to breathe."

"The decision is always yours to make," I said with an admiring smile.

"It is yours as well," she said.

"There are mindreaders in the North Country," I thought to myself.

Taking the space you need to consider what you really want for yourself can be the beginning of the end or a new start together. It is hard to make the right decision for yourself when you have a frightened partner continually dogging your footsteps, asking for reassurance that he or she is still loved. It is impossible to make the best decision for yourself unless you are free to entertain all your options, even those you think are impossible or silly. Getting away just to be alone with your thoughts and ponder what is best for you is a wonderful experience.

Unfortunately, couples often wait until they've already decided to separate for good or want to be with a lover before they take the necessary time to reconsider their lives. It would be far more helpful if, like my Norwegian friend, more people could spend regular time away alone to take a personal inventory. How wonderful to know that you are always free to chose what your life will become.

Having control over your life is the sign of a free person.

Good Reasons for Getting Away Alone

Some good reasons for taking time by yourself away from your relationship:

Because you can't stand it anymore and want to figure out what you want to do.

Because you are confused.

Because you are not sure if you are still in love.

Because you feel too close to the relationship and too distant from yourself.

Because you want to leave.

Because you are trying to figure out the conditions under which you will agree to stay.

Because you love someone else.

Because it is difficult to love yourself where you are.

Because you are just tired and bored with the other person's problems and want to see what the world feels like without them, at least for a while.

Because you are not taken seriously and need to show your partner that you mean it when you say you want to make things better.

Because you are abused.

Because you need a new perspective on life.

GUIDELINES TO MAKING
A SEPARATION

If you decide to separate from your partner, it is important to set some guidelines. There are no rules for this. You are the one who must create these guidelines. Don't ask permission. It is up to you to decide what you want and need.

If you are just leaving for a weekend to think things over, the rules are that you trust each other and don't need rules. You expect to be back on Sunday night. If you are running to avoid being battered or abused, seek safety first. Make the rules when you are out of danger. If you are taking a month's vacation alone, you may want to define the limits of each other's behavior during your separation. Finally, if you are separating to reevaluate yourself and your relationship, you must grant your partner the same freedom.

Here is a summary of some of the important points that need to be considered and agreed upon in planning a separation.

Why Are You Separating?

What do you want: peace of mind, a brief vacation, the opportunity to see what you've been missing, safety, sanity, tranquility, excitement, adventure?

Is the separation really necessary? Are you motivated by the wish to get even or to torment your partner? If so, you'd do better talking to the other person about your angry feelings. If you must go, search your heart and find better reasons. When you leave for spite there is a tendency to keep the anger alive to motivate you. This works against you by diverting energy. Should the anger subside you may find yourself lacking resolve and doubting yourself and mistakenly return to a relationship that may not be good for you.

Whom Should You Tell?

You should not only decide whom to tell but what to tell them. Remember, a separation is a period of reevaluation. If you end up back together, you don't want to be fighting over the distortions that you told others in order to justify your position. In-laws especially can be unforgiving. Disclosing negative personal details at a time like this is like arming an intruder. If you paint the other person as worthless and later return or accept him or her back, what does that say about you, your judgment, or your credibility? The best approach is to say that there are personal differences and you are trying to work them out.

How Long Should You Be Apart?

You can go away for a day, a weekend, a week or two to resolve the acute stresses of a difficult situation. Shorter separations are helpful to regain your strength so you can return and deal with problems that have overwhelmed you. They are cooling-off periods, changes in scenery to regain perspective. Longer separations are for serious reconsideration of your life together, especially your decision to return or leave.

During shorter separations, it is best that you keep apart and have no contact except for emergencies. Define what an emergency is before you leave or else emergencies will be invented to disrupt your solitude. Even a slight intrusion into a short separation can ruin the positive effects of being apart. One needy phone call from an angry or insecure partner will serve to remind you of all the bad things that make you want to leave and can precipitate a premature decision to make the separation permanent. So if your partner wants to be alone, grant him or her the space without interruption. Your understanding and maturity will work in your favor more than your pleading or acting sullen and morose.

If you are seriously reconsidering your commitment, a longer separation is suggested. Obviously, that requires a certain amount of planning, perhaps finding a roommate or making a living arrangement that if necessary can be converted from temporary to permanent. Staying with parents for a long time is not as productive as being on your own. Still, when children are involved and finances wear thin it may be the only way at first. Even so, being in your own is best for you. Don't go from one dependent situation into another.

Separations that last over a year are often unproductive and usually reflect a deep conflict between needs and values, profound ambivalence or guilt over leaving, or a refusal to work on the relationship's problems. You should reach a decision about your relationship in under six months.

Talking It Over

When you discuss a separation, insist on total honesty from your partner and express precisely how you feel. This is no time for accusations or playing the helpless victim. You are asking for time to decide whether you want to go on together and if so under what conditions.

You separate ultimately so you can be real, to speak your own mind, to share what you feel, to think your own thoughts and be yourself again. Ideally, you should decide what freedoms you wish to reinstate in your relationship. If your relationship is right for you, it will permit you what you need.

Planning Your Finances

If you are planning what is euphemistically called a trial separation—really a trial divorce—you need to test your independence and ability to make it on your own. Falling back on the other for support every time you get into trouble is not in either of your best interests. It is best to make some kind of support agreement to begin with and then follow expenses closely so you can make adjustments should you wish to make the agreement permanent. You should have some general idea of your financial requirements before you leave. Keep a financial diary for this purpose and record your monthly expenses just to be sure you understand what it costs to support yourself.

What About Sex?

Do you intend to remain faithful, to date your partner and have sex together? Dating your partner while separated can sometimes re-create the romance that got lost in your marriage, but it often ends up in terrible arguments, pleas to return, and the same attempts to manipulate that made you leave. Of course, if after a while the feeling of love returns with the distance, it is a sign that the separation is accomplishing its purpose and you should let your heart guide you.

What Do You Tell the Kids?

Don't try to restrict a partner's access to children during a separation unless you believe your partner is causing them real harm. Unfortunately, this tactic is used mostly by weak and resentful partners who wish to punish their mates. Husbands who are so restricted usually seek to retaliate by withholding their support. Restricting access to children is a two-edged sword. Think of the children's needs. No matter what happens, how angry or justified you feel, you and your partner will always be your children's parents. Making the situation as easy and as natural as possible for the children at a time of such disorganizing stress and uncertainty is the right move. Children do not need to hear either parent's story of the conflict. Both views are incomplete and distorted. You and your partner should act toward your children during a time of separation the way you would if you were getting along lovingly. Tell them that the two of you are not getting along right now and

244

need to be apart to think clearly. Be truthful but don't unload your unhappiness on them and don't blame your partner.

Dealing with the Family

Should you go together to important events, such as funerals and weddings? Or should you go alone or avoid them completely? If an important family event is coming, talk about it. Don't wait until the last minute.

Just because you are separating does not mean that you should encourage your family to shun or abandon your partner. Giving each other the freedom to pursue and enjoy family ties goes a long way toward reconciliation. Again, manipulating family members to support your case is not a good idea. Be as natural as possible and allow others to be themselves without attempting to influence their behavior.

Conditions for Reconciliation

If being together feels like being pinned down on a battlefield, cessation of hostilities should be the minimum prerequisite for returning. If you are leaving because your partner does not want to work with you on your relationship's problems or insists that he or she is perfect, a change in that position is the requirement for coming back. Don't be prompted by loneliness, fear, or financial stress to sell out for anything less than a commitment to fix what is wrong. Chances are you'd be making the same mistake that got you where you are now.

A TIME TO GROW

There are few things more difficult than facing the imminent dissolution of a relationship. Each partner wishes to preserve his self-esteem, be right, and blame the other. A separation neutralizes old manipulations. A partner's attempts to control, to create guilt by acting helpless, or to restrict finances become seen as reasons to stay apart where before they had the power to hold partners in place. This is a time for growing, for giving up the restraints your relationship placed on you, for learning to trust yourself and to realize that your relationship only has a chance if both of you are free to disagree and decide for yourselves.

You may not like the idea that your spouse wants to be alone, but try not to take it personally. Use the separation for your own advantage. It's your separation, too. Think about your own needs. You cannot be in a relationship with someone who is deeply ambivalent about staying without having some reservations of your own. A relationship can't be terrible for one partner and wonderful for the other.

Don't panic or attempt to resist your partner's decision. Don't make threats about what you will do if he leaves. It will only propel your partner into impulsive behavior or lead him to defy you. If the worst is going to happen and your deepest fears are going to be realized, there is nothing you can do to stop it. Certainly opposing the inevitable will only strengthen your partner's resolve.

Agreeing to separate without prejudice or blame, even under circumstances that seem against you, can mark the turning point in your relationship. Rise to the occasion. Be understanding and supportive. Recognize that it is not going well. Welcome the opportunity to be apart. Remember, each of you has to do what is right for yourself. Admitting this may give your partner real hope for reconciliation. Indicate that you want it to work out if that is what is best for both of you. Empathizing is a far better approach than threatening or trying to manipulate or control.

GETTING BACK TOGETHER

There should be no punishment or guilt-producing behavior when partners reunite. If your partner wants to return, see this as an opportunity to make your relationship more open, more of a partnership. Talk about everything. Why is he returning? Why does she want to start over? What have you learned about yourself in this time? What were you unhappy about? What do you want to change? Express your needs. Try to reach a new understanding.

Reconciliation is not a time to sweep problems under the table.

It is the time to bring up everything that you feel needs to be worked on. So be flexible, accept your role in the problem, but insist on coming to an understanding about the conflict between you. Superficially forgiving the other person out of desperation without raising the level of truthfulness between you may make things feel better for a time, but it does nothing to make the relationship work.

SEPARATING FOR GOOD

Should you decide to make the separation permanent, announce your decision as soon as you are sure. If the decision is the right one, it will give you strength. Even so, don't be surprised if you suddenly have intense feelings of sadness even though you are leaving the cruelest spouse for the life you have always dreamed of. Closing a chapter on our errors is a sobering experience. Be sure you do not confuse your feelings of regret over making mistakes with your decision to leave. Don't make this announcement in anger, but with resolve. The last thing you want to do is start a fight. There will be tears. There may be bitterness. Your goal is to remain on friendly terms even if you can no longer be lovers.

SOME ADVICE ON GETTING
A DIVORCE

If you are married and agree to make the separation permanent, you should wait a few months before hiring a lawyer. You need this time to think and be sure. The legal process has a momentum of its own and some divorce lawyers have a way about them that discourages reconciliation, their protests to the contrary notwithstanding. Decide on a temporary support program beforehand. No matter what your lawyer tells you, supporting yourself is in your best interest. It may not be in his.

If possible, proceed with the no-fault route. The adversary approach is needlessly destructive and often requires that the partners abandon their goodwill in order to give their lawyers freedom to attack. This is nonsense. Being punitive or retaliatory at this point only reflects your earlier inadequacy in expressing your feelings. Trying to get the court to punish your partner is mostly an expensive pipe dream. Unscrupulous lawyers will encourage you to pursue the law to the limits to obtain your rights. Your real rights are to be free of anyone's undue influence; settle this matter as quickly as possible so you can live a life of your own.

If you choose a lawyer on a percentage of settlement basis, you are making a big mistake, especially if children are involved. It is true that some mates need legal restraints to get them to provide minimal support, but these people are by far in the minority. If you perceive your mate as this kind of person, ask if your anger has anything to do with this before assuming the worst. Using a court of law to repay you for your own poor judgment in getting involved in the first place is the sign of someone who has a poor self-image.

During the period of legal proceedings, carry an envelope with you and each time you get an idea about your case, write it down and put it in the envelope and bring it up with your lawyer. It will be one less item to preoccupy you. Speak to your lawyer as little as possible. Keep notes, have an agenda of what you wish to accomplish in each meeting.

Remember, your goal is to get past your anger, to forgive and start over again. The last thing you want is to make the same mistake twice. Accepting responsibility for your half of the problem is your best insurance against this.

Whether you are together or apart, if the path is now open to grow, you have won an important victory.

Part Four

BEING YOUR
BEST TOGETHER

CHAPTER FIFTEEN

Creating Your Own Sex Manual

I T HAS often been said that when sex is bad it is a very large part of a relationship and when sex is good it is a very small part.

THE MOST COMMON MALE SEXUAL PROBLEM

Sexual spontaneity reflects the openness of the communication between partners. For example, nearly all impotence in otherwise healthy men is the result of withheld anger. It is an unusual man who has never had a little difficulty with this problem, but such difficulties are usually temporary. Impotent men often feel guilty and fear risking rejection by revealing their anger and thus proving they are bad. Instead, they deprive their partner of sexual pleasure while claiming it isn't their fault. It is as if they are saying "How could I hurt you? I'm so powerless I can't even get an erection." Rather than admitting their deeper feelings, they express remorse over their inability to perform sexually, seeking support and reassurance from their partners at the same time as they punish them.

Since the emotions involved are usually hidden, the problem

frequently feels obscure and hopelessly complex. For example, the nicer their partners are, the more guilty these men feel about hurting them by withholding sex. In addition, because impotence is also a threat to the woman's sexuality, she wonders what is wrong with her and why she cannot excite her man; frequently she tries to arouse him just to prove herself. When her giving is motivated by such insecurity rather than desire, it adds to the man's hurt, thereby increasing his anger and making the situation worse. In spite of the woman's best efforts, the man remains impotent just to prove her sexually unattractive. Impotence is a contradiction in which the man wins by sacrificing his sexuality.

Just as with other problems in a relationship, the first step in overcoming impotence is to admit the anger and reveal the hurt that caused it. This is difficult for those men who equate admitting they are hurt with being weak. When a man feels weaker than his woman, impotence can sometimes be the only expression of anger with which he feels comfortable.

Becoming involved in sexual activity, where both vulnerability and aggressiveness are required at the same time, threatens these men. Where they feel afraid to be aggressive, they will also be impotent. They must therefore prove their virility elsewhere. Especially if they are unwilling to admit that they have a sexual problem, impotent men can be overly aggressive and competitive in "safe" areas, such as business and sports.

There are many paradoxes here. Men are frequently able to perform with one partner and not with another, with "bad women" who deserve to be treated badly but not with their mates. If a man is impotent but has erections in his sleep or on arising, the problem is most likely emotional, for in the dream state those defenses that operate when one is conscious are lowered.

Men become preoccupied about impotence and quickly lose perspective, thinking only about their wounded egos and their inability to perform. Frequently, the man's self-absorption totally overshadows his partner's feelings. While men acknowledge that the woman is not being satisfied, they believe they are the one who is really suffering.

Some impotent men avoid all physical contact under the pretext that they do not wish to hurt their partner by leading them on—an excuse for giving even less. Other men become cuddly as if wishing to be nurtured, consoled, and forgiven by being treated like a child.

Besides coping openly with the hidden anger, reducing stress with rest, taking a vacation, combatting boredom by variations in technique, position, time, and place can all help relieve impotence stemming from psychological causes. Depression that causes impotence is mostly a result of withheld anger as well. Unfortunately, to resolve this problem men sometimes use drugs and/or seek relationships with more attractive or caring partners. Don't be confused by impotence. Assume it is inhibited anger and deal with the underlying hurt.

THE MOST COMMON FEMALE SEXUAL PROBLEM

Frigidity is a little more complicated because women cannot point to a flaccid penis as an excuse for not participating in sex. They need to make more elaborate excuses when they are unwilling to admit their hurt and anger. Women, like men, have moments when their sex drive evaporates. This is common after the birth of a child, especially when the woman feels overwhelmed about fulfilling her new role and feels that her husband and child are both babies needing her care. Some women feel uninterested in sex during certain days of their menstrual cycle, at certain periods of their lives, and when they are afraid of something. Women are much less able to have sex for its own sake, unlike men, who can suddenly get in the mood just by remembering something sexy that happened twenty-five years ago. Women are more likely to be taught by an unhappy mother that it isn't nice to enjoy sex or that sex is unfulfilling or dirty, a perverse attempt to discourage them and protect their chastity.

It is a woman's attitude about herself that determines her sexuality. Low self-esteem, fear of losing control, and anxiety over being lovable are the main reasons women have problems with sex. A woman who does not feel good about herself cannot feel truly sexy. Although some women use sex to feel loved, such sex feels manipulative and draining. It's not exciting. When a woman feels she must perform to please her partner, the experience may be sexy by the man's standards, but it's often a bit distanced and staged, and not very fulfilling.

The frigid woman is not interested in the man and usually for good reasons. She may feel he is insensitive, demanding, controlling, or filled with self-importance. Unable to express her anger, she retaliates by not participating in sex. The man tends to lose patience with her, finding her too difficult to deal with. Instead of trying to understand her, he often just demands his rights. This further damages the equality between the partners.

A woman who is not permitted to say "no" without feeling guilty will never say "yes" with abandon.

A woman who is stripped of her own career and identity, who feels dependent and powerless, also feels resentful even if she is unwilling to admit it to herself, even if she protests the opposite to the world. Often she is not taken seriously, not listened to, and not treated as an equal. So when her partner asks for sex, he empowers her to refuse. When that is the only power a woman has over her mate, you can be sure she will use it.

Most frigid women aren't sexually unfeeling. They are just so hurt and angry that there is no way that tender, receptive feelings can express themselves. If a woman is angry at a man for bottling her up and not caring for her, the last emotion she will express is sexual desire. A woman's sexuality depends on her ability to feel vulnerable, trusting, and loved. Millions of dollars' worth of psychotherapy have been spent trying to make this point to frustrated husbands. Men betray themselves when they want sex on command because spontaneous sex is the by-product only of an open, feeling relationship where the partners are both free.

A happy sexual life is an extension of a happy, free life together. If you are not happy together, why should you expect your sex life to be good?

While insecure men are likely to label their sexually uninterested mates psychologically impaired, or point to an unhappy childhood to explain why they are not aroused, they are just fooling themselves. For all the problems in self-esteem or mistaken beliefs about sex, when sex isn't working the problem is usually in the relationship. Many so-called frigid women have easily warmed to passion in the arms of a caring partner.

Men cannot imagine love without sex.

Women cannot imagine sex without love.

The frigid woman is not cold by nature but by reaction. She wants tenderness and love but is reduced to withholding sex to keep from losing her identity. She avoids participating in sex because it makes her even more dependent on the man, exactly what she is trying to avoid.

Frigidity is a perverted symbol of independence.

FACTORS AFFECTING SEXUAL RESPONSE

Orgasm requires trust and the willingness to be vulnerable.

In order for orgasm to be shared and not merely one partner masturbating in the other's presence, the partners need to be open, loving, aware, sharing, expressive, trusting, caring, accepting, committed, and free. Partners who are controlling, demanding, impatient, hurtful, sarcastic, mistrustful, closed, angry, critical, and suspicious are less likely to have sexually fulfilling relationships.

To have the ideal sexual life, both partners need to be awake to each other's feelings inside and outside the bedroom. You can no more fake an orgasm than you can hide hurt. The price you pay is in lost sensitivity to yourself and to your partner's feelings.

COMMON SEXUAL PERVERSIONS

Anything that happens between two partners that makes them both happy is good.

It is a perversion to make love without caring. It is a perversion to force another person to have sex with you in ways that give only you pleasure. So is threatening punishment if the other person refuses.

WHAT IS NORMAL?

It is normal to have sex one to four times a week. It is also normal to have sex once in two or three weeks and to have sex five times on a weekend away. It is as unusual to have sex once a month as it is to have sex every day, but neither is especially abnormal. If your partner continually needs sex to feel loved, worthwhile, given to, or appreciated, it is a reflection of his or her own neediness and is an addiction.

Intense, frequent sex over short periods can be exhilarating, but when sex is insisted upon several times every day, it no longer has much to do with love, but is obsessional. Sex for its own sake is self-generating. There is a state of irritability that occurs with prolonged daily sex that participants mistake for heightened arousal. In fact, creating and relieving this irritability is mechanical. The effect is in the doing, not the result. This state is hard to maintain except in fantasy. Some partners may leave a relationship to find this sort of sex, but if they find it they easily become lost in it.

WRITING YOUR OWN
SEX MANUAL

The best sex creates a state of satisfaction that lasts for days because it is love manifested as physical caring. You are there for each other because you are so in touch with your partner's feelings and because giving pleasure is as wonderful as getting pleasure. You become your partner's feelings. The reason many couples do not have an intense sexual life is because they do not have an open, feeling relationship. You cannot have a profound sexual experience together unless you can cry and fight together, unless you can forgive each other, and unless you can be there for each other in illness and adversity. The level of trust that is needed to transcend the sexual experience and raise it to the level of your love requires a state of ongoing acceptance and commitment. Maintaining this openness is the continuing work of a relationship.

Transient relationships, those where strangers share intense passion, are largely a fantasy. Technically, the physical aspect of love-making can be shared by people who have good instincts about such things and who are sensitive to their partners. The deepest sexuality, however, is incomplete without understanding. The closest you can be to another person comes as an expression of the joy you feel in being with each other.

Penetration is not closeness. Technique is not understanding. Experimentation is not courage, and frequency is not caring.

If you have little desire to air the differences between you, you and your partner will have short and indifferent sexual contact. If you are unwilling to share the difficult times, the good times will be limited. You need to create an iridescent private world that reflects the full range of your understanding and feelings.

Every couple writes its own sex manual, a living text of experiences woven together from two lives. It is possible to make your sexual life more fulfilling by enhancing the sharing and communication between you. What follows is a guide to constructing your own sex manual by making it easier to discuss your needs and your fantasies. Sometimes you don't get what you want until you ask for it.

These exercises, essays, and lists are designed to make your sexual life fuller and more fun. Complete them one at a time independently of your partner. Share your responses afterward. It is suggested that you do this at a time and place where it is possible to show as well as tell your partner what you mean.

YOUR EROGENOUS ZONES

No two people are anatomically alike. Some people derive sexual pleasure and high erotic excitement from seemingly innocent contact, such as having one's face held in another's hands or having your partner kiss your ears. The biggest mistake you can make with a lover is to assume that what you are doing is pleasurable because you think it should be pleasurable. Ask for feedback. When in doubt, ask for instructions. While doing to others what you want to have done to yourself is a good rule and usually works in sexual contact, the opposite is also good to keep in mind. Don't do to your partner what would hurt you. Watch your partner's face and follow his or her expression. There is nothing like pain to convert a sexy evening into a fight over whether or not you really care.

EXERCISE 1
Charting the Map of Love

Make a list of every part of your body where you like to be touched. For each indicate:

Where you want to be touched

When: before making love, during, after?

How: lightly, firmly, playfully slapped?

With what: hands, lips, tongue?

What I want you to do and the order in which I want you to do it

How this will feel to me if you do it right

Exchange notes with your partner when you have completed this list. Then, using your partner's notes as a map, explore your partner's erogenous zones one at a time. If you have any doubts, ask your partner for precise instructions to help you. You need to know how your partner wishes to be touched, what is pleasurable, sensitive, and creates the greatest arousal. Tell your partner how it feels to touch and be touched. Take your time. You may not get to all the items on each other's list. You can go back to what you missed another time. Give specific advice. Be helpful. Take turns.

It is important to be a good teacher. Be encouraging, patient, appreciative, and willing to allow the exercise to progress to the point where the two of you are both involved. It is also important to be a submissive and willing pupil. So practice and study are recommended.

EXERCISE 2
What Excites Me

List everything you can think of that arouses your sexual interest. This can include seeing your partner silhouetted in a certain light, the smell of your partner's hair, being nuzzled on the neck while standing on line at the movies.

In completing this list, focus your attention on your senses. What sights, sounds, smells, tastes, touches give you pleasure? Don't worry if you sometimes feel aroused by a person other than your partner. Every man and woman who is sexually alive is attracted to other people. This does not mean that you want to become involved. It is merely a sign that you have vital sexual energy. You need to know all of the things that excite you so you can bring this excitement into your relationship.

For each item on your list indicate:

What you find sexy about it and why.

How you can include more of this in your life together.

When you have completed your list, share it with your partner. Talk about your needs. How often are these needs fulfilled? Are you free to show these needs? Are you willing to satisfy your partner's needs? If you and your partner changed places, how would you go about pleasing him or her? Talk about the ideal experience that would arouse this person. Have you ever had this experience? If so, why not have it again? If not, why not create it?

EXERCISE 3
Express Your Romantic Feelings

Anytime you feel aroused or in the mood, share the feeling with your partner. You should not expect anything more than to share your feeling of loving closeness. A smile or a light squeeze of your hand needs to be as important to you as having sex. If it is, you'll be making love all the time.

Romance is a light, airy, free thing born of fancy and fantasy, encouraged by little loving promises and lusty appreciations. These promises are not legal tender warranting payment on demand. If you can allow romance to flourish easily, you keep it alive. If you insist on your rights and what is due you, your account is soon empty.

In the middle of a dinner party you can whisper something naughty in your partner's ear. The more formal the surroundings, the more exciting the notion will seem. It is also wonderful to make a short and torrid telephone call to your partner during the day, full of suggestions and desires. Leaving little love notes in your partner's clothing, briefcase, or lunch pail is another way to enliven romance.

Greet such salacious utterings with mock shock, gratitude, and acceptance. Pretend to be offended, hard to get, but make it obvious you are pretending. You don't want to shut your partner off. Let the anticipation build. Occasionally, during the time the feeling builds, there should be additional remarks commenting on the progress of your growing interest. If this seems silly or undignified to you and you wonder what has happened to the sexual excitement in your life, I'll tell you. Your attitude has aged you. It's time to be playful again.

Sandy called my radio program feeling embarrassed about her declining sexual interest. She was only thirty years old.

S: I've been considering going to a sex therapist because I have problems. I guess you would say sexually. I've been married four years. It's not the first time I've had these feelings.

V: What feelings?

S: I feel embarrassed, sexually.

V: What's embarrassing?

S: I just can't dress up sexy without getting embarrassed. I can't do any of the things I did when our relationship was new. The way I feel just doesn't make any sense. I want to do what I used to be able to do and enjoy it.

V: Do you feel sexually toward your husband?

S: Yeah, I do, but . . .

V: Who wants you to dress up sexy?

S: Me. I do. He does, too, but I just don't feel like it.

V: What does dress up sexy mean?

S: Wearing a teddy or something or garter belt and stuff like that. It gets embarrassing for me once you get to know somebody and live with them day to day.

V: Okay, so the idea of putting on a teddy doesn't make you feel sexy. But why are you being so rough on yourself? Why don't you assume that you are all right and nothing bad has happened to you?

S: Well, I guess because I still can do it by myself when I'm alone and feel sexy. But I don't do that as much as I used to. Since my daughter was born I hardly have a sex drive. It's like a fourth of what it used to be.

V: And you think there's something wrong with you?

S: Well . . . right, I guess I do.

V: What changed after your daughter was born?

S: Well, I used to work full time and now I don't work at all.

V: That's important. You're home all day, not stimulated as much.

S: Oh, yeah. That's for sure!

V: That's for sure? Hmm? You're embarrassed all right, but it doesn't sound like it's mostly over sex. You're embarrassed for not liking the home situation as much as you think you should. You don't feel sexy anymore because you feel bound to being a mother.

S: Yeah!

V: You need to fix up your life. Do you go out as much?

S: Oh, no!

V: How much did you get out before the baby was born?

S: Oh, about once a week. At least once every two weeks.

V: When was the last time you went out?

S: Oh, we went to a concert. I guess it was two months ago.

V: You see, you've stopped being romantic together.

S: When we do go out, it is . . . it's just like being kids again.

V: Sandy, listen to you. You have allowed your love life to slip away from you. Anybody, the sex kitten of the Western world, stuck into your life would turn out to be Miss Dowdy-Two-Shoes in a year. How do you expect to be sexual and put on teddies and come in with a feather boa and dance a tap dance on the bed nude when you feel like someone who never goes out to enjoy herself? You have turned into an old woman.

S: Yeah, I know.

V: So fix it.

S: I guess I need to have better communication with my husband.

V: You need to tell him how you feel about being stuck in the house, but mainly you just need to go out more. You need to plan time together. No relationship can endure a lack of recreation together without deteriorating.

S: Really?

V: That's right. You need to go out at least once a week.

S: That would be heaven!

V: Do it. You need to spend time with each other. When was the last time you went window-shopping or sat in a sidewalk café together watching people go by and just talked? The only time you're intimate is when you're in bed. Isn't that dumb? Would you ever "do it" with someone who treated you like that before? You need some romance. You're not a machine. Tell your husband you love him dearly but you've both been terrible to the relationship. You want to put new life into it, to make it better. You want to do the things for yourself that you used to do. Just because you have a kid you didn't stop being a person. Being a mother doesn't mean that you stop being a siren. You shut it all off and now you're saying "I wonder why I'm embarrassed? Maybe I should go to a sex therapist." Take the money you would give to a sex therapist and go out one night a week and go away overnight at least one night a month.

S: Oh, boy. That would be wonderful.

V: Make it part of your life. You need it, and what's more you deserve it. Are you going to do it?

S: I'm going to talk to him about it.

V: No, just do it.

S: I'm going to do it.

V: Have fun.

Sexual spontaneity is easily bruised. It takes time to deaden the romantic urge. When a partner thinks "What's the use?" whenever he or she feels romantically inclined and shuts the feeling off, the damage grows, depositing layers of doubt and disillusionment over the sexual feelings. By pushing the hurt of disappointment and the anger of unfulfillment away as well, the feelings become even more deeply buried. Opening each other up to feel again is the correct direction to reawaken and preserve romance.

EXERCISE 4
What Turns Me Off

This is a delicate subject in any relationship. Make a list of everything that turns you off sexually, all the things you don't like. Your list can include matters of taste, style, approach, a particular sexual act, a manner of addressing a sexual issue, a technique, the setting for lovemaking, and the like. Things that also belong on this list include anything about your partner's personal habits or sexual style that make you want to avoid sex. Don't eliminate something because you think it is petty, insignificant, or might hurt your partner's feelings. If something diminishes your pleasure, it is already hurting your feelings. Whatever interferes needs to be mentioned.

Next to each item on your list indicate:

Specifically what offends you? Why?

Have you told your partner? Why not?

Were your objections taken seriously?

Is your partner demanding or uncaring about your feelings?

Do you feel rushed, used, or treated like a sexual object?

Are your feelings or pleasure ignored?

Does the point in question feel unnatural or perverted, dirty or unwholesome, silly, stupid, or just unsexy?

Does it embarrass you or make you angry?

Why do you feel the way you do about this issue?

In general, the disgust a partner feels about performing a sexual act is related more to feelings about the other person than about the particular act. Some sexual acts symbolize conquest and submission or surrender and possession, and to partake in them wholeheartedly requires that the partners are both free to do so. If you have problems expressing your feelings to your partner, expecting exotic expressions of passion is unrealistic. It should not come as a surprise to discover that a partner is often willing and eager to perform with another person the same sexual act that they steadfastly refused their mate. What turns people off the most is feeling they have given too much of themselves away while getting little in return. Searching for love, proving one's adequacy, and defying one's partner also play a part. Men are different from women about this. After a terrible argument in which the most damaging comments are made, men are apt to ask for sex, for reassurance that they are still lovable.

After you have made the list of items that turn you off, ask yourself the following questions:

Which of your negative reactions is a representation of your anger at your partner? How were you hurt? Is your partner aware of this? Are you trying to punish him or her? Disguising your anger, claiming that you are really angry at yourself and are undeserving of sexual pleasure is an unsatisfactory solution. It portrays you as defective rather than angry, not good for your self-esteem and not honest.

If one of the items on your list is something your partner brings up over and over again, begging you to participate, consider how much your resistance to participating is a power game. If the way in which the subject is brought up offends you, such as your partner beginning the subject by including a recital of all his or her disappointments from the past, playing on your guilt, or questioning your sexual adequacy, indicate that this attitude is more of a problem for you than the act itself.

Fulfilling sex can only be given away. You should want to make each other happy. It is hard to do this if you feel resentful for being judged unromantic or frigid.

Finally, share your list with your partner. Express the feelings you've been hiding. If your partner has also made a list, discuss that, too. You will be surprised to find that once these matters are out in the open, they can usually be resolved.

EXERCISE 5
Romance

The object of this exercise is to define your notion of a romantic time together and share it with your partner. While it is wonderful for your partner to anticipate your needs, it is always important to share them. Making your needs known is the first step to getting them fulfilled.

To do that, describe to your partner in as much detail as you can what you consider an ideal time. The following points are to guide you:

The time of day and the places you consider most romantic.

The actions of your partner that you consider most romantic.

The activities you'd like to share with your partner.

Everyone has a different version of what is romantic. For me, romance is sharing the anticipation of discovery and adventure together, exploring new roads, meeting new people, having the time to be us. Romantic means to be glad to be sharing our perceptions of the world together.

There may be little sexuality in your description of romance. While romantic times may become lost in sexual ardor, some of the most romantic times have very little sex in them. The essence of romance is the kiss that is an end in itself. You kiss because you like being there. You kiss absorbed in the touch of faces and the soft murmur of closeness and breathing. A romantic kiss is not concerned with where it will go. A romantic kiss seals a moment forever. Its hallmark is its completeness, not necessarily its innocence. It transforms a rainy evening under streetlamps into a cherished memory. A kiss at a momentary stop at a scenic roadside turnout turns a mountain range into a personal possession. Under the spell of a kiss, observing the curvature of the earth together becomes a reflection of the cosmic expansiveness of your feelings for each other. A kiss is the whole world.

Romance doesn't happen all the time because there are other

matters that intrude. You need to take care of your emotional loose ends before you can be romantic. This is why romance is so much more common in relationships that are just starting. The partners have no old unexpressed emotions blocking their feelings. If you wish to rekindle the romance in your relationship, you first need to be able to speak your feelings.

Romantic love is the stuff of a well-managed relationship. It can be yours if you are willing to plan for it. Romance needs time and space. Romance is a framing of reality in a particular attitude, the belief that everything out there in this world is there solely for the two of you. The world is your stage and your love is the great performance. It is heady business and requires two free people willing to celebrate being together, committing to being each other's, and resolving whatever comes between you in anticipation of more good to come.

EXERCISE 6
Planning Spontaneity

This may sound like a contradiction in terms, but planning is the essence of a happy romantic relationship. Consider how much of the time the outside world intrudes on your intimate life, how often concern over bills or children, career or the house manage to get in the way of your being together. All relationships walk a fine line here. You need to take care of the business of your life in order to be free to love. You cannot love with a lot of unfinished business on your mind. Neither can you allow every piece of business to take precedence over loving. Don't allow work to pile up. Don't brush problems under the rug, but still plan for time together, time free of mundane concerns.

During this time there will always be some mention of problems, just don't make problem solving the continual focus of these precious moments. Don't react to the problems that are brought up in the easy freedom of expression that comes when you are relaxed. Think of it this way: If you were running away from the cares of your relationship and having an affair with your partner, and he or she brought up these same points, you would react sympathetically; you would not make it an additional problem by being hurt or by complaining that these concerns were ruining your good times. Enjoying your aloneness together is the romantic part of love. Find this mutuality in all the moments you share and cherish it. It is all a matter of attitude. You can say "There he goes talking about work again" or just allow the moment to pass without resentment and focus on being there together, holding hands and smiling. Remind yourself that the free expression of whatever is on your mind keeps the way clear. Trust in romance and it will reward you by appearing.

If you have nothing special planned, try walking. Parks and gardens are free. So are window-shopping, people watching, museums, and galleries. But if you have someone you love to share them with, the time is precious. You need to convey your delight at having your partner to play with. If you feel you don't have time for these sorts of things, you have to make room for them. These are the things you used to do before you were so busy, successful, famous, important, needed, or indispensable.

Life reaffirms life, but you have to be present for it. Sharing the simple moments of life together is as full as life ever gets. Coming to life with an open heart and the desire to be there together is what a relationship is all about. You need to make room for your love to flourish. You need to show your love in the world. It will give others courage and restore their faith.

Bert, a fifty-two-year-old businessman, called my program.

B: I just thought I'd like to pose a question or perhaps share an emotional experience that I had a couple of hours ago [that was] quite different from anything I've experienced in my lifetime. I had an appointment in Newport Beach and after I finished, driving down Balboa Boulevard during the lunch hour, just out of the corner of my eye I spotted a restaurant and it said, The Fifties Place. I said, "Now, I have to stop in there for lunch." I went in and was totally transformed back to high school. Everything was the same as a coffee shop we frequented right down to the jukebox, the menu, the songs, the decor. Even the waitresses wearing . . .

V: What was the emotion you had?

B: I sat down and started looking at the menu and my life was like passing or flashing in front of me.

V: What was the emotion?

B: Tears were just running down my cheeks.

V: What was the emotion?

B: Well, I don't know if it was nostalgia, if it was yearning . . .

V: Yearning for what?

B: I guess maybe just to be back there.

V: With who?

B: Friends.

V: Specifically whom?

B: In actuality I thought of my first high school sweetheart.

V: And you were thinking about her. And what was it about her you were remembering?

B: Well, she was pretty, always laughing, smiling.

V: What happened to her?

B: Oh, I went into the army. I don't know, she eventually married someone, but . . .

V: Were you in love?

B: I was at the time, yeah. As a high school senior I guess I was in love.

V: Did you ever feel that kind of love again?

B: No, I never have.

V: Is that what's missing from your life?

B: Well, I love my wife and my children very dearly.

V: I understand that, but what I'm saying is, is that what's missing from your life?

B: It just might be. At this point it's just been so current, within the last two hours, I'm really not certain.

V: You're feeling like you're missing that kind of excitement and love in your life.

B: And the whole concept of what it was like thirty, thirty-five years ago.

V: The newness.

B: Yes.

V: The being wanted.

B: Yes.

V: The being afraid to get close, all of that. What's her first name?

B: Her name was Kathleen. When it came to the point when the waitress came to take my order, the tears were rolling down my cheeks, and I was so embarrassed that I apologized. Then, when she served my food, which was absolutely scrumptious, I could only take about two or three bites and I was so overwhelmed with emotion that I had to get up and leave.

V: Did you ever lose your appetite over Kathleen?

B: No, not that I ever recall. We enjoyed hamburgers and french fries.

V: What did you have for lunch?

B: I had a cheeseburger and french fries.

V: Sometimes the old feeling comes back like that, and it's a reflection that you haven't permitted enough time in your present life to be as free and open with your wife as you need to. I think you have to regain some of what you lost so you don't feel that the past is the only place that you found love. I think you need to find more time to play. When was the last time you and your wife took a Saturday afternoon off to walk around the galleries or go down to the beach or just to do something without your pressured schedule?

B: You mean, with her schedule and my schedule . . .

V: When was the last time?

B: Gosh, it's been a while. I don't think we've had fun like that for several years.

V: Every week I want you to take three hours together, just her and you. You'll find the fifties again right there in your own heart because she misses it as much as you do.

269

B: Yes, she has been saying to me lately, "You just don't give me enough love and affection anymore."

V: And you can't be getting love back if she feels that way. Take three hours a week or a Saturday afternoon. Make it a custom. Make it a present to your life. As a matter of fact, take the whole Saturday afternoon and make it yours.

B: Sounds like a wonderful idea.

V: It'll be the best present you ever gave yourself.

Your love is part of a universal plan and statement, but you need to give it the time and room to breathe. Share your versions of romantic times with your partner and talk about ways of making them come true. Then set aside a time for being alone together each week and make these plans a reality. More importantly, set aside a few moments each day when you take the time to be present for each other in a loving way. The rewards of this simple advice are enormous. Remember, love is a gift. Expect nothing in return. Just be tender, sweet, and sincere.

EXERCISE 7

How I Need You to Love Me

Write out a short paragraph describing what you consider to be the most fulfilling and loving sexual experience. Start with how and where you would like to be approached. Go into some detail in depicting the entire process—before, during, and afterward. Indicate what you would like to do and what you would like done to you.

When you are done, take turns whispering your paragraphs in each other's ears. Such a whispered exchange of feelings will become a frequent occurrence in a truly romantic relationship.

It is wonderful to get lost in the sexual experience and to be one with the feelings that you share, but you need to remain in contact with each other and to be present for your partner's experience. If you are not especially aroused, encouraging your partner's arousal is a powerful source of excitement. You do this by making complimentary sounds and saying little words of encouragement. These words always sound downright silly if you take them out of context and use them in any other situation, but the eroticism of the sexual moment makes them ring with a special truth. Be outlandish but supportive. Lavish praise on each other's sexual endowments and performance. Don't be afraid of being laughed at. Moaning, laughing, and talking crazy all add to the excitement of the moment.

If something feels good, tell your partner. You can say "Mmmmmm!" or "Don't ever stop" or "You found my place" or "You're making me crazy!" but say something. If you want more of the same, tell your partner directly. Remember that as much as your partner cares about you, during the period of building toward climax the focus is on completion. It's easy to get lost in the passion.

Be tender, be obscene, be silly, but be what you feel.

EXERCISE 8
Sharing Fantasies

The purpose of this exercise is to heighten your sexual awareness and inventiveness. People have sexual fantasies all the time. Many people are embarrassed by them, some feel guilty because these fantasies involve people other than their mates and sometimes even members of the same sex, so there is a fear of revealing these thoughts. Everyone has a wide range of sexual thoughts, but this does not mean anything other than your mind is active and you are stimulated by a wide variety of interests. A large percentage of the population has homosexual thoughts. This does not mean that these people are homosexual. We all had mothers and fathers and therefore learned to love people of both sexes. Often when we are lonely and introverted, we tend to wish for a closer relationship and are likely to sexualize feelings of closeness just to intensify them. If we are fearful we can panic at the unwelcome prospect of having such feelings. The best idea is to permit yourself the freedom of feeling and imagining anything you want. Trying to inhibit such feelings always causes them to grow and then you fear losing control of these fantasies.

Sharing your fantasies with your partner is a wonderful way of building intimacy and trust. To help you do that, keep a notebook for several weeks in which you put down all of your sexual fantasies. Here are some suggested titles under which to group your entries:

Fantasies that excite me.

Things we have done that made my fantasies come true.

Things that would make you more sexy to me.

Places I would like to make love.

Rewards I have up my sleeve.

The strange things I think about.

Things I would like to try at least once before I die.

Leave your notebook where your partner can find it.

SEXUAL EXPERIMENTATION AND GROWTH

Positions and Practices: Ovid said love has a thousand positions. Variety in your sexual relationship is important, although there is a lot to be said for going along with what you are comfortable with and what satisfies you. Still, for excitement and a change of pace, it is fun to look at copies of classical love manuals. *The Perfumed Garden,* an Arabian manual, and *The Kama Sutra* are good places to start. These are fun to read aloud in bed to each other and to try to follow in practice. The main thing to bear in mind is that no one has the perfect answer for your individual needs. If a position is uncomfortable or hurts, avoid it. Adapt the best for yourself. Be careful not to make this an academic, intellectualized pursuit. Keep it fun and a tiny bit prurient.

Appliances: Vibrators are useful to experiment with, especially when the woman has difficulty reaching orgasm. Keep them clean and use the lower speed. Overstimulation can take men and women past the maximum point of excitement to the post-orgasmic phase without even experiencing orgasm, very disappointing after all that buildup. Be gentle, watch your partner's expression. Follow your feelings. Again, ask for feedback. The best way to experiment with a vibrator is to allow your partner to use it on herself while manually stimulating her to climax. As that approaches, entry can be made and you can complete the act together. This is especially useful to men who have trouble maintaining an erection or who tend to climax prematurely. If a woman uses a vibrator while the man is inside her, it can cause the man to have a lower grade orgasm almost involuntarily.

Mirrors: Mirrors are a wonderful and natural stimulation. It's like having an orgy with yourselves, but safely and warmly. I recommend mirrors for their simplicity and feedback.

It's also a good practice to have a conversation standing in front of a mirror watching your expressions as you talk. You'll be amazed at how much new information you'll get.

Lighting: Sex in the dark is warm and snuggly, but is less erotic than with the lights on. Try changing the lighting. Use candles or spots. Seeing what is going on is a lot of the fun.

Music: Turn on some music, but keep it as background. You want to get lost in the moment, but you want it to be romantic, exciting. Loud sounds will blast you right out of the mood.

Massage: Buy a book on massage and take turns practicing on each other. It is good to use a high quality moisturizing lotion and to offer the massage without the expectation of sexual gain. Pay special attention to the soles of the feet, the lower back and buttocks, and the neck. To relieve stress, gently rub the neck, shoulders, and upper arms for a minimum of five minutes.

If you wish to give a sexual massage, use a massage oil, flavored if you like. These massages should be slower and gradually involve the erogenous zones. A light touch is desirable. Focus your touch on whatever area your partner indicates feels good. Move away from the area and then return slowly and lightly, teasing almost to the point where your partner moves the body part to meet your hand, a kind of physical begging. Go closer and closer to the center of the excitement, using a little more pressure. Don't rush. Be the model of restraint, tease, and then give it all away.

Massaging is a good way to enhance your sexual instincts. You do this by paying attention to your partner when you touch. It's a bit like the childhood game of discovery where you direct another person, indicating whether their approach is getting warmer or colder, closer or further away from the goal. Do the same with your partner when you give a massage and follow his or her response to the most sensitive places. Again, developing an open channel of feedback is your goal. No matter how long you have been together, massaging with such directions is a good way to deepen your ties to each other.

Incense: Incense is an inexpensive and exotic addition. Few things can make a mood the way incense can.

Water: Hot tubs, showers, or a hot bath together are great for relaxing and for getting clean enough to please the most fastidious lover. Especially good if you are thinking of experimenting with new positions or practices.

Home Movies: Taking videos or using the camera can be a risky business. There is always some anxiety about the pictures falling into the wrong hands. A mirror is cheaper and safer.

Pornography: Pornography can be stimulating, but if used to excess it can get boring. Pornography is generally more stimulating to men, who can isolate love from sex more easily than women. Ideally, pornography is best used as an ice-breaker for sexual arousal. Sustaining that interest is up to you.

WHEN TO MAKE LOVE

Always making love as a nightcap just before bedtime is a common practice but not an especially sexy one because the expectation is that you will fall asleep afterward. And what often happens is that at bedtime both of you are too tired to get involved in serious lovemaking or the man may not be able to control himself long enough to satisfy the woman.

Making love in the morning seems natural to many men merely because they have an erection on arising. Sometimes the stimulation for this is a full bladder, sometimes a dream. Capitalizing on this fortuitous occurrence makes more sense to men than women, but there is no denying that many women like to start off the day by making love. Men are often hurt when they are refused at such times, not realizing that their mates are concerned with getting the kids ready for school, starting their work day, and getting into another gear altogether.

You cannot plan when to have sex with any reasonable guarantee of success. The worst is to set up a time and then not be in the mood and have your mate complain "But you promised." Again, try to find times and places in your life where you can follow your instincts. If your are in the mood, whisper to your partner and be affectionate. You can steal a few torrid minutes in the middle of the day every so often. It does wonders for a relationship, giving you a little secret to share.

REFUSING SEX

The most demeaning and least sexy times in a relationship are likely to occur when one partner wants sex and the other doesn't. Instead of pushing and making your partner defensive, ask your partner why he or she doesn't want to get involved. Don't interrupt. Just ask till you understand. Ask your partner what he or she feels and remember that headaches, fatigue, depression all have common source: withheld hurt feelings. You do not want to get into an argument or a deep discussion of the psychodynamics of your relationship with the lights out, lying flat in bed. It's an invitation to disaster. Turn the light on if you are going to talk. Say you know something is bothering your partner and you would like to understand. Offer to discuss it then if he or she wishes, if not, certainly in the morning.

Don't fight in bed. Don't go to sleep without expressing your anger or hurt.

Don't take a sexual refusal personally. Just accepting your partner's feelings as legitimate without demanding sex can be the sign of the love and acceptance he or she needs to be given.

Remember, it is okay not to want to have sex.

If your partner does not want to have sex with you, do not roll over angrily, pull fretfully at the covers, mutter self-deprecatory statements, compare your partner to another person, or recite a litany of previous such injuries. Instead, give your partner a gentle kiss, stroke his or her hair, rub his or her back, and hold him or her close, but not tightly. Make it all right to refuse sex and the situation will get better.

If you beg for sex, you sound very unsexy. It is also guilt-producing to have a partner beg. Don't make your partner into a villain.

Mercy sex—having sex just to get your partner off your back and to get you out of the debit column—is another bad practice but not uncommon in deteriorating relationships. Usually, it is the wife who bestows a half-hearted sexual gift on the husband to smooth things over. It is far better to admit that there are problems and to say that as a result of these problems your sexual feelings are momentarily obscured. Work on the problems instead and allow each other's sexual feelings to resurface naturally.

Much of mercy sex has to do with reassuring a frightened partner that he or she is still lovable. It is better to reassure in words and gentle discussion.

BEING A GOOD SPORT

Giving to your partner when your partner is needy is an act of kindness. You don't need to be in the mood to have meaningful, warm sexual relations, but you do need an ongoing understanding and commitment that allows such giving to be free. When a relationship is good, such one-sided giving is permissible and usually ends up with both partners enjoying the moment. The very same act in a relationship in difficulty will feel like a trespass and being used.

There are acquired tastes in sexual practice just as in anything else. The very act that you may have regarded with fear and revulsion when you first heard of it can become an abiding source of comfort and intimacy. Nothing is perverted if it gives both partners pleasure and enhances their relationship. If you have the ability to provide a new source of excitement and pleasure for your partner, try to get involved in the pleasure you give. That is at least as rewarding as anything else. Often having control over your partner's arousal and passion is a highly exciting feeling in its own right.

Try to follow these feelings and to participate in them any way you can. Saying yes to new experiences and going a little further with your involvement will help build a new level of intimacy.

Attitude counts nearly as much as performance. Wanting to please, being demonstrative with your feelings, sharing your arousal and your excitement openly is a very big turn-on. A partner who is responsive and reveals his or her excitement confirms his or her partner's ability to arouse and increases the partner's arousal. Sex without such response is of much lower intensity and much less satisfying.

QUIET TIMES

Every relationship goes through phases ranging from greater to lesser sexual activity. Mostly, these phases are irregular and reflect the changes in the partners' openness in dealing with problems. Not surprisingly, when the children are having problems or during times of financial preoccupation and career stress, sexual frequency usually decreases. If the partners use their sexual relations to make up for what is missing in the rest of their life or as a tranquilizer, they tend to desensitize themselves, seeking relief rather than pleasure in being together. Consequently, their enjoyment decreases.

This is a frightful age to adjust to. Time seems so condensed. The demands of the world are hard and the pressure to give more wears us out. We seek solace from all this with the person we love. It becomes a great temptation to lean on each other and drain each other's good feelings to say afloat. Where love is given freely this drain is kept to a minimum, but it is still possible to abuse sex and destroy its magic. You have to put back what you take out of the relationship.

Allow your relationship to be what it is. Do not feel that you must be lovers all the time in order to be in love. Everyone goes through periods when they feel less sexual than at other times. Each of us is evolving and the role sex plays in that process differs at different times. Know that there will be these quiet times in your partnership. Do not blame, but seek to understand and accept.

The rewards of loving and being loved are everything.

CHAPTER SIXTEEN

Thoughts on Love and Togetherness

REMEMBERING WHY YOU ARE TOGETHER

When a relationship is not going well it's easy to forget why we ever joined forces in the first place. We feel sorry for ourselves, complain about our partner, and catalogue our disappointments. We become immersed in negativity to convince ourselves that our situation is hopeless, that we should leave, and that we are no longer obliged to be our best.

All partners need to learn to trust the love between them and to remember how good it was when they were in love. Still, suddenly falling out of love feels so devastating that partners want to give up before they have really given their love a chance to prove itself.

Your memory of the good times is your strength, but it is also your potential undoing. You cannot use your memory of the happy times to coat your anger with numbness. Your love must be real to be full. So you must permit yourself to feel your disappointments, to see your partner in ever clearer focus, and to learn to accept and finally to love the real persons you see emerging before and within you.

A good relationship brings you closer to yourself as well as the person you love, makes you more lovable, and gives another dimension of being to your life, being alone together.

Remember why you are together: to live your life from both sides.

FEELING THE POWER OF
YOUR LOVE

Our weaknesses and strengths are all part of the same trait. Which side we show is mostly a reflection of how lovable we feel.

Love gives us the courage to be our best. When we doubt our lovability we are always less. Love inspires us to realize our potential. With love, a dependent person can become independent, a controlling person can become free, and a competitive person can learn to nurture others.

Our partner's love is a reminder that we are lovable even when we are not our best, but it cannot replace self-love.

Love is a support, but although it is freely given it is not a permanent loan. Love is a flow of feeling. To keep it moving in both directions the partners have to be worthy of the love bestowed on them.

The most satisfying part of loving another person is seeing your love make a change for the better. There is nothing more dismaying than loving someone who never seems to grow, who stays trapped in the same fears, nurtures the same negativity, and so invalidates the worth of your love. Such a person does not love himself enough to return the love he receives.

It is tempting to point out your partner's failings under times of stress. And you will be prompted by frustration and bitterness to do so. Just remember you always have a choice. Decide to look for the good without being blind to your partner's faults.

Be encouraging, but not unrealistic.

Be truthful, but don't use the truth as a way to punish.

Be consoling, but still allow your partner to feel the pain of his or her disappointment.

Love to support, not to dominate. If your partner becomes dependent on your love, neither of you is free.

BEING YOUR BEST TOGETHER

Love needs to be returned. Take the love you are given and allow it to show.

Love gives you the courage to be yourself in the presence of the person who loves you. Use this courage to be your best.

PATIENCE

During stressful times in a relationship, the natural inclination is to vent emotions destructively. Give your partner and your relationship the benefit of the doubt. Allow a little more time before you react. You lose nothing by being quiet and allowing the madness around you to go its own way.

Rise above it.

Find yourself in all the confusion.

Let your calmness be the island of reasonableness that brings both of you back in balance.

If you go with the turmoil, it will surely get worse.

Expect the situation to improve.

Remember, it takes time to heal.

Look for evidence that there is still good between you.

Nurture it by welcoming the positive feelings that arise.

Let negativity float past you. Do not attract it to you by resisting or holding on to it. Don't play hurt. Don't be a container for anger.

Keep your best self company in the face of abuse and accusation. Let the answers come to you.

Decide what is best for you as you listen, but do not react while you are deciding.

Implement your decision in peace.

Be patient.

PAYOFFS

What are you getting out of all this? What you have gotten is what you are likely to get.

Are you happy with it?

Is this what you hoped for?

Is it enough?
Is it real?
Is it what you want?
What is all this struggle worth?
If you are unhappy, say so.
If you are discouraged, show it.
Declare yourself.
Claim your feelings.
Ask for what you want.
Be yourself.
Create better times by being your best together.
You cannot live for the future. Your payoff is the way you feel right now.

COMING FROM LOVE

The secret of love is to come from love.
   In times of adversity, remember your love.
   When there is a choice, come from love.
   Coming from love is not avoiding pain, but insisting on healing.
   Coming from love is allowing others to be one with their sadness so they can mourn and clear the way to feel joy again.
   You cannot shoulder the burden of a friend.
   You cannot take up the grief of a loved one.
   Coming from love is being your best in the presence of others.
   The love that flows through you is only partly a response to the people you love.
   It is the life force seeking expression, filling you, attaching itself to what is lovable, nurturing the good.
   If you are in doubt, come from love and you will understand.
   If you are in pain, come from love and you will grow.
   If you are forsaken, come from love and you will find happiness again.
   You are the world. Fill it with love.

THE HAPPIEST COUPLES

The happiest couples share a unique view of the world.
The happiest couples are partners in a destiny they create together.
No one is bound to be what the other cannot achieve.
Each is his own person and free.
The present is without debts.
The moment is without fear.
The answer is I love you.
The question is unimportant.

Epilogue

LOVE MEANS to care about the feelings of another as if they were your own.

If you do not love yourself, it is impossible for your love for another to be deep. If another person does not regard your feelings as important, then what is it he claims to love when he says he loves you?

Love is the acceptance that comes with knowing all of a person's faults and not rejecting the other for what you discover, but rather living in expectation of good. The great peace of love is that there are no surprises you can discover that will cause you not to love the other. The love that lasts is based on the partners' acceptance of themselves as they truly are.

Love is trust. You trust that good abides in you and that you are worthy of being loved. You trust that you are being treated directly and fairly and you trust that your partner feels the same way.

This is the rule of love, that love is open and love is free.

This is the rhyme of love, that love is answered and accommodated, that crowded schedules change and opportunities for togetherness are created out of pressure and chaos, that distances are bridged, absences endured, and joining celebrated.

Love has priority. Love is first. Love is now. Love is best. Love is also next and last.

This is the rhythm of love. It is an inner motion seeking to dance among the stars.

The perspective of love is ever closer and larger, warmer and freer. It is open and giving, expanding and encompassing. It is a generosity of feeling because it recognizes the sameness of feelings between you. It is a passion among equals or it is nothing at all.

The dance of love is a quickening of heart, a belief in the impossible because it is suddenly real.

Love is honesty made visible.

Love is giving made acceptable.

Love helps the needy grow from envy to self-acceptance, from possessiveness to self-confidence, and from jealousy to trust in ourselves.

We need love the way we need air. We need love the way we need food. We need love the way we need love.

When you are in a relationship that nurtures and accepts you, you stop striving for the symbolic rewards that comfort a troubled soul. You feel peace because you have the thing you need. A house is empty without love, but a soul is empty if it does not love its oneness. You cannot love another person unless you can abide your own singularity, your aloneness, your being with yourself.

A life without love of self is a lonely life.

A life without love of another is an unreflected life.

Love is openness and wonder. Love is relief, spawned of sharing intimacies and self-doubt with childish candor. Love is simple and love is easy, when love is easy.

But when love is confounded, when doubt stands in its way, when the open demonstration of feelings gives way to suspicion and love is removed, trust falters and the spirit of love hides. It does not die. It just conceals itself behind the dark feelings that prevent its expression.

Where once love was offered openly without measure, it is now expressed warily, a wounded part, groping to see if it is safe to love again. The climate is tested, the landscape measured, the partner evaluated through doubting and sore eyes. Any questionable behavior, word, or glance reopens the painful dispute. The hurt seems immeasurable, for the pain of not loving is the cruelest punishment of love. Withholding love is a burden to a loving heart.

Learning to accept ourselves through our lover's acceptance is the healing that comes with love.

The recollection of the love that lies beneath the turmoil gives courage and helps lovers risk loving again.

We are all here as partners in life. To find a partner with whom we can grow more honest and more alive is the goal of a healthy relationship.

Working out life together is what makes a relationship sacred, love holy, and the world feel ever young.

Acknowledgments

I WOULD like to thank Lena Tabori for her support in conceptualizing the manuscript and for her friendship and affection and direction over the years of its writing.

Much appreciation is due Elizabeth Beier and Fred Hills for their editorial suggestions and untiring patience with me, for their continued faith in and enthusiasm for the manuscript, and for their sensitive and caring editing that was itself an act of love.

Thanks to Bill Grose for his continued support of the project at Pocket Books and in the Simon and Schuster organization.

Special thanks to Graydon Goss for his insightful suggestions.

Much appreciation to Sandra Vassil for her help with the manuscript and for giving up weekends, usually on short notice, to do so, and for being a good sport and meticulous helper during it all.

Thanks to Lee Holloway for allowing me to read sections of the book to her at all hours of the day and night and for her showering me with love, knowing how much I needed it at those moments of doubt.

Finally, it would be difficult to overestimate how much Candace Bowman, my assistant, contributed to this book. Her patience in hearing me read and reread sections through the tenth revision and coming to each version with freshness, enthusiasm and intelligence, offering supportive suggestions and passionate criticism made the difference. Her faithfulness to the manuscript and her tireless good energy, patience, and caring with the frustrating work of inserting additions, making deletions and corrections, and reinserting deletions is deeply appreciated. Her love and affection were the glue that held much of this together.

About the Author

In addition to his enormously popular radio program on the ABC Talkradio Network, and his new, nationally syndicated television show, "Getting in Touch," David Viscott is the founder of The Viscott Institute in Sherman Oaks, California, where his revolutionary short-term psychotherapy method has had great success.

He is the author of several best-selling and highly praised books, including *How to Live with Another Person, The Language of Feelings, Risking,* and *The Making of a Psychiatrist,* which was a National Book Award and Pulitzer Prize nominee. A graduate of Dartmouth College and Tufts Medical School, Chief Resident at University Hospital's Psychiatric Clinic and Fellow of the Boston University Medicine Institute, Dr. Viscott has served as Senior Psychiatrist and consultant for the State of Massachusetts. He now lives in Los Angeles, California, with his wife, Katharine Random, a fashion designer. He has four children and four cocker spaniels.